S0-DTB-182

Attitudes
and
Consequences
in the Restoration Movement

Homer Hailey

Truth
Publications

Taking His hand,
Helping each other home. ™

© **Truth Publications, Inc. 2018.** All rights reserved. No part of this book may be reproduced in any form without written permission from the publisher. Printed in the United States of America.

ISBN 10: 1-58427-334-8

ISBN 13: 978-158427-334-9

Truth Publications, Inc.
CEI Bookstore
220 S. Marion St., Athens, AL 35611
855-492-6657
sales@truthpublications.com
www.truthbooks.com

DEDICATION

To all those noble souls of today who find courage and
inspiration from the spirit and zeal of the pioneer
preachers of the gospel; men who are "set for
the defense of the gospel" "once for all
delivered unto the saints"; men who
are content to point the lost of
this age to the "good way" of
"the old paths," this work
is affectionately dedi-
cated.

THE AUTHOR.

CONTENTS

PART ONE

THE FORMATION OF AN ATTITUDE
1809-1849

CONTENTS

PART TWO

THE MIDDLE PERIOD: ORGANIZATION, CONTROVERSY, DIVISION
1849-1875

CONTENTS

PREFACE

The aim of this work has been to trace the development of two attitudes toward the Scripture authority in the Restoration Movement: that of the early spirits in the movement, and another which grew up within it, leading ultimately to division.

It may be charged that the book is too largely a compilation of quotations rather than an original vigorous discussion of the subject. The charge is admitted. The effort of the writer has been to let the men speak for themselves, thus breathing their own spirits into the work rather than that of the author. The very purpose of the Old Path's Book Club is to preserve and make available to the reading public of today the writings and positions of the pioneers of the movement.

Some quotations may appear lengthy and cumbersome, susceptible of having been shortened or in some cases even omitted. The author's defense is that he considered their message worthy of a place in presenting the trend of attitudes and their development, and also worthy of being made available to present-day students of such literature. In all quotations the spelling, punctuation and methods of expression have been preserved as found.

The writer is greatly indebted to his intimate friend, Olan L. Hicks, Editor, *The Christian Chronicle,* for valuable suggestions offered in the arrangement and material in the book, and for help rendered in correcting the manuscript.

May the God of hosts give to the church of today the courage and convictions of the Apostles of the New Testament era, and of the pioneers of the present glorious movement; that spirit of holding fast the word of Christ, so essential in meeting the present-day wave of infidelity. Infidelity rages without, while within the church there is seen on the horizon a cloud of modernism looming in certain sections. Victory is to be found in the truth as it is in Jesus; defeat in the fanciful deceptions of modern philosophies and psychologies, which consider the Bible as merely a product of human experience. It is hoped that the contents of these pages will help the gospel preachers of today to see which way the wind is blowing by the way the leaves are now falling, as viewed in the light of past experiences.

HOMER HAILEY.

October 18, 1945. Los Angeles, California.

INTRODUCTION

The sponsors are to be highly commended for bringing this book by Mr. Hailey to the members of the Old Paths Book Club. It has been a pleasure to follow the work done by the author during the preparation of the materials in this volume, and now to see it brought before the brotherhood for a wider reading.

Few men in our ranks have a better conception of the important position entrusted to preachers in the church today. He has spent many months in the collection and preparation of the materials here presented. Some of the material here used is well known to many, but some, both old and young, are not fully aware of the implications of our religious position, and will find in this book a clear definition of the issues and gain a clearer view of the great responsibility that falls upon them. Much of the material here has not been presented before, while all of it is used in a different direction and to a new advantage in emphasizing our position and problems today. Every preacher of the gospel will find his love for the gospel increased by the reading of this volume.

So-called Christendom today faces the awfully important responsibility of choosing between a return to faith in the Bible as being the word of God, and as containing the revelation of His will to man or simply abandoning any serious convictions regarding it and depending entirely upon the wisdom, desires, and impulses of man. There is no middle ground. All efforts at a synthesis between the two ideals is futile.

During the last seventy-five years (thanks to the so-called higher criticism of the Bible) there has developed a number of widely divergent attitudes toward the Bible. They have all sprung from the same basic assumptions, in spite of the various outward forms they have assumed. In this field where

3

the Bible loses its Divine authority, every man becomes a law
unto himself, and whims, fancies, and dogmatic assumption
have all the currency of legal tender. Thus there develop
almost as many shades of belief as there are individuals.
In his study of the development of attitudes toward the
Bible Mr. Hailey has not been so much concerned with the
full current of these developments as with what has taken
place within the movement commonly known as the Restoration Movement. His study has to do with the developments
within the ranks of those who started out with the avowed
purpose of restoring the New Testament Order of things—
in name, worship, faith, and practice.

At the outset of this movement there were high and
noble purposes. There was a mighty and unifying desire to
restore the primitive simplicity and purity of the New Testament and to raise again the fallen structure of the Church of
the Lord Jesus Christ as it is set forth within the pages of
the New Testament. This lofty ideal fired the imaginations
and inspired the hearts of thousands and gave the original
bearers of the plea a glorious battle cry. The effect was elec-
trifying, and historians have never given just credit to the
permanent effects of this movement on religion and society
generally. Many thousands were captivated by the obvious
justness and glory of such an appeal and while the plea was
maintained in its integrity, it swept all before it. But alas!
Such a glorious state was not to continue.

As is too often true with noble movements, some were
brought into the circle who were never completely aware of
the implications of the new ideal of restoration. They were
enamored by its novelty and the first flush of its popularity, but
failed to understand its fullest bearings. Of these early out-
croppings of dissatisfaction with the original plea Mr. Hailey
speaks in this volume. Men like D. S. Burnett, whose eloquence and political acumen did perhaps as much as any
other thing to bring into reality the missionary society, and
L. L. Pinkerton, whose bold and relentless battle against

such men as Moses E. Lard and J. W. McGarvey found its
fruition in his introducing the first melodeon into the worship
of the churches espousing the restoration ideal, were not in
full sympathy with the spirit of the movement.

Such men in the first and second generation of the movement were followed by whole schools of men who embraced
similar liberal attitudes to those held by them. They were
not the same type as the present-day modernist, who denies
the inspiration of the Scriptures altogether, although by 1895
we find many of them expressing sympathies with the new
ideas preached by the German and English higher critics.
These sympathies and many other factors revealed that there
was rapidly developing within the ranks of the movement a
new group which understood neither the spirit nor the letter
of the plea. Their ideas were undermining to the whole original purpose of the movement. These were the ones who
promoted innovations upon the original idea. And once the
floodgate of innovation was opened—though that opening be
ever so small—there was no way of closing it. The pressure
of the tide could never be overcome, but rather grew to flood-
stage and found its culmination in such developments as the
ultra-modernistic wing of the so-called Disciples of Christ
and the Campbell Institute of the present.

Once the way was opened for it, there could be no limit
to this departure from the plain teaching of the New Testament. Thus there have developed among the alleged advocates of the restoration principle three or more clear-cut attitudes toward the Bible. First, there is the thoroughgoing
modernistic group, led by such men as Dr. Edward Scribner
Ames of the Disciples Divinity House, Chicago, Ill., and
other younger men, aided and abetted by such schools among
them as Bethany College, founded by Alexander Campbell,
and the first school produced by the movement, Berea College, Berea, Ky.; The College of the Bible, Lexington, Ky.;
Texas Christian University, Fort Worth, Texas; Drake University, Des Moines, Iowa, and others.

This group assigns no authority to the New Testament over other books and creeds of christendom, and many of them advocate the non-superiority of Christianity over the ethnic religions. They consider the New Testament simply a human, intellectual formulation thrown off by the church in one of the stages of its religious evolution, and not by any means a norm or standard to guide men today. They insist we must not permit it to anchor us down today with its antiquated and restrictive influences. To them the New Testament is no more than a glossator's note on the margin of the church. With them, we should add also, the church is not composed simply of those who are striving to live in strict conformity with the New Testament, but is made up of the complete historic stream and development within the pale of christendom.

A second group occupies a more moderate ground. These have through the years been very closely identified with the fortunes of the *Christian Standard*. The attitude assumed by them has rather consistently been that espoused by the founder and first editor of the Standard, Isaac Errett. The position of the group in the development of attitudes toward the Bible is perhaps even more embarrassing for them than that of the thorough-going modernists mentioned above, for, in the first place, the modernists in group sprang from their midst. They were the first ones to make an open break and departure from the original position and plea made by Alexander Campbell and his co-laborers. They were the first advocates of innovation, and the first to open the floodgates. The position occupied by the ultra-liberal group is simply the natural and logical climax to the position of the second group.

This group is today waging a stern battle against the liberals, in America, but strangely enough is courting the favor and claiming the membership of the liberals in England, particularly those supporting and endorsing the modernistic Overdale College there. In this they have shown themselves thoroughly inconsistent, apparently for the sake of numbers. They have often urged that the original plea, "We speak where the Bible speaks, and keep silent where it is silent," should be interpreted to mean that where the Bible has specifically forbidden a thing we must forego it, but that we are at liberty to introduce things not specifically forbidden in the New Testament.

They are accustomed to speak of their more conservative brethren as "legalists" and "negative authoritarians." In this they have shown a strange lack of perception, not realizing they are the ones who have in reality assumed a negative attitude toward the New Testament, when they deny its furnishing a sufficient pattern of faith and practice in all matters or religion. We may, indeed, call them "negative authoritarians," for they believe somewhat in the authority of the New Testament, only they deny that it furnishes an all-inclusive picture of how to work for and worship the Lord, and leave for themselves plenty of room for the introduction into their work and worship things not specifically prohibited in its pages.

With them the New Testament serves as a cane for a blind man; as an antidote for two extremes. This principle, pushed to its ultimate conclusion, will admit anything men may desire into the service of God, so that every man again may become a law unto himself. If the Gospel is to be preached and the church preserved in anything like their pristine purity, such a principle as this is absolutely inadmissable.

Lastly, there remains a group which believes in the abiding, "positive" authority of the New Testament. They conceive of it neither as an evolution of man nor as a half-complete guide to erring man, but rather as a glowing light, leading them positively all the way—that it furnishes the man of God completely unto every good work and needs no additions or subtractions. With them the simplicity of the

New Testament worship was no mere accident, but was expressive of the Will of God.

With this third group Mr. Hailey stands. In a time when nearly the whole world has succumbed to the gods of liberalism and modernism it is a happy event when a work of this type is brought before the brotherhood to whet our awareness of our responsibility. There are many in the generation now coming into responsibility who may not know the story of the struggle and vigilance necessary to maintain the integrity of New Testament worship and work. This book will help many to a clearer conception of our responsibility. Those who believe in the New Testament as the word of God will have to bear the burden not only of converting the world, but also of combating infidel teaching from every side. They alone can furnish men the "words of Life." Only men who believe in the Authority of the New Testament can preach it to others for what it is.

Let us burn into our hearts the lesson to be learned from the disloyalty of men to God's word. If there are those in our midst who have felt enamored with the new theories of either innovation or infidelity, they do not understand the great cause they have espoused. They should consider again the weighty issues involved, and choose this day whom they will serve. There is no middle ground.

Our strength and prosperity lies in way of complete adherence to the teachings of the New Testament, and the restoring of the church portrayed therein in all respects. If the church of the Lord Jesus Christ is a divine institution, then the restoring of it is a divine task, and such a task we have assumed.

OLAN L. HICKS.

PART I

THE FORMATION OF AN ATTITUDE
1809-1849

CHAPTER I

ATTITUDES TOWARD THE SCRIPTURES
DEVELOPED THROUGH THE CENTURIES

One of the most thrilling chapters in the history of
religion is that of the great Restoration Movement of the
nineteenth century here in the Western Hemisphere. As a
matter of fact, it is exceeded only by that of the first century when Christianity was launched by its Founder, Who
entrusted to the hands of a few humble souls His great
message of salvation, charging them to go preach it to the
whole world. Those few disciples, filled with fervent love
for their Master and His great cause, carried that message
of redemption into all parts of the civilized world, "turning
the world upside down" from a religious and social stand-
point.•

Those men believed implicitly in the authority of their
Master, and in the message entrusted to them. They believed
the Scriptures inherited by them from their forefathers to
have been the Word of God, inspired by the Holy Spirit.[1]
They considered themselves ambassadors of Christ, speaking
for Him.[2] Their word was the word of God.[3] The churches
planted under their ministry were "churches of God,"[4] over
which Jesus Christ ruled as head and Lord.[5] The preachers
themselves were not "clergymen" but "ministers," servants
of the Lord through whom the people believed; it was God
who gave the increase.[6] Brethren were to live together in

---

[1]2 Peter 1:20-21.
[2]2 Corinthians 5:18-20.
[3]1 Thessalonians 2:13.
[4]1 Corinthians 1:2.
[5]Ephesians 1:22, 23.
[6]1 Corinthians 3:5,6.

11

unity, division being sinful,[7] while in all things God should be glorified.[8] In the strength and power of His might, clad in a spiritual armor of divine workmanship, they went forth to conquer and to save.

Thus equipped and commissioned, those early disciples of .the Lord invaded all lands, winning souls to Christ, planting churches of Christ, and making Christians of the individual converts. They were opposed, ridiculed, beaten, stoned, called upon to suffer and oftentimes to die for the faith, but God led them in their battles for right and gave to them strength for the conquest and victory for their reward. But alas! that the day should come when men began to depart from the simple faith of the Gospel and to allow heathen philosophies to take the place of simple faith, and pagan pageantry to be substituted for simple worship and fellowship. As lust for power moved men from spiritual overseers of the flock to Bishops and Patriarchs over congregations and dioceses, exercising temporal and spiritual power, and creeds became substitutes for the word of God, Christianity began to go into an eclipse destined to hide the lustre of its beauty and the purity of its simplicity for centuries to come.

Not until we reach the nineteenth century do we find sweeping movements and efforts to restore the original plan and purpose of God in all its points. There had been many attempts at "reformation," noble and far-reaching in their influence, but there has been only one concerted effort at "restoration." Christianity had and has suffered more from human leadership and human philosophy than from any other curse. Before the original could shine in all its brilliance and lustre, these must needs be abolished and set aside, and the gospel and authority of Christ made to stand out in the thinking of men. This was the grand objective of the nineteenth

---

[7] 1 Corinthians 1: 10.
[8] 1 Corinthians 10: 31, 32.

century reformers on the American continent. They sought to get back beyond the leadership, philosophies and traditions of men to Christ, His Word, and the church which He established by the labors of His specially selected apostles.

The attitude of those first-century Christians was that God had acted for their salvation and through Christ had spoken the final word for their redemption. The attitude toward that word should be one of reverence and respect. Where God had spoken, man could not legislate, for His word was the conclusion of the whole matter. The purity of the church, the unity among brethren, ultimate victory over the world, rested upon the attitude of those who had espoused the great cause. This also was the attitude of the men of the nineteenth century. But as time passed and innovations crept in, as untaught individuals became *nominal* Christians, changes began to be made. The pattern was altered, attitudes were no longer as of former years, until gradually the pristine simplicity was marred and covered, until the original simple plan of God could no longer be recognized. Ambitions began to manifest themselves, pagan philosophies became substitutes for the word of God, until darkness descended upon the face of the earth and the light of truth was covered by ignorance and superstition.

The object of this work is not to trace in detail the history of Christianity from those early years through the centuries, but to consider the attitude of the nineteenth century reformers toward the Scriptures, and to trace that attitude through the growth and development of the movement known as the Restoration Movement, until finally another attitude developed, parallel with it, repeating the history of the early centuries, which resulted in a division in that great brotherhood who were so nobly leading the religious thinking of this country. Before considering the work of these recent reformers, however, it would be well to trace briefly the attitude toward the Scriptures developed in the Roman Church, the German Reformation and in some of the early American

denominations as a background to the attitude manifested by
the men of the past century and of our own special study.

1. *The Attitude Within the Roman Catholic Church.*

Augustine, who was born November 13, 354, in Tagaste,
a small municipality in Numidia, is considered the "Father
of Roman Catholicism."[9] To him, the church stood as a
symbol of all external authority. Scripture must be authoritative because the church declares it so. Not only was the
church the final appeal of authority, but it was such an institution that all men must be brought into it, even to the extent
of using force, that the elect might be saved. Augustine had
taken the church as he found it. He had accepted the teaching of Cyprian that outside the church there was no salvation;
that to have God as one's Father, one must have the church
as his mother. In commenting upon Augustine's attitude at
this point, Alexander Allen says:

> The church was here by divine appointment, and if
> so it was the divine will that all men should come into
> it; and if they would not come of themselves, they must
> be forced to do so; and if the church lacked the power of
> compulsion, it was the sacred duty which the state owed
> to the church to come to its rescue, and by the might of
> the sword "compel them to come in," that the church
> might be filled.[10]

This doctrine led in later years to persecutions which
appealed to the authority of Augustine's writings—persecutions far more drastic than anything to which Augustine
himself would have subscribed. Of Augustine's position in
the matter of forced membership, Philip Schaff says, "The
great authority of his name was often afterward made to

[9]*Encyclopedia of Religion and Ethics:* Art., "Augustine," by B. B.
Warfield.

[10]Alexander V. G. Allen, *The Continuity of Christian Thought,*
pp. 152, 153.

justify cruelties from which he himself would have shrunk with horror."[11]

It is to Augustine that the credit must go for crystallizing the dogma of the place that the Church was to hold throughout the following centuries. His labors were unceasing and his influence was immeasurable. However, the question with which we are concerned is, "What was the final result of his services to the Church?"

Augustine's position was that truth is a "deposit" entrusted to the episcopate for preservation. It is to be found only in the church, and to the church even Scripture owes its authority. This definitely is the beginning of that attitude which found its climax in the Papal Decree of Infallibility of 1870. Dr. Harnack gives a most complete summary of Augustine's contribution in the shortest statement when he says:

Precisely in the best of his gifts to the church, Augustine gave it impulses and problems, *but not a solid capital.* (Italics mine. H. H.) Along with this he transmitted to posterity a profusion of ideas, conceptions, and views which, unsatisfactorily harmonized by himself, produced great friction, living movements, and finally, violent controversies.[12]

The influence of Augustine in religious thinking, and in the forming of religious doctrine, cannot be overestimated. His influence did not stop with the Catholic Church, nor is he quoted by them alone, but it passed on into the Reformation, where among many, his name carried great weight and his opinion great authority.

In his early days, the youthful Augustine found nothing of interest in the Scriptures; they were not to be compared with the writings of Tully. It was in the "Hortensius" of Cicero that he found his earliest inspiration to seek knowl-

---

[11]Philip Schaff, *History of the Christian Church,* Vol. III, p. 145.
[12]Adolph Harnack, *History of Dogma,* Vol. V, pp. 5, 6.

edge and to find wisdom in philosophy. After his conversion, and as a bishop in the Church, the Scriptures became to him the authority for religious doctrines and practices, but on the basis of the church's declaration of the authority of the Scriptures. "Now faith will totter if the authority of Scripture begins to shake," he said.[13] But of this authority of Scripture, Schaff quotes him as saying, "I would not believe the Gospel, if I were not compelled by the authority of the universal church." But he immediately adds: "God forbid that I should not believe the Gospel."[14] Clearly, here is recognized the basis of that view of church authority which later placed the traditions of men on an equality with the Word of God: the authority of the church gives authority to the Gospel.

In the matter of faith Augustine was convinced that everything in Scripture was valuable, and that any thought was at once justified, ecclesiastically and theologically, by being proved to be Biblical; yet, Dr. Harnack says of him:

He ultimately regarded Scripture merely as a *means,* which was dispensed with when love had reached its highest point, and he even approached the conception that the very facts of Christ's early revelation were stages beyond which the believer passed, whose heart was possessed wholly by love.[15]

Augustine's own words are:

And thus a man who is resting upon faith, hope and love, and who keeps a firm hold upon these, does not need the Scriptures except for the purpose of instructing others.[16]

[13]Augustine, "On Christian Doctrine," Book I, Ch. 39, *Nicene and Post-Nicene Fathers.*

[14]Schaff, *op. cit.,* p. 343.

[15]Harnack, *op. cit.,* p. 99.

[16]Augustine, *op. cit.*

Having spoken of Augustine's regard for the Scriptures merely as a *means*, Harnack says further, "A means indeed which is finally dispensed with like a crutch."[17] Which position, as summarized by Harnack and as stated by Augustine himself, is sure to be fatal so far as truth is concerned. In the "Confessions" one sees the depth of soul and love for God of the great Augustine; in his other writings is discovered the doctrines which most affected later religious thinking. His life has wielded a tremendous influence, but of the whole of his work this writer is prone to agree with Harnack, when he said of Augustine, that he gave to the Church impulses and problems, "but not a solid capital." This attitude was the beginning of the introduction of traditions and church interpretation destined to lead away from the Scriptures which the great theologian thought to disseminate. While doing much good, he at the same time set in motion doctrines and theories destructive to primitive Christianity, and which ultimately led to the great apostate church of the middle ages, and the present.

What was begun by Augustine in the forming of an attitude in the early Catholic Church was completed by Thomas Aquinas, the "angelic Doctor" of the Schoolmen of the Middle Ages. Born of noble parentage, Aquinas refused a place in the service of his country that he might devote his life to the Church. He received his earliest training from the Benedictine monks of Monte Cassino, having been placed there at the age of five. He was later sent to Naples, from which place he was to have been sent to Paris or Cologne; but the plans were interrupted by his parents and brothers, who had him taken by soldiers and held for two years a virtual prisoner in the fortress of Rocca Secca. At the end of that time he was sent to Paris, where his education was continued. Before he was twenty years of age, he had received the habit of the Order of St. Dominic. The

[17]Harnack, *ibid.*, p. 100.

exact year of the birth of Thomas is uncertain, the end of
the year 1225 being the date usually assigned, although
some think 1227 the more probable date. He died in 1274,
being not yet fifty years of age. It is almost unbelievable
the amount of work he accomplished in such a brief lifetime.
Aquinas possessed two outstanding abilities, namely, a
remarkable talent for systematizing, and a great power of
simple and lucid exposition, his own writings oftentimes
being simpler than the explanations and commentaries written about them. As his life's work, Thomas attempted to
set forth a solution of all the ecclesiastical claims of antiquity.
He undertook to accomplish that of which the Roman Church
had long dreamed, the formation of a complete system of
dogma. The theology of this new Augustine was the development, in its full splendor and practical realization, of that
which the Latin Church had begun to dream of from its
infancy. Harnack sums up the effort of the great School-
man, when he says of him:

> He set himself to solve the vast problem of satisfy-
> ing under the heading and within the framework of a
> church dogmatic all the claims that were put forward
> by the ecclesiastical antiquity embodied in dogma, by the
> idea of the Church as the living, present Christ, by
> the legal order of the Roman Church, by Augustine's
> doctrine of grace, by the science of Aristotle, and by
> the piety of Bernard and Francis.[18]

In general, more than any other, the "angelic Doctor,"
as he is called by the Latin Church, labored to harmonize
the principles of Aristotle with the teachings of the Church,
of whose maturity, including the supreme authority of the
Popes, he was a devoted champion. He was able to accomplish more toward the end of such a stupendous program
than would seem possible in such a short span of life.

---

[18] Harnack, *op. cit.*, Vol. VII, p. 4.

"Under his hand," writes Philip Schaff, "the Scholastic doctrines were organized into a complete and final system."[19] Although the great work of this Scholastic theologian may not have resulted in lessening the strain of the mutually antagonistic forces at work in Roman Catholicism or in securing a satisfying unity (nay, to some degree it may have produced the opposite result), it must be claimed for him that he so formulated and assembled the teaching of the Roman Church that the work of the Council of Trent centuries later was little more than a simplification and endorsement of his work. He was able so to combine Aristotle the politician and Augustine the theologian in his own theology that the two became allies, thus laying the foundation for the decree of papal infallibility which came later. "In that," says Harnack, "consists the importance of Thomas in the world's history."

The Catholic Encyclopedia claims that Aquinas composed more than sixty works in his lifetime, some of them brief, some very lengthy. Of these works the more important are: "Quaestiones disputatae (Disputed Questions)"; "Quodlebeta"; "Summa de veritate Catholecae fidei contra gentiles," in which he strives to show that no demonstrated truth (science) is opposed to revealed truth; "Oposculeum contra errores Graecorum," in which he refuted the errors of the Greek Catholic Church, as viewed by the Roman Church, discussing such questions as the procession of the Holy Spirit from the Father, the primacy of the Roman Pontiff, the Holy Eucharist, and purgatory; and "Summa Theologica." The last named, "Summa Theologica," was the most important of his many works; it filled twenty-two volumes in the English translation. The "Summa" is divided into three principal parts, which parts are broken into divisions and subdivisions. The first part treats of God, including the nature of God, the Trinity, and the relation of God to the World. The

---

[19]Schaff, *op. cit.*, Vol. V, Part 1, p. 661.

second treats of man and ethics, ethics after the Aristotelian philosophy. The third part deals with Christ, the Sacraments, and with Eschatology. The work was cut short by the death of Aquinas while he was working on the doctrine of the Sacraments.

Of the estimate placed upon Thomas by the Catholic Church today, it may be said that to them he stands as the theologian *par excellence;* they feel that he not only advocated a system of thought adequate for the thirteenth century in which he lived, but likewise suited for the twentieth. The Dominical Order, of which the learned theologian was a member, has made his works a necessary requirement of study among their students today. Walter Farrell, a Catholic writer of the present time, says of him and his works, "This is a man and a book providentially designed for the needs of the twentieth century."[20]

Although one might agree with some of the things said by Mr. Farrell as to the needs of the modern age and of the general shortcomings of the century, but does Thomas Aquinas and his philosophy meet the needs of the day? This is most questionable, and is denied by Protestant writers. Alexander Allen revolts against the thought of one man so completely grasping and summarizing the whole field of religious thought as to make "conquest of human reason." Of such an effort to present to the world a complete system of absolute truth and to thus bind human reason, Allen says:

> Indeed, it is inevitable in the interest of freedom and of progress that the human mind should rebel against a system like that of Aquinas, which definitely fixed all things in heaven and earth without the need of any further inquiry, and stamped the whole result with the assumption of infallibility.[21]

---

[20] Walter Farrell, *A Companion to the Summa,* Vol. I, p. 32.
[21] Allen, *op. cit.,* p. 229.

Of the work of Aquinas in contributing to the formation of an attitude toward the Scriptures in the Roman Catholic Church, only one thing more needs to be mentioned, namely, his teaching concerning the infallibility of the Roman pontiff. For centuries the trend of Catholic teaching had been toward the doctrine of papal infallibility; the teaching of the infallibility of the Church in her religious teaching would inevitably lead to the doctrine of infallibility of the Pope. There must be a final infallible voice in determining points of doctrine; it was only natural that the head should become that unerring voice. Up to the time of Thomas such a dogma had not been uttered; as a matter of fact, until his day, belief in the infallibility of the Pope had not been demanded as an article of faith necessary to salvation.

It is true that the doctrine had long been recognized, that through a special divine protection the Roman Church could not entirely fall from faith, and was the divinely appointed refuge for doctrinal purity and unity, but beyond the groups under the influence of the Dominical Order, the doctrine of infallibility did not command acceptance. On this point, Harnack says:

So far as I know, Thomas was the first to state the position roundly in the formula: "(Ostenditur etiam), quod subesse Romano pontifici sit de necessitate salutis" (It is also shown that to be subject to the Roman pontiff is essential to salvation).[22]

More than three hundred years before the convening of the Vatican Council, in which Council the decree of Papal Infallibility was announced, the Council of Trent (1543-1563) had formulated the doctrines of the Roman Church into one body, called "The Canons and Degrees of the Council of Trent." The convening of this Council had been forced upon the Roman hierarchy by the Catholic peo-

---

[22]Harnack, *op. cit.,* Vol. VI, p. 122.

ple themselves as a result of the Protestant Reformation; they felt they must have a clear and comprehensive statement of what they believed if they were to meet the rising tide of Protestantism. This is no place for a study of these Councils; only one point concerns us, i.e., a consideration of the attitude toward the Scriptures expressed in the canons of this particular Council, and the attitude that would naturally result from the decree of the Vatican Council.

Traditions originating throughout the centuries had been received by the Church as equal in authority with the Scriptures themselves. The exact words in which the decree is expressed by the Council of Trent are translated from the Latin by Schaff as follows:

> . . . and seeing clearly that this truth and discipline are contained in the written books, and the unwritten traditions which, received by the Apostles from the mouth of Christ himself, or from the Apostles themselves, the Holy Ghost dictating, have come down even unto us, transmitted as it were from hand to hand: (The Synod) following the examples of the orthodox Fathers, receives and venerates with an equal affection of piety and reverence, all the books both of the Old and of the New Testament—seeing that one God is the author of both—as also the said traditions, as well those appertaining to faith as to morals, as having been dictated, either by Christ's own word of mouth, or by the Holy Ghost, and preserved in the Catholic Church by a continuous succession.[23]

Schaff says, "Next in authority to the decrees of the Council of Trent, or virtually superior to it, stands the Professio Fidei Tridentinae, or the Creeds of Pius IV." This "Profession of the Tridentine Faith," issued in 1564, consists of twelve articles, giving a clear summary of the

---

[23]P. Schaff, *Creeds of Christendom*, Vol. II, p. 80.

doctrines set forth by the Council of Trent, with an additional declaration that the "Roman Church is the mother and mistress of all churches" and an oath of obedience to the Pope of Rome. This "Profession" was subscribed to by all Roman Catholic priests, bishops, and teachers in Catholic schools of all types. Two articles of the "Profession" pertain to the theme of this study, as they reveal the attitude toward the traditions and the Scriptures, including the Scriptures almost as an afterthought.

I most steadfastly admit and embrace apostolic and ecclesiastic traditions, and all other observances and constitutions of the same Church.

I also admit the holy Scriptures, according to that sense which our holy mother Church has held and does hold, to which it belongs to judge of the true sense and interpretation of the Scriptures; neither will I ever take and interpret them otherwise than according to the unanimous consent of the Fathers.[24]

The top-stone to the pyramid of the Roman hierarchy was placed by Pope Pius IX, when on July 18, 1870, the decree of Papal Infallibility was proclaimed at the fourth session of the Vatican Council.

Although the call for the convening of the Council had been issued in June, 1868, it did not open until December 8, 1869. With varying numbers present throughout the ten months the Council was in session, 764 appears to have been the largest number ever present, which diminished rapidly after the proclamation of the decree of Papal Infallibility, until there were only between 180 and 200 by the time it was dismissed.[25] This proclamation was the crowning act of blasphemy of all the blasphemies which had proceeded from the Vatican since the beginning of the

[24]*Ibid.*, p. 207.
[25]Schaff, *op. cit.*, Vol. I, pp. 140-141.

Roman Catholic Church. In it, apostasy reached its absolute completeness. In order to complete this brief study of the development of an attitude within the Roman Church, a portion of Chapter IV, "Concerning the Infallible Teaching of the Roman Pontiff," of the "Dogmatic Decrees of the Vatican Council," is here given:

> Therefore faithfully adhering to the tradition received from the beginning of the Christian faith, for the glory of God our Saviour, the exaltation of the Catholic religion, and the salvation of Christian people, the sacred Council approving, we teach and define that it is a dogma divinely revealed: that the Roman Pontiff, when he speaks *ex cathedra,* that is, when in discharge of the office of pastor and doctor of all Christians, by virtue of his supreme Apostolic authority, he defines a doctrine regarding faith or morals to be held by the universal Church, by the divine assistance promised to him in blessed Peter, is possessed of that infallibility with which the divine Redeemer willed that his Church should be endowed for defining doctrine regarding faith or morals; and that therefore such definitions of the Roman Pontiff are irreformable of themselves, and not from the consent of the Church.[26]

After declaring that "the Church is the divinely appointed Custodian and Interpreter of the Bible," and discussing the proposition "That God never intended the Bible to be the Christian's rule of faith, independently of the living authority of the Church," Cardinal Gibbons states the real attitude of the Roman Catholic Church in this matter when he says,

> We must, therefore, conclude that the Scriptures *alone* cannot be a sufficient guide and rule of faith because they cannot, at any time, be within the reach of

---

Ibid., Vol. II, pp. 270-271.

every inquirer; because they are not of themselves clear and intelligible even in matters of the highest importance, and because they do not contain all the truths necessary for salvation.[27]

From a slow and gradual departure from the Bible as the Word of God, and the authority for all things pertaining to the church in its spiritual conduct and doctrine, the position of the Roman Church must be the ultimate end. It must be either the Bible as the standard and guide in all matters, or human wisdom as the standard, whether that human wisdom finds its expression in an alleged infallible head, as in Roman Catholicism, or in the individual human reason as in Modernism. With an honest confession from Gibbons, who said, "A Pope's letter is the most weighty authority in the Church,"[28] we turn to consider briefly the attitude of the sixteenth century Reformers toward the Scriptures, before taking up the thread of our study in the Restoration of the nineteenth century.

2. *The Attitude of the Sixteenth Century Reformers.*

After wading through the writings of the Scholastics of his day, in which they appeal to the fathers and schoolmen of former days, it is most refreshing to turn to Martin Luther and there find in all of his works a challenging appeal to the Scriptures. With Luther, there was an absolute supremacy of the Word of God over all the words of men, regardless of their position. "To reform the church by the fathers," said he, "is impossible; it can only be done by the Word of God."[29] Throughout the years of his reforming and preaching, he followed the policy that the Scriptures must do the reforming, if reformation were to

[27]James Cardinal Gibbons, *Faith of Our Fathers*, 94th edition, 1917; pp. 89, 90.

[28]*Ibid.*, p. 93.

[29]Schaff, *History of the Christian Church*, Vol. IV, p. 36.

be effected. In the controversy with Eck, in the early years of the Reformation, Melanchthon laid down a fundamental principle of difference between the authority of the Scriptures and the fathers, when he said, "We must not explain the Scriptures by the Fathers, but explain and judge the Fathers by the Scriptures."[30]

This attitude of Martin Luther toward the Bible has played one of the most conspicuous roles in the whole of the Reformation. In every matter of dispute, the Scriptures were to the Reformer the final court of appeal, the final voice of authority.

The question of authority is one constantly coming up in religious discussions and disputes. No question can be settled until men have agreed on a final voice of authority. Writing on the subject, Harnack well said,

> There has never yet existed in the world a strong religious faith, which has not appealed, at some *decisive* point or other, to an *external authority*. It is only in the colorless expositions of religious philosophers, or the polemical systems of Protestant theologians, that a faith is constructed which derives its certitude exclusively from its own inner impulses. . . . Only academic speculation thinks that it can eliminate external authority; life and history show that no faith is capable of convincing men or propagating itself which does not include obedience to an external authority, or fails to be convinced of its absolute power. The only point is to determine the rightful authority, and to discover the just relationship between external and internal authority. Were it otherwise, we should not be weak, helpless beings.[31]

In the statement of "determining the rightful authority," and "discovering the just relationship between external and

---

[30]*Ibid.*, p. 204.
[31]Harnack, *op. cit.*, Vol. V, p. 82.

internal authority," Harnack touches the crux of the whole matter. It is upon this point that men differ; all will admit the absolute need for some final voice of authority in questions of difference.

Luther saw that previous to his time, questions as to what is Christian, and what is the church, "had been determined in a way quite arbitrary and therefore uncertain." "He accordingly," says Harnack, "turned back to the sources of religion, to the Holy Scripture, and in particular to the New Testament."[32] With Luther, all things had to be determined by the Scripture, by the Word of God. "The Word of God which he constantly had in his mind, was the testimony of Jesus Christ who is the Saviour of souls," says Harnack. Luther sought, in his appeal to Scripture, to divide, or better, to describe, the whole of Christianity under the terms *law* and *gospel;* but with him the Gospel was redemption itself, while the law was simply a burdensome husk.

Luther did not free himself entirely from the letter of Scripture, nor does it seem that anyone can and still appeal to the Scriptures. Of that lack to free himself completely from the authority of the letter, Harnack further says, "the lack was still greater on the part of those who came after him." However, of the outward authority of the written word, Harnack says, this "was certainly occasionally disregarded by him in his Prefaces to Holy Scripture, and elsewhere as well."[33]

Writing on this same subject, Sabatier says of the Reformers, "Their faith, being of the purely moral and religious order, clung before all things to the moral and religious substance of the Bible, and not to its letter and outward form, which are matters not of faith, but of history."[34] This position, however, appears to be contradicted by the conduct

---

[32]*Ibid.*, Vol. VII, p. 188.

[33]Harnack, *op. cit.*, Vol. VII, p. 246.

[34]Auguste Sabatier, *Religions of Authority*, p. 157.

of Luther at Marburg. In the meeting with Ulrich Zwingli, in which the two reformers met to discuss their differences pertaining to the Lord's Supper, Luther wrote on the table before him the words, "This is my body" (in Latin), to which he constantly returned. With him it was a literal interpretation from which he refused to yield an inch. Zwingli repeated John 6:63 many times, but to no avail. Had Luther considered the spiritual significance of the Supper, or given a spiritual interpretation to the language, the Lutheran doctrine of the Lord's Supper would never have come into being. It was his strict adherence to literalness that forced the gulf between the two great reformers.

A comparison of the work done by these two distinguished reformers is most interesting, but impossible in a work of this nature. D'Aubigne has well summarized the attitude of the two men toward the Scriptures, in which it will readily be seen that of the two, Zwingli's position is more nearly the forerunner of that held by the leading spirits of the nineteenth century reformation. D'Aubigne says:

> The Swiss Reformation here presents itself to us under an aspect rather different from that assumed by the Reformation in Germany. Luther had severely rebuked the excesses of those who broke down the images in the churches of Wittemberg;—and here we behold Zwingle, presiding in person over the removal of images from the temples of Zurich. The difference is explained by the different light in which the two Reformers viewed the same object. *Luther was desirous of retaining in the Church all that was not expressly contradicted by Scripture, while Zwingle was intent on abolishing all that could not be proved by Scripture.* (Italics mine. H. H.) The German Reformer wished to remain united to the Church of all preceding ages, and sought only to purify it from everything that was repugnant to the word of God. The Reformer of Zurich passed back over every intervening age till he reached the times of the apostles;

and, subjecting the Church to an entire transformation, laboured to restore it to its primitive condition.

Zwingle's Reformation, therefore, was the more complete. The work which Divine Providence had entrusted to Luther, the re-establishment of the doctrine of Justification by Faith, was undoubtedly the great work of the Reformation; but when this was accomplished, other ends, of real if not of primary importance, remained to be achieved; and to these, the efforts of Zwingle were more especially devoted.[35]

Sabatier is correct in attributing to Luther the beginning of a new criticism of Biblical writings.[36] In this Luther departed from the current custom, to challenge the historical position, and the relative value of certain books. It is also true that Luther succeeded in removing "the seat of religious authority from without to within, from the Church to the Christian consciousness,"[37] but in so doing, Luther always recognized that the conscience must appeal to the Scriptures themselves for that final endorsement which constituted the authority in all matters.

Schaff says of the matter, "Luther did not appeal to his conscience alone, but first and last to the Scripture as he understood it after the most earnest study. His conscience, as he said, was bound in the word of God, who cannot err. There, and there alone, he recognized infallibility."[38]

As has been suggested, Luther did not hesitate to pass judgment on certain portions of the Bible, designating some as of greater value than others, and some as being unworthy of a place in the canon. "He called the Epistle of Jude," says Schaff, "an 'unnecessary epistle,' a mere extract from

[35]J. H. Merle D'Aubigne, *History of the Great Reformation of the Sixteenth Century in Germany, Switzerland, etc.*, p. 342.

[36]Sabatier, *Religions of Authority*, p. 158.

[37]*Ibid.*, p. 160.

[38]Schaff, *op. cit.*, p. 313.

Second Peter and post-apostolic, filled with apocryphal matter," and worthy of being rejected.[39] He found little in the book of Revelation worthy of acceptance, until he saw in it a value in fighting Rome; when this was conceived by him, its value was greatly enhanced. The Epistle of James stood lowest in his estimation of all the parts of Scripture; he called it an epistle of straw as compared with the genuine apostolic writings. Because the Epistle to the Hebrews seems to deny the possibility of repentance after baptism (Chapters 6, 10, 12), he found objection to it.[40]

At Worms (April 17 and 18, 1521), before the Diet convened by Charles V, Luther offered to repudiate his writings if they could be refuted by the Word of God; if not, then he would be forced to stand by what he had written. Not only did he provoke the Roman Catholics there gathered when he refused to decant anything he had written, but he added to their indignation when he affirmed that popes and councils had made mistakes in the past. With Luther, the Holy Scriptures were the only writings to which appeal could be made; they were infallible.

When von Hutton desired to make war on the Peasants, Luther sought to detain him, and to deter him from his course by an appeal to the Scriptures, on the ground that in a spiritual warfare carnal weapons had no place; the Word of God must be the instrument of reformation.

In reforming the worship, Luther again appealed to the Scriptures, and sought to return to a simpler worship, more nearly patterned after the apostolic procedure. This should consist of the Lord's Supper after the original simplicity, more reading of the Scriptures, and the service in the language of the day so that it would be intelligible to the people assembled. He rejected five of the seven sacraments, retaining only baptism and the eucharist. Ceremonies, robes, candles, and the attitude of the minister in prayer, were

---

[39]*Ibid.*, p. 36.
[40]*Ibid.*, p. 36.

matters of indifference with Luther.[41] In all of his discussions, Luther's constant appeal was to the Scriptures, whether in defending his writings, in exposing the corruptions of others, or in defense of his positions which were called in question.

No doubt one of the most important works of Luther's busy life was that of translating the Scriptures into his native German. He began this work while imprisoned in the castle at Wartburg, in 1521. Taken to the castle on the 4th of May, 1521, by Elector Frederick, he remained in seclusion nearly eleven months, known as "Junker Georg." During this time he translated the New Testament, which was joyously received by the people. In this translation, Luther made use of all the materials available in his day, especially of the Greek translation of Erasmus. In his excessive zeal for the newly discovered ancient doctrine of justification "by faith," he inserted in his translation of Romans 3:28 the word "only." The error was inexcusable, for such an addition forced a contradiction between the passage and James 2; besides, the Scriptures plainly teach justification by faith, but just as plainly do not teach justification by faith "only." This became a weapon against Luther in the hands of his enemies.

This work, begun at Wartburg in 1521, was completed in 1534 (with much of the work on the Old Testament being done while he was a second time in prison at Coberg, 1530), "although he made emendations until 1545." Schaff says, "He prepared five original editions, or recensions, of his whole Bible, the last in 1545, a year before his death. This is the proper basis of all critical editions."[42] All Protestant scholars are profuse in their praise of the language used by Luther in his translation; the language of his translation has become the basis of a classic German.

---

[41]Schaff, *op. cit.*, Vol. VI, pp. 484-489.
[42]*Ibid.*, p. 348.

Philip Schaff, who has been so often quoted in this section, pays a fitting tribute to the great German Reformer and scholar, when he says:

> The richest fruit of Luther's leisure in the Wartburg, and the most important and useful work of his whole life, is the translation of the New Testament. . . . He made the Bible the people's book in church, school and house. If he had done nothing else, he would be one of the greatest benefactors of the German speaking people.[43] . . .

and we might add, "of the entire religious world."

The whole world is indebted to Martin Luther; even the Catholics, his bitterest enemies, owe him a debt of profound gratitude. The protestant world is indebted to him for unchaining the Bible from the pulpits of the clergy and placing it in the hands of all; the Catholic Church is indebted to him for lifting the mask from the Church of that day, exposing the corruptions attached to it, and forcing it to cleanse itself of some evils by which it had been corrupted. One need not try to hide Luther's imperfections; he was a man; but he was a man to be admired and loved by all generations for what he has done, in spite of those imperfections and shortcomings. Martin Luther is another monument to the ability of God to take man in his imperfections and use him to His own matchless and eternal glory.

If Luther's movement rested so emphatically upon an appeal to Scripture, why such a vast difference between his work and that of the nineteenth century reformers? The answer is that Luther never attempted a complete restoration of Apostolic Christianity. He never comprehended such a movement, which is made more evident by the fact that the Augsburg Confession contains doctrines and dogmas which are purely of Papal origin. Writing of Protestants generally,

---

[43]Schaff, *op. cit.*, p. 341.

Professor Briggs has well answered the question asked above when he says,

> The great initial movements by which the Christian church advanced in the combination of the variety of forces into harmonious operation, in every case gave way to reaction and decline, in which the various forces separated themselves, and some particular one prevailed. So it was in the seventeenth century after the Reformation. . . . The Scriptures once more became the slaves of dogmatic systems and ecclesiastical machinery, and were reduced to the menial service of furnishing proof texts to the foregone conclusions of polemic divines and ecclesiastics.[44]

Passing from the errors into which Protestants have fallen, Briggs goes on to discuss the work of Biblical theology in his day, now fifty years ago, in which summary by the Professor is recognized the very thing which was in the minds of the men associated with the nineteenth century reformation, which will become more evident as we continue. With the statement from Professor Briggs on the work of Biblical theology, applicable today, we leave the attitude of Martin Luther and his day to consider the attitude of two early American groups.   Mr. Briggs says,

> It (Biblical Theology) has a four-fold work: of removing the rubbish that Scholasticism has piled upon the Word of God; of battling with Rationalism for its principles, methods, and products; of resisting the seductions of Mysticism; and of building up an impregnable system of sacred truth.   As the Jews returning from their exile built the walls of Jerusalem, working with one hand, and with the other grasping a weapon, so must Biblical scholars build up the system of Biblical Theology, until they have erected a structure of Biblical

---

[44]Charles A. Briggs, *Biblical Study*, p. 371.

truth containing the unity in the variety of Divine Revelation, a structure compacted through the fitting together of all the gems of sacred truth according to the adaption of a divine prearrangement.[45]

3. *The Attitudes of Early American Congregationalists and Baptists.*

The Congregationalist Churches of New England grew out of the Pilgrim and Puritan movements of the early colonial period. Church government was the problem especially confronting the people of that period; wherefore they were most concerned about getting back to the Scriptural plan in this particular point. One of the most important Synods of those early churches was that which convened in Cambridge, in the years 1646-48. Out of this Synod came the "Cambridge Platform," called by Bacon the "Platform of Church Discipline Gathered out of the Word of God."[46] Their form of congregational church government was their most distinguishing characteristic, and in this they sought to get back to the New Testament plan.

In their earliest period Congregational churches possessed no formal confessions of faith. Those early congregations had what they called a "confession" or a "covenant." Barton writes:

. . . But the general habit of including a creed in the constitution of a Congregational church originated in the early part of the nineteenth century, when the Unitarian controversy sharply defined, and in some instances overemphasized, the lines of Christian dogma, dividing the adherents of that communion from their brethren in the historic Congregational churches.[47]

---

[45]*Ibid.*, p. 390.

[46]Leonard Woolsey Bacon, *The Congregationalists*, p. 65.

[47]William E. Barton, *Congregational Creeds and Covenants*, p. 9.

They later came to accept the Savoy and Westminster Confessions, of which Barton also writes:

> The Savoy Confession was practically identical with the Westminster standards, excepting as to church government. These two symbols were readily accepted for substance of doctrine in New England, partly because Congregationalists for the most part were Calvinists and essentially like-minded with Presbyterians, and with English Congregationalists, but none the less because they were ready to assent in general terms to almost any orthodox creed.[48] . . .

It was only in the matter of Congregational church government that the Congregational Churches of New England resembled the Reformers of the nineteenth century who came after them. It appears doubtful if they were affected to any marked degree by the movement so far to the southwest of them at that late date.

The religious bodies of the period touched most intimately by the new Reformation were the Baptist Churches. The Baptist Churches were congregational in their government, opposed to infant baptism and to affusion or aspersion as baptism. More will be said of the relation of the Reformers to these in later chapters. Their acceptance of the Scriptures as the standard of all their practices is stated by A. H. Newman, a Baptist historian, as follows:

> The Baptists of all parties have, from the beginning, persistently and consistently maintained the absolute supremacy of the canonical Scriptures as a norm of faith and practice. They have insisted on applying the Scripture test positively and negatively to every detail of doctrine and practice. It has never seemed to them sufficient to show that a doctrine or practice, made a matter of faith, is not contradictory of Scripture; it must be dis-

---

[48] Barton, *op. cit.*, p. 15.

tinctly a matter of Scripture precept or example to command their allegiance or secure from them a recognition of its right to exist.[49]

Standing on such a platform as this, it seems that when the Campbells came before the world with their position, "Where the Scriptures speak, we speak; and where the Scriptures are silent, we are silent," the two should have combined and gone along together in a most harmonious way. It is to be wondered at that they did not, but history reveals a deadly antagonism between the two groups from the earliest days of the Reformation. Mr. Newman offers his understanding of those things which hindered such a combining of forces when he says:

> ... A large proportion of the Baptists of the Southwest were so perverse in doctrine and so unamiable in spirit that milder and more evangelical types of Christianity were imperatively called for, and those who had once been repelled by the extravagances of so-called Baptists were more likely to be attracted by non-Baptist parties than by Baptists of a more evangelical type. It is probable, moreover, that if the Baptists of the Southwest had been thoroughly evangelical the secession under Alexander Campbell would never have occurred. A contemporary writer, in attempting to account for the prevalence of anti-missionary sentiment in Tennessee up to 1845, remarks: "Some of the prime friends of missions among the Baptists became converts of Mr. Alexander Campbell's system, and joined him. Thus missions became beyond measure odious." The spread, if not the rise, of the Disciples, as a sect, was undoubtedly due far more to the excrescences that had well-nigh destroyed the life of the Baptist denomination throughout extended regions than to anything inherent in the Baptist system;

---

[49]A. H. Newman, *A History of the Baptist Churches in the United States* (American Church History Series), pp. 1, 2.

and some of the erroneous features of the Disciples' system may have been a result of extreme reaction against the errors of unevangelical Baptists.[50]

Mr. Newman charges Baptists with having conformed themselves too rigidly to the Calvinistic theology, which made it possible for Alexander Campbell and those associated with him to find such a following among them.[51] Finding it impossible to work with the Baptists, many of the Baptists left their particular denomination to unite with the Reformers. Mr. Newman remarks further:

> . . . It is not improbable that the influence of this party (the Campbell movement) has been one among many causes that have led to the prevalence among Baptists of a more evangelical type of doctrine and the proper subordination of confessions of faith to Scripture.[52]

With this as a brief background of developed attitudes toward the Scriptures, and the efforts of bodies to get closer to the New Testament pattern of things, we pass to the movement of the nineteenth century, and the development of an attitude within the group known as "the Restoration Movement" of that particular period.

---

[50]Newman, *op. cit.*, pp. 440, 441.

[51]*Ibid.*, pp. 487, 494.

[52]Newman, *op. cit.*, p. 492.

CHAPTER II

"BACK TO THE OLD PATHS"

Jeremiah's charge to Israel in ancient times, "Stand ye in the ways and see, and ask for the old paths, where is the good way" (Jer. 6:16), seems to have been finding a new realization and fulfillment at the close of the eighteenth and beginning of the nineteenth centuries. General religious unrest was to be found on every hand. The people were standing "in the ways" and asking for "the old paths" as they sought to find "the good way" of the Scriptures. Popular sectarianism was becoming too narrow, bigoted and formal; reformers were springing up among nearly all religious bodies. A brief review of some of these will help the reader better to appreciate the attitude toward the Scriptures of the "Restoration Movement" as it began under the preaching of Barton W. Stone, the Campbells, Walter Scott and others.

1. *James O'Kelly, Methodist.*

Among the Methodists, James O'Kelly of North Carolina and Virginia raised a disturbance toward the close of the eighteenth century, resulting in the establishment of a faction which later called itself "The Christian Church." At the General Conference held in November, 1792, Mr.O'Kelly introduced a motion which would seriously affect the power of the episcopate, and which indirectly reflected on the administration of Bishop Asbury, the first Bishop of the Methodist Episcopal Church ordained in America. There was an effort to avoid the bill introduced by O'Kelly, but to no avail, as he was determined that if possible it should be passed. According to Stevens, a historian of the Methodists, the bill introduced read as follows:

. . . After the bishop appoints the preachers, at conference, to their several circuits, if any one thinks himself injured by the appointment he shall have liberty to appeal to the conference and state his objections; and if the conference approve his objections the bishop shall appoint him to another circuit.[1] . . .

The bill was defeated, and O'Kelly and the preachers influenced by him, who were also from Virginia, left the conference. However, the attitude of O'Kelly toward the episcopate was not the only thing held against him by his co-preachers of Methodism. As the humiliated preacher left the conference with those who stalked out with him, a Mr. Lee says, as quoted by Stevens, that he and a preacher standing with him watched O'Kelly and his company walking down the street, whereupon

. . . The preacher then informed me (said Lee) that O'Kelly denied the doctrine of the trinity, and preached against it, by saying that the Father, Son, and Holy Ghost were characters, and not persons; and that those characters all belonged to Jesus Christ. . . . The preacher further said, that it was his intention to have had O'Kelly tried at that conference for the false doctrines which he had been preaching.[2]

This charge, however, was never brought against him, as he withdrew from the conference when his bill was defeated.

After returning to his field of labor, O'Kelly later revolted against certain practices of the Methodist church, leaving it, to organize his associates into what he called "Republican Methodists."[3] The main point with O'Kelly and his group was the question of church government; who should

[1]Abel Stevens, *History of the Methodist Episcopal Church*, III, 21.
[2]*Ibid.*, p. 26
[3]*Ibid.*, p. 32.

govern the church, and in what manner should it be governed? However, the group finally came to the point of discarding anything the Discipline should say on the matter, determining to be governed by the New Testament. Stevens writes:

> In 1793 they held a conference in Mannakin Town, Virginia, the scene of a former dissentient Methodist Assembly, in the famous "Sacramental controversy." They there framed a constitution, and O'Kelly, as their leader, ordained their preachers. In 1801 they discarded their laws and title and assumed the name, "The Christian Church," renouncing all rules of Church government but the New Testament, as interpreted by every man for himself.[4]

According to W. E. MacClenny, biographer of James O'Kelly, a general meeting of the "Republican Methodist Church" was held August 4, 1794, at Lebanon Church, Surry County, Virginia.[5] The first and most important matter before them "was by what name they should be known to the world." With this, and other considerations demanding their attention, a committee of seven was appointed to work out something definite to bring before the whole body. Writing of the committee of seven, MacClenny says,

> Finally Rev. Rice Haggard stood up in the meeting with a copy of the New Testament in his hand and said: "Brethren, this is a sufficient rule of faith and practice, and by it we are told that the disciples were called *Christians,* and I move that henceforth and forever the followers of Christ be known as Christians simply." The motion was unanimously adopted, since which time they have had no other name for their organization.[6]

---

[4]Stevens, *op cit.,* p. 34.
[5]W. E. McClenny, *The Life of Rev. James O'Kelly,* pp. 114-115.
[6]*Ibid.,* p. 116.

The next matter of concern before the group was that of a creed; on this point, MacClenny continues, "Next a Rev. Mr. Hafferty, of North Carolina, moved to take the Bible itself as their only creed, and this, too, was carried, and has so remained to this day."[7]

These considerations were reported to the conference next day where they were passed upon and accepted. Five principles were adopted during the conference as the doctrinal foundation of the "Republicans." These were:

1. The Lord Jesus Christ is the only Head of the Church.
2. The name Christian to the exclusion of all party and sectarian names.
3. The Holy Bible, or the Scriptures of the Old and New Testaments our only creed, and a sufficient rule of faith and practice.
4. Christian character, or vital piety, the only test of church fellowship and membership.
5. The right of private judgment, and the liberty of conscience, the privilege and duty of all.[8]

From occurrences such as this, one realizes that tendencies to find the way "back to the Bible," to reject human creeds, and to wear the simple name "Christian" had been stirring religious action for a number of years before the Campbells came to America, and altogether independent of them. This incident from the history of O'Kelly is particularly interesting to this study, as Rice Haggard later became associated with Barton W. Stone. It was he who made the suggestion to Stone concerning the name "Christian." John Rogers, the biographer of Stone, says that within a year of the time that Stone and his group rejected the name "Springfield Presbytery" (June 28, 1804),

---

[7]MacClenny, *op cit.*, p. 117.
[8]*Ibid.*, pp. 121, 122.

. . . We took the name Christian—the name given to
the disciples by divine appointment first at Antioch. We
published a pamphlet on this name, written by Elder Rice
Haggard, who had lately united with us.[9]

Other than this, there seems to have been no connection
between the movement of Stone and that of O'Kelly, for
Stone had been preaching his doctrine of reformation some
time before Haggard united with him and his co-laborers.

2. *Elias Smith and Abner Jones, Baptists.*

Before considering the Stone movement in Kentucky, it
will be profitable to pay slight attention to a movement similar to that of O'Kelly which took place among the Baptists
of New England about the same time. The work of these
men in no way touched that of either O'Kelly or Stone, but
it reveals the temper of the times and the disposition to return
to the Bible. Elias Smith was ordained into the Baptist ministry in 1792, but W. E. Garrison says of him, that later, "He
abandoned Calvinism, adopted Universalism, which he immediately gave up again, and began anew to search the Scriptures. Presently he joined with Abner Jones in organizing at
Portsmouth, New Hampshire, a "Christian Church," and
withdrew from the Baptist fellowship. . . . He died in 1840
in the fellowship and ministry of the Christian denomination.
An unstable and in some respects unheroic character, he was
a pioneer not only in the wilderness of Vermont, but in the
effort to discover in the New Testament a program for simple
and undenominational Christianity."[10]

Abner Jones, who labored with Smith and who was no
doubt influenced by him, organized an independent church at
Lyndon, New Hampshire, in 1801, with others organized by
him later. Of him, Garrison writes, "Jones was ordained by

---

[9]John Rogers, *The Biography of Elder Barton Warren Stone*, p. 50.
[10]W. E. Garrison, *Religion Follows the Frontier*, p. 60. (See also
Robert Richardson, Memoirs, Book II, p. 186.)

three Freewill Baptist preachers, but not as a Baptist, simply as a Christian."[11] Here again is found that same spirit, the disposition to return to the simplicitiy of the New Testament order and to throw overboard party names and party creeds.

3. *Barton Warren Stone, Presbyterian.*

The most important counter-movement among religious bodies, as it affected the work of the Campbells, is that of Barton Warren Stone of Kentucky. Mr. Stone was born near Port-Tobacco, in the State of Maryland, December 24, 1772. Upon his graduation from an academy in Guilford, North Carolina, he was licensed to preach in the Presbyterian Church. It was not, however, until the fall of 1798 that Mr. Stone entered the ministry in earnest. At that time he received a call from the united congregations of Cane Ridge and Concord, Kentucky. It was with some misgivings, he tells us in his autobiography, that he appeared before the Presbytery of Transylvania for ordination, as he had some doubts about many of the things taught in the Confession of Faith. He was determined to accept the Confession only so far as it agreed with the word of God, committing himself no further than that. Of the occasion, Mr. Stone says,

> ... They (the Presbytery of Transylvania) asked me how far I was willing to receive the confession. I told them, as far as I saw it consistent with the word of God. They concluded that was sufficient.[12]

Whereupon this highly interesting character, destined to become the leader of no mean movement to lead people "back to the Bible," was ordained to preach as a minister of the Presbyterian Church.

In his biography (the first part of which is autobiographical) Mr. Stone tells us that he became wearied with

---

[11]W. E. Garrison, *op. cit.*, p. 61.

[12]Rogers, *op. cit.*, p. 29.

the doctrines of men, and constantly sought the guidance of the Bible. He found himself faced with insurmountable difficulties as he endeavored to call sinners to repentance, while the Confession taught that such was a work of God. He himself was in love with the souls of men, and would save all of them if he could. Surely, if he was so in love with them, God must be infinitely more so, he reasoned. He could not reconcile his own feelings and the word of God with the Calvinism of Presbyterianism. He says,

> From this state of perplexity I was relieved by the precious word of God. From reading and meditating upon it, I became convinced that God did love the whole world, and that the reason why he did not save all, was because of their unbelief; and that the reason why they believed not, was not because God did not exert his physical, almighty power in them to make them believe, but because they neglected and received not his testimony, given in the Word concerning his Son.[18]

This splendid reasoning was the beginning of the way out of confusion into the light of gospel truth.

It was during the "Great Revival" of 1801 that Stone began to break with the Presbyterians. The period was one of great religious enthusiasm and fervor, much of it reaching the stage of fanaticism. During this "Revival" Stone preached enthusiastically God's willingness to save sinners, and man's responsibility to act in that salvation. Shortly after this, in September, 1803, Stone and four friends withdrew from the Presbyterian synod, but not from the Presbyterian Church, forming what they called the "Springfield Presbytery."

Between the time of forming the Springfield Presbytery and its dissolution, June 28, 1804, Stone and his co-laborers wrote and published *The Apology of the Springfield Presbytery*. Stone says of it later:

---

[18]*Ibid.*, pp. 32, 33.

... In this book we stated our objections at length to the Presbyterian Confession of Faith, and against all authoritative confessions and creeds formed by fallible men. We expressed our total abandonment of all authoritative creeds, but the Bible alone, as the only rule of our faith and practice.[14] ...

In their effort to return to the apostolic church, taking the Bible as their only guide in matters of faith and practice, these men soon realized that their Springfield Presbytery had no more sanction in Scripture than did any other "presbytery" of its kind, or than did any of the peculiar tenets of the Presbyterian Church. Therefore, they resolved to disband the Presbytery, whereupon they met and drew up what they called "The Last Will and Testament of the Springfield Presbytery." A few extracts from this last named document will reveal the attitude of these reformers toward the Scriptures:

Imprimis. We *will,* that this body die, be dissolved, and sink into union with the Body of Christ at large; for there is but one body, and one Spirit, even as we are called in one hope of our calling.

Item. We *will,* that our power of making laws for the government of the church, and executing them by delegated authority, forever cease; that the people may have free course to the Bible, and adopt *the law of the Spirit of life in Christ Jesus.*

Item. We *will,* that candidates for the Gospel ministry henceforth study the Holy Scriptures with fervent prayer, and obtain license from God to preach the simple Gospel. . . .

Item. We *will,* that the people henceforth take the Bible as the only sure guide to heaven. . . .

"Rogers, *op. cit.,* p. 49.

Item. Finally we will, that all our *sister bodies* read their Bibles carefully, that they may see their fate there determined, and prepare for death before it is too late.[15]

The document was dated June 28, 1804, and was signed by Robert Marshall, John Dunlavy, Richard M'Nemar, B. W. Stone, John Thompson, and David Purviance, Witnesses.

This reveals a Restoration movement under way in Kentucky several years before Thomas Campbell sailed for America, which was wholly unknown to him. These people were calling themselves "Christians," rejecting human creeds and party names, and appealing only to the Bible for their guidance in faith and conduct. The subject of baptism came up during this period of revival and return to the Scriptures, which led Stone and many of his co-laborers to be immersed. Stone says of the matter:

The subject of baptism now engaged the attention of the people very generally, and some, with myself, began to conclude that it was ordained for the remission of sins, and ought to be administered in the name of Jesus to all believing penitents. . . . Into the spirit of the doctrine I was never fully led, until it was revived by Brother Alexander Campbell, some years later.[16]

Stone did not meet Alexander Campbell until 1824, although the two men had heard of each other for some years before that time. After meeting, a warm and mutual friendship developed between the two.[17] The uniting of the two bodies, that led by Stone and that led by Campbell, began in 1832,[18] resulting finally in the merging of nearly all congregations influenced by the reformatory efforts of these two men, so nearly in perfect agreement were the two groups,

---

[15]Rogers, *op. cit.,* pp. 51-53.

[16]Rogers, *op. cit.,* p. 61.

[17]*Ibid.,* p. 140.

[18]*Ibid.,* p. 141.

though completely independent of each other in their origin and development. This need not appear unnecessarily strange, though the two men were so different in disposition and background; for the harmony of views was simply the result of studying the same book, with the same desire to learn and do its bidding and to return in all things to the New Testament pattern.

4. *The Campbells, Thomas and Alexander, Seceders.*

Thomas Campbell was born in County Down, Ireland, February 1, 1763. His father was a member of the Church of England, but Thomas united with the Presbyterians, preferring the simpler worship of the Seceder Presbyterians and Covenanters to that of the Anglican communion. Mr. Campbell was serving as pastor of the Seceder Church at Ahorey, County Armagh, at a place called Rich-Hill, when Alexander was born. During this time he joined the "Society for Propagating the Gospel at Home," organized by the Haldanes; he felt that the religious need of the times was a union of all the people of God.

The Seceder Church, of which Thomas Campbell was a member, had been torn asunder in 1747 by political questions, into Burghers and Anti-Burghers. These two factions were bitter in their attitude toward each other, which condition was most painful to the kind and benign spirit of Mr. Campbell; such bigotry and narrowness had the effect of moving him to seek unity wherever he labored.

Among the religious bodies of Rich-Hill, where Mr. Campbell and his family resided, were the Independents, whose teaching had originated in Scotland with John Glas, who was deposed in 1730 for teaching that "there is no warrant in the New Testament of a national church," and that a National Covenant and Solemn League are without Scriptural authority. Mr. Glas rejected the accepted position of the Anglican Church, that laws pertaining to the church could be carried out by secular powers. He gathered about him a

ATTITUDES AND CONSEQUENCES

group of people who shared his views; in all his teaching he adopted the principle that the Scripture is the only standard of both doctrine and practice.

Among other things adopted by Mr. Glas was the weekly observance of the Lord's Supper, plurality of elders over each congregation, and community of goods, all of which he claimed to have derived from the primitive church. Mr. Glas was followed in his work by Robert Sandeman, his son-in-law; the followers of these two men were called Glassites or Sandemanians. While residing in Rich-Hill, Mr. Campbell and his family attended the services of this group, many of whose practices they incorporated in their work in America.[19]

Many other sects arose during the years, 1750 to 1800, sharing common ground on a number of similar points. Of them, Mr. Gates writes: "The features which they shared in common were independency in church government and a more strict adherence to the Scriptures in faith and practice." In the congregation of Independents attended by the Campbells were to be heard such men as J. A. Haldane, Rowland Hill, Alexander Carson, and John Walker. Writing of John Walker, Alexander Campbell declared in 1815: "I am now an Independent; of that faith and view of the gospel exhibited in John Walker's *Seven Letters to Alexander Knox,* and a Baptist so far as regards baptism."[20] In the midst of such religious surroundings, characterized both by an effort to return to the New Testament order of worship and practice, and by strife and division among those attempting to arrive at the teachings of the New Testament, the Campbells imbibed some of the attitudes later manifested so strongly in their religious movement in this country.

After spending several years teaching at Rich-Hill, in addition to his labors as "pastor" of a congregation there,

[19]Errett Gates, *The Disciples of Christ,* pp. 27-29.
[20]Gates, *op. cit.,* p. 31.

Mr. Campbell's health began to fail. Finally, after having been warned by his physician that he must make some change in his program of work, he was persuaded by his friends and son, Alexander, to seek health in America. On the first of April, 1807, Mr. Campbell, with a small company of friends bent on coming to the new world, bade farewell to his family and friends, as he set out for the port of embarkation. On the eighth of April he sailed for America, leaving forever his beloved native land.

Following the departure of his father for America in 1807, Alexander spent the term of 1808-09 as a student in Glasgow University, where, according to B. B. Tyler, he received his first impulse as a reformer. It was during his stay in Glasgow that Mr. Campbell met Greville Ewing, an intimate friend of the Haldane brothers, Robert and James Alexander. This acquaintance made with Mr. Ewing and others of like mind, while he was in school, had a marked effect upon the American Reformer in later years. Tyler quotes from a letter written by Mr. Campbell in 1835, in which he said,

"I am greatly indebted to all the Reformers, from Martin Luther down to John Wesley. I could not enumerate or particularize the individuals, living and dead, who have assisted in forming my mind. I am in some way indebted to some person or other for every idea I have on every subject. When I begin to think of my debt of thought, I see an immense crowd of claimants."[21]

Consequently, when, in 1809, Alexander Campbell sailed for America, accompanied by his mother and sisters, he was already imbued with the spirit of reformation, having become dissatisfied with Presbyterianism and Anglican doctrines and having met and heard many men in England and Ireland who were advocating such reforms as later characterized his own. When he reached America he found his father had

[21]B. B. Tyler, *History of the Disciples of Christ*, p. 43.

broken with the Presbyterians and that the "Declaration and Address" was just coming from the press. He was delighted with the document and found that it coincided with the views he had been forming and the decisions he had been making. Not long thereafter, the son resolved to devote his life to the promulgation of the principles set forth in the "Declaration and Address." From henceforth it should be father and son, united in a great crusade for unity and for the restoration of the Scriptures to their rightful place in the religion of Jesus Christ, with every effort at reform based on a "thus saith the Lord." This position rigidly followed would destine these two men to occupy a distinctly unique position among religious reformers, a position that would bring down upon them the wrath of the religious world of that day, as it would challenge the traditional positions, creeds, and doctrines of men formulated throughout the years. Such proved to be the result.

Shortly after his arrival in America in 1807, Mr. Campbell was called upon to visit a few members of the Seceder Church who were living in the Allegheny Mountains above Pittsburgh. A Mr. Wilson, a member of the same denomination, accompanied him on the journey. The special purpose of the visit among the scattered members was to spread the Lord's table that they might partake of the communion service, it being generally believed that an "ordained" person should preside over such worship. Out of the bigness and liberality of his great heart, and according to his conception of Scripture teaching, Mr. Campbell invited all those present at the service to partake of the supper, even those not in the Presbyterian communion. This being contrary to the Presbyterian principles of that day, Mr. Wilson considered it his duty to report to the Presbytery the "heresy" of the elder preacher. This resulted in the trial of Mr. Campbell before the Presbytery and finally before the Synod, where he was forced to enter into an agreement contrary to his liberal spirit. Looking upon this act of the Synod as one of narrowness and bigotry, which would restrict his preaching, he felt it would be impossible for him to continue laboring with the Presbyterians under such circumstances, whereupon he formally withdrew from them.

Withdrawing from the Presbyterian communion in no wise meant stopping his labors as a preacher. Such narrowness and prejudice as had been expressed by the Synod only fanned into a brighter fire the longing of his heart for peace and union among the religious people of his day. Mr. Campbell continued to preach regularly, attracting to himself an assembly of men and women, who like himself, yearned for a closer union of the children of God, where fellowship in Christ and freedom from such sectarian narrowness, could be enjoyed.

As these continued to meet, and Mr. Campbell continued to preach for them, there was a growing consciousness of the need for a clearer statement of their purpose and the end sought. Union based upon the Scriptures was the desire and aim of all, but there had been no definite statement formulated which would clarify their position in the minds of the people. The entire group deplored the bitter partisan and sectarian spirit existing among the various denominations, which spirit resulted from ignorance of the Word of God and the substitution of human traditions. Consequently a day of meeting was appointed in which there should be a discussion of the need, and a definite aim formulated.

On the day appointed the assembly met at the house of Abraham Altars, a man friendly to the group and its aims, but who was not a member of any church. Most of the number were members of some religious group, while a few, like Mr. Altars, were members of no party. All were intent on finding "the good way" of "the old paths," if such could be discovered. Mr. Campbell spoke at length upon the divided condition of Christendom and its attendant evils, upon the general unchristian spirit which characterized sects, and the desire and urgent need for unity among all professed

Christians. He emphasized the necessity of that unity's resting upon the Scriptures, and that it was their duty to urge a general reformation upon all religious bodies. But in that reformation they should be governed by the rule or principle that they had been following. As he neared the conclusion of his speech, Mr. Campbell is reported to have said, "That rule, my highly respected hearers, is this, that where the Scriptures speak, we speak; and where the Scriptures are silent, we are silent"—an expression which became the slogan of a movement destined to sweep the country and to exert an influence upon the religious thinking of a nation to a far greater extent than has been admitted by historians of the religious thought of America.

Mr. Richardson says, "Upon this annunciation a solemn silence pervaded the assembly. Never before had religious duty been presented to them in so simple a form." Henceforth they should be guided only by the word of God; it should be spoken faithfully, and opinions should be held in silence. Quoting Mr. Richardson again, he said of their attitude toward the Scriptures,

> "Thus the *silence* of the Bible was to be respected equally with its revelations, which were by divine authority declared to be able to 'make the man of God perfect and thoroughly furnished unto every good work.' Anything more, then, must be an encumbrance. Anything less than 'the whole counsel of God' would be a dangerous deficiency. Simply, reverentially, confidingly, they would speak of Bible things in Bible words, adding nothing thereto and omitting nothing given by inspiration.[22]

The rule was adopted unanimously by the assembly; however, questions were raised before they adjourned, among them that of infant baptism. Andrew Munro is reported to have said, "Mr. Campbell, if we adopt *that* as a basis, then

---

[22]Robert Richardson, *Memoirs of A. Campbell*, Book I, p. 237.

there is an end of infant baptism," whereupon Mr. Campbell replied, "Of course, if infant baptism be not found in Scripture, we can have nothing to do with it.[23]

Even though some may have sensed that such a rule would raise many questions, no one could have appreciated fully the far-reaching significance of what was done on that memorable occasion. Only time could reveal that. The significant point for our study is that an attitude had been definitely declared, an attitude that should go far toward finding the "good way" of "the old paths," for which so many were groping in those days.

[23]Robert Richardson, *op. cit.*, p. 238.

CHAPTER III

BIRTH OF THE RESTORATION MOVEMENT
(1809-1823)

1. *The "Declaration and Address."*

Mr. Richardson says of the occasion when Mr. Campbell uttered his famous Rule, "Where the Scriptures speak, we speak; where the Scriptures are silent, we are silent,"

> . . . It was from the moment when these significant words were uttered and accepted that the more intelligent ever afterward dated the *formal and actual commencement of the Reformation* which was subsequently carried on with so much success, and which has already produced such important changes in religious society over a large portion of the world.[1]

Immediately following this meeting, Mr. Campbell set himself to the task of drawing up what became the most important document of the movement, "A Declaration and Address." The object of the "Address" was to set before the public in a clear and definite declaration the object and purpose of the Association. It was not a "creed," the very thing from which Mr. Campbell was determined to escape, but it was simply a "declaration" of purposes and an "address" setting forth the ground on which these purposes should be attained. When the writing of the "Declaration and Address" was finished, Mr. Campbell called a special meeting of the chief members of the group and read it to them for their approval and adoption. The sentiments of the paper were unanimously agreed to, and it was at once ordered to be printed, September 7, 1809.

---

[1]Robert Richardson, *Memoirs of Alexander Campbell*, I, p. 237.

Thomas Campbell had no intention, and certainly no desire, to begin a new religious body when he penned the document for which he afterward became famous. He had a consuming passion for unity among professed followers of Christ, and it was his desire that such unity be effected among the people of that section as would lead to a more tolerant attitude by all religious groups, and develop a more Christ-like spirit among them. Motivated by this passion for unity, he was of the firm conviction "that the basis of that unity could be found nowhere 'but in Christ and His simple word.'" The will of Christ, as expressed in the Scriptures, should be the sole basis of such unity, regardless of the consequences such a position should have upon doctrinal conclusions formerly held. Mr. Campbell's conception of the will of Christ as revealed to man was, as has been well stated by W. E. Garrison:

> . . . first, that the will of Christ included the revelation and imposition of a definite doctrinal and ecclesiastical program. Second, that the Scriptures give an inerrant report of the teachings of Jesus and His apostles and the procedure of the church of the first century, so that any verse in the New Testament could be quoted with perfect assurance of its historical accuracy. . . . Third, that the teaching authority of Jesus had passed over undiminished to the apostles, so that both the injunctions and the examples of the apostles possessed complete authority over the church for all time, that their teachings were as the commands of God, and that the practice of the church of the apostolic age constituted a pattern which the church must permanently follow.[2]

A few extracts from the "Declaration and Address" clearly reveal these three positions. The entire document filled fifty-four closely written pages: the "Declaration" a little less than three, the "Address" eighteen, followed by an

---

[2]Winfred Ernest Garrison, *Religion Follows the Frontier,* pp. 95, 96.

Appendix and Postscript of thirty-three pages. In the last named, Mr. Campbell sought to forestall any misunderstanding of the things set forth in the first two parts by a lengthy explanation of the principles revealed in them.[3]

Having declared that every man must be measured by "The Divine Standard," and judged by God, the "Declaration" continued, "We are also of opinion that as the divine word is equally binding upon all so all lie under an equal obligation to be bound by it, and it alone; and not by any human interpretation of it." Human judgment was declared to violate the law of Christ; division and partyism were denounced, while the restoration of "unity, peace, and purity, to the whole church of God" were earnestly desired. However, they could reasonably expect to find this desired rest and peace nowhere "but in Christ and His simple word." It was further declared,

> . . . Our desire, therefore, for ourselves and our brethren would be, that rejecting human opinions and the inventions of men, as of any authority, or as having any place in the church of God, we might forever cease from farther contentions about such things; returning to, and holding fast by the original standard; taking the divine word alone for our rule; The Holy Spirit for our teacher and guide, to lead us into all truth; and Christ alone as exhibited in the word, for our salvation that, by so doing, we may be at peace among ourselves, follow peace with all men, and holiness, without which no man shall see the Lord.

Nine resolutions followed, in which it was stated that the Association had been formed "for the sole purpose of promoting simple evangelical christianity, free from all mixtures of human opinions and inventions of men." Each

---

[3]The following quotations are from the *Declaration and Address*, Centennial Edition, 1909; published by Centennial Bureau, 203 Bessell Block, Pittsburgh, Penn.

member should, "according to ability, cheerfully and liberally subscribe a certain specified sum" for the carrying on of the work of the Association. Other societies similar to this one should be organized. Resolution Four declared, "That this society by no means considers itself a church, nor does at all assume to itself the powers peculiar to such a society; nor do the members, as such, consider themselves as standing connected in that relation . . . but merely as voluntary advocates for church reformation." Since the promoting of simple evangelical christianity should be its objective, Resolution Five declared, the Association should support only such ministers "as reduce to practice that simple original form of christianity, expressly exhibited upon the sacred page; without attempting to inculcate anything of human authority, of private opinion, or inventions of men, as having any place in the constitution, faith, or worship, of the Christian church —or, anything, as matter of Christian faith, or duty, for which there cannot be expressly produced a thus saith the Lord either in express terms, or by approved precedent."

The remaining four resolutions pertained to the appointment of a standing committee to look after its various interests, the times of meeting throughout the year, the order of the meeting, and the support of the ministers of the Association. It was now clearly stated that the Association was not another church; its purpose was that of reformation and union of Christians on the basis of a "thus saith the Lord"; and its objective the restoration of peace and holiness, through Christ and His word, to the hearts of men everywhere.

The entire spirit of the Address which followed was one of love and humility, activated by love for men and for the word of God. Divisions were tearfully deplored; the word of God containing the promises of God was appealed to; peace and unity were prayed for. "With such encouragements as these (promises of God), what should deter us from the heavenly enterprise; or render hopeless the attempt, of accomplishing, in due time, an entire union of all the churches in faith and practice, according to the word of God," was the spirit of the Address. Mr. Campbell believed that it was only necessary to come before the world with such an appeal as he was making through the Association to accomplish the end sought. The cause was not peculiar to themselves; it was not a party cause; "it is a common cause, the cause of Christ and our brethren of all denominations." Further, because it was God's will that all should be one, he felt that union should be easily persuaded. Only one thing was necessary, the adopting of the New Testament pattern, and this they were determined to do. Said he,

> Dearly beloved brethren, why should *we* deem it a thing incredible that the church of Christ, in this highly favored country, should resume that original unity, peace and purity, which belongs to its constitution, and constitutes its glory? Or, is there anything that can be justly deemed necessary for this desirable purpose, but to conform to the model, and adopt the practice of the primitive church, expressly exhibited in the New Testament? Whatever alterations this might produce in any or all of the churches, should, we think, neither be deemed inadmissible nor ineligible. Surely such alteration would be every way for the better, and not for the worst; unless we should suppose the divinely inspired rule to be faulty, or defective. Were we, then, in our church constitution and managements, to exhibit a complete conformity to the Apostolick church, would we not be in that respect, as perfect as Christ intended we should be? And should not this suffice us?

Mr. Campbell believed that all professed Christians who truly loved the Lord and sought to do His will would readily subscribe to such a program of religious conduct. "Who," he asks, "would not willingly conform to the original pattern laid down in the New Testament, for *this* happy purpose?" Admitting that he and his brethren, as well as others about them, had their educational prejudices and peculiar customs, he continued, "But this we do sincerely declare, that there is nothing we have hitherto received as matter of faith or practice, which is not expressly taught and enjoined in the word of God, either in express terms, or approved precedent, that we would not heartily relinquish, that so we might return to the original constitutional unity of the Christian church; and in happy unity, enjoy full communion with all our brethren, in peace and charity." Surely, such an attitude and platform advocated, should have accomplished the end sought; if not, can human wisdom devise another? It must be admitted that this attitude toward the Scriptures and toward the unity for which Jesus had prayed, was unique in its difference from those advocated by other reformers.

In explaining his meaning of certain statements in the "Address" Mr. Campbell said in the Appendix of this statement of relinquishment, "By the proposed relinquishment, we are to be understood, in the first instance, of our manner of holding those things, and not simply of the things themselves: for no man can relinquish his opinions or practices, till once convinced that they are wrong; and this he may not be immediately, even supposing they are so. One thing, however, he may do, when not bound by an express command, he need not impose them upon others, by any wise requiring their approbation; and when this is done, the things, to them, are as good as dead; yea, as good as buried, too; being thus removed out of the way." So, in the policy advocated, one could hold an opinion so long as it was an opinion, but could not attempt to force it upon others, and when convinced that it is an opinion contrary to Scripture teaching, he should willingly give it up. He said further, "And here let it be noted, that it is not the renunciation of an opinion or practice as sinful, that is proposed or intended; but merely a cessation from the publishing or preaching of it, so as to give offense. . . . Neither is there here any clashing of duties, as if to forbear was a sin, and also to practice was a sin; the thing to be forborne being a matter of private opinion, which, though not expressly forbidden, yet are we, by no means, expressly commanded to practice,—Whereas we are expressly commanded to endeavor to maintain the unity of the spirit in the bond of peace." It was at this point that trouble came in later years, and contention and debate waxed warm, which shall be properly considered in due time.

It was the specific policy and general agreement of the "Address" that nothing should be binding upon the Society for which there cannot be expressly produced a "Thus saith the Lord," either in express terms or by approved precedent. And in no wise should the propositions of the "Address" become a creed, or function as such. This also was emphasized:

Let none imagine that the subjoined propositions are at all intended as an overture towards a new creed, or standard, for the church, or, as in any wise designed to be made a term of communion;—nothing can be farther from our intention. They are merely designed for opening up the way, that we may come fairly and firmly to original grounds upon clear and certain premises; and take up things just as the Apostles left them.—That thus disentangled from the accruing embarrassments of intervening ages, we may stand with evidence upon the same ground on which the church stood at the beginning. . . .

With this denial of any relation to a creed, the "Address" continued by submitting thirteen propositions; all of them are interesting and instructive, but since only four of them deal directly upon the theme before us, the development of an attitude, these four Propositions, 3, 4, 5 and 6, are here inserted:

3. . . . nothing ought to be inculcated upon christians as articles of faith; nor required of them as terms of communion; but what is expressly taught and enjoined upon them, in the word of God. Nor ought any thing be

admitted, as of divine obligation, in their church constitution and managements, but what is expressly enjoined by the authority of our Lord Jesus Christ and his Apostles upon the New Testament church; either in expressed terms, or by approved precedent.

4. That although the scriptures of the Old and New Testament are inseparably connected, making together but one perfect and entire revelation of the Divine will, for the edification and salvation of the church; and therefor in that respect cannot be separated; yet as to what directly and properly belongs to their immediate object, the New Testament is as perfect a constitution for the worship, discipline and government of the New Testament church, and as perfect a rule for the particular duties of its members; as the Old Testament was for the worship discipline and government of the Old Testament church, and the particular duties of its members.

5. That with respect to the commands and ordinances of our Lord Jesus Christ, where the scriptures are silent, as to the express time or manner of performance, if any such there be; no human authority has power to interfere, in order to supply the supposed deficiency, by making laws for the church; nor can any thing more be required of christians in such cases, but only that they *so* observe these commands and ordinances, as will evidently answer the declared and obvious end of their institution. Much less has any human authority power to impose new commands or ordinances upon the church, which our Lord Jesus Christ has not enjoined. Nothing ought to be received into the faith or worship of the church; or be made a term of communion amongst christians, that is not as old as the New Testament.

6. That although inferences and deductions from scripture premises, when fairly inferred, may be truly called the doctrine of God's holy word: yet are they not formally binding upon the consciences of christians far-

ther than they perceive the connection, and evidently see that they are so; for their faith must not stand in the wisdom of men; but in the power and veracity of God— therefore no such deduction can be made terms of communion, but do properly belong to the after and progressive edification of the church. Hence it is evident that no such deductions or inferential truths ought to have any place in the church's confession.

Although Mr. Campbell believed that unity could and would be attained to a considerable degree upon such a platform as he was advocating, he himself was definitely committed to the side of truth rather than popularity, if none should accept it. The strength of their appeal should rest in its truth and soundness. "It is not the voice of the multitude," said he, "but the voice of truth, that has power with the conscience—that can produce a rational conviction, and acceptable obedience. A conscience that awaits the decision of the multitude, that hangs in suspense for the casting vote of the majority, is a fit subject for the man of sin." He concluded, as he drew toward the close of the "Address," "For if holding fast in profession and practice whatever is expressly revealed and enjoined in the divine standard does not under the promised influence of the divine spirit, prove an adequate basis for promoting and maintaining unity, peace and purity, we utterly despair of attaining those invaluable privileges, by adopting the standard of any party. To advocate the cause of unity while espousing the interests of a party would appear as absurd, as for this country to take part with either of the belligerents in the present awful struggle, which has convulsed and is convulsing the nations, in order to maintain her neutrality and secure her peace." A complete re-statement of the principles advocated by Thomas Campbell in the "Declaration and Address" is not amiss in the present time, although nearly one hundred forty years have elapsed since the penning of that memorable document.

Thus it was proposed that the union of professed followers of Christ be formed upon the ground, not of fallible human leadership or human dictation, but upon the original ground of Apostolic authority and Divine leadership. That Divine leadership must be found in the Scriptures, and union must be realized by the complete submission of all Christians to that authority and to it alone, while "longsuffering" and "forbearance" should be practiced by each toward his fellow-Christian.

Mr. Gates, in viewing the background of Thomas and Alexander Campbell and the spirit of the elder Campbell toward division and toward unity, was able to say of the "Declaration and Address," "It was forged out of the experience and charged with the spirit of Thomas Campbell. It is free from bitterness or vindictiveness, but is passionate with the eloquence of one who had felt all the misery and meanness of sectarianism."[4] It proved to be the greatest contribution made by Thomas Campbell to the movement which he inaugurated. Professor Garrison says,

> After the "Declaration and Address," Thomas Campbell never wrote a line, delivered a speech, or made a decision which had any marked effect on the faith or fortunes of the movement which he had started. But the production of that document was, under the circumstances, a sufficient title to gratitude and fame.[5]

The attitude toward the Scriptures set forth in the "Declaration and Address" was the attitude held by the two Reformers, Thomas and Alexander Campbell, throughout the period of their labors. Mr. Richardson says of Thomas Campbell:

> . . . It was his conviction that, if men would adopt the Bible as the only standard of religious truth, and

---

[4] Errett Gates, *The Disciples of Christ*, p. 45.
[5] W. E. Garrison, *Religion Follows the Frontier*, p. 88.

accept the meaning of words as determined simply by the rules of language, its true sense would be sufficiently obvious, and there would be universal agreement in relation to the things which it revealed.[6]

Not only was this true of Mr. Campbell, but it was also the conviction of all united with him in the movement: *with them, a simple appeal to Scripture was regarded as decisive in relation to every matter on which it treated.* Quoting a statement made by Alexander Campbell years after the movement was launched, Mr. Richardson writes:

"The Bible alone," said he, "must always decide every question involving the nature, the character or the designs of the Christian institution. Outside of the apostolic canon, there is not, as it appears to me, one solid foot of terra firma on which to raise the superstructure ecclesiastic."[7]

The newly organized "Christian Association of Washington" was made up of individuals who had been attracted to Mr. Campbell by his earnestness, piety, and consecration to the principles taught in the Scriptures. Motivated by an intense desire to bring unity among the people of God, the little group launched out upon an uncharted sea, trusting the providence of God and the light from His word to guide them. Mr. Richardson, the biographer of Alexander Campbell, sums up the position of the Christian Association and its attitude toward the Scriptures, when he says:

. . . It trusted to the Bible, therefore, and to the Bible alone, as furnishing the entire plan and all the necessary specifications of the Divine Architect, and, though delayed and hindered by the necessity of removing often the accumulated rubbish of human speculations, it steadily

---

[6]Richardson, *op. cit.*, Book II, p. 11.
[7]*Ibid.*, p. 495.

pursued its original design, until it succeeded at length in developing the entire structure of primitive Christianity.[8]

2. Union With the Baptists.

Because many of the members of the Association lived in the valley of Brush Run, about two miles above its junction with Buffalo Creek, a meeting-house was erected there in 1810. In the summer of 1811 it was decided that the congregation should organize themselves into an independent church because of continued hostilities to the Association by different religious parties. Mr. Richardson says, "It was with great reluctance that he (Thomas Campbell) finally concluded to take this step, and to separate himself from those whom he desired to recognize as brethren."[9] In organizing a church from the members of the Association, Thomas Campbell was appointed elder, four men were chosen deacons, and Alexander was licensed to preach the gospel.

Not only did the adoption of such an attitude as that expressed in the "Declaration and Address," and subscribed to by the members of the Association, bring the reformers into violent conflict with the religious parties of the day, but it also brought them into conflict with positions which they themselves formerly held; among the first questions to arise was that of baptism. Having been reared in the environment of Presbyterianism and in accordance with its teachings, none of the Campbell family had been immersed. By a diligent study of the Scriptures, Alexander soon realized that he had not been baptized scripturally. This led to the baptism of Alexander and his wife, his father, mother and sister, Dorothea, along with two others, Mr. and Mrs. Hanen, on June 12, 1812, upon a simple confession of their faith in Jesus as the Christ the Son of God. This became a very important

---

[8]Richardson, *op. cit.*, p. 350 (Book I).
[9]*Ibid.*, p. 365.

event in the work of the two men, as observed by Mr. Jennings, who writes:

> The importance of this baptismal service is hard to overestimate. It reversed the position of father and son. Up to June 12, 1812, the father had been the leader. He had penned the *Declaration and Address*, to whose principles the son had given allegiance; he had led in the organization of the Brush Run church. The son, however, was the first to recognize the place of baptism, and from that time became the real leader. He was the right man in the right place.[10]

At the next meeting of the Brush Run church, thirteen others followed the example of the seven who had been immersed the week before. It was not long until others had followed the examples of these, and practically the entire congregation was made up of immersed believers. In this two things impress one: progress was being made in the direction of reformation and restoration, while leadership was gradually passing from father to son. Appeal to the authority of Scripture continued to be a paramount issue with the leaders and group; every step was slow and guarded, based on a "thus saith the Lord."

Inasmuch as the desire for unity had given impetus to the movement, it seemed out of harmony with such a program and appeal to continue existing as an association separate from any other group, as there was danger of becoming another denomination among denominations. The position of the Brush Run church on the action of baptism had brought them into favor with the Baptists of that section, although there was a very fundamental difference in the opinions of the two groups as to the purpose of baptism. Because of these two circumstances, the fear of becoming a "denomination" should they remain to themselves, and the

---

[10]W. W. Jennings, *Origin and Early History of the Disciples of Christ*, p. 94.

favor they had gained with the Baptists, the question of union with the Baptists was laid before the Brush Run church in the fall of 1813. It was agreed that a petition should be made to the Redstone Association of Baptist Churches for admission, but with the following provision:

> . . . Provided always that we should be allowed to teach and preach whatever we learned from the Holy Scriptures, regardless of any human creed or formula in Christendom.[11]

On these conditions the Brush Run church was admitted into the Redstone Association of Baptist Churches. The attitude of the Campbells toward their own liberty of teaching under the guidance of the Scriptures is the really significant thing in the terms of this union. Already they had begun to shift the emphasis from the obligation of Christian union to the authority of primitive Christianity, whether or not they were conscious of this shift.

Such a union could be neither successful nor happy, as there were too many differences between the Brush Run congregation and the Baptist Association. Difference existed and continued to grow more pronounced with respect to the Lord's Supper, the authority of the Old and New Covenants for Christians, the meaning and value of ordination, baptism, and the conceptions of faith held by the two groups. Because of the unpleasantness of the union over these differences and the break that finally came between the groups, it is sometimes charged that the Campbells were expelled from the Baptist Association. This charge, however, is false. Mr. Tyler says:

> The Campbells were never expelled from any Baptist church nor from any association of Baptist churches. In the course of time life in the Redstone Association became so unpleasant that they voluntarily

---

[11]Errett Gates, *op. cit.*, p. 94.

entered the Mahoning Association. In 1827 this Association adjourned, as such, *sine die,* the majority believing that there is no warrant in Scripture for such organization of churches.[12]

3. *The Development of an Attitude.*

Throughout the years 1809 to 1823, "primitive Christianity" and what it means to "speak where the Scriptures
speak, and to keep silent where the Scriptures are silent,"
were undergoing a process of definition. This definition,
as has been mentioned, could not but lead to an inevitable
break with the Baptists, and result in a wider breach between the Reformers and other religious bodies. The two
Campbells were coming more and more to realize that
union among the religious bodies of that time was a hopeless task and must be postponed until their faith and practice
should be made conformable to the Divine Standard.

It shall be our purpose, not to give a detailed history
of the movement launched by Mr. Campbell and "The Christian Association of Washington," but to follow the attitude
which grew out of the slogan, and to examine some of the
trials which followed. As the plea for New Testament
precedent was advocated with growing zeal and enthusiasm,
and men came to realize more fully the changes such a plea
would necessitate as they turned from the sectarianism of
the day to the New Testament pattern, the sentiment gradually transferred itself from "union" to "restoration"—the
restoration of the ancient order of things.

From the beginning the disciples of the new movement
have passed through periods of controversy. At first it was
controversy with their religious neighbors, which resulted
in adding converts to the new movement. But as the body
of believers grew, and social customs changed, there appeared those who believed that in its method of working,

---

[12]B. B. Tyler, *History of the Disciples of Christ,* p. 70.

the church should adapt itself to the changing conditions of the times. Others continued to hold to the original attitude that the New Testament reveals a fixed pattern for the church of all time, and that it is the business of disciples of Christ to hold to that pattern, regardless of consequences. With these two attitudes developing, one holding to a rigid interpretation of Thomas Campbell's famous slogan, and the other to a liberal interpretation of its sentiments, conflicts were inevitable. It is with these two attitudes which ultimately led to division, that we specially concern ourselves in this work.

Chapter IV

EARLY YEARS OF THE REFORMATION
(1823-1829)

1. *From Union to Restoration.*

By 1823 the Reformation was definitely under way. Alexander Campbell's famous *Sermon on the Law,* delivered in 1816, had caused much dissatisfaction and prejudice toward him among the Baptists. By the year 1823, it had been printed for distribution, giving grounds among the Baptists for charges of heresy against him. The same year he and thirty-one others had asked to be dismissed from the Brush Run church in order to organize a congregation at Wellsburg. The purpose behind this move had been to get out of the Redstone Association before being expelled for heresy. The Wellsburg congregation then joined the Mahoning Association, which was later dissolved for lack of Scriptural authority for its existence.

This was the year in which Alexander Campbell met Mr. McCalla of Kentucky, a Presbyterian, in debate, having already gained some recognition as a debater in his debate with Mr. Walker in 1820. In this year also, 1823, Mr. Campbell began the publication of a monthly magazine which he called *The Christian Baptist.* Mr. Campbell stated the purpose of the new publication in the Preface to the first edition. "We now commence a periodical paper," he wrote, "pledged to no religious sect in Christendom, the express and avowed object of which is the eviction of truth and the exposure of error." The design of the new paper should be that "of maintaining the Apostles' doctrine only, in opposition to every system, how specious soever." In coming out of the errors of the sectarianism of that day, he declared, "We have learned one lesson of great importance in the pursuit of truth; one that acts as a pioneer to prepare the way of knowledge—one that cannot be adopted and acted upon, but the result must be salutary. It is this: Never to hold any sentiment or proposition as more certain than the evidence on which it rests; or, in other words, that our assent to any proposition should be precisely proportioned to the evidence on which it rests." This evidence, in the words of Mr. Campbell, should be "the most satisfactory evidence from reason and revelation." In the Original Dedication of the new periodical, the editor wrote:

> To all those, without distinction, who acknowledge the Scriptures of the Old and New Testaments to be a Revelation from God; and the New Testament as containing the Religion of JESUS CHRIST: Who, willing to have all religious tenets and practices tried by the Divine Word; and who feeling themselves in duty bound to search the Scriptures for themselves, in all matters of Religion, are disposed to reject all doctrines and commandments of men, and to obey the truth, holding fast the faith once delivered to the Saints—this work is most respectfully and affectionately dedicated by The Editor.

The thing that strikes the reader most forcefully in this new program of action is the complete absence of all reference to Christian union. No mention of that original purpose is found. The emphasis now rested upon the principle of scriptural authority and primitive precept and example. It was now to be restoration, not union. Beginning with the February 7, 1825, edition, and concluding with the September 7, 1829, edition, there appeared thirty-two articles entitled "The Ancient Order of Things," which completed the fixed definition and essential elements of primitive Christianity for those who attached themselves to the new reformation.

Publication of *The Christian Baptist* continued for seven years; it proved to be a powerful instrument in the hands of such an able editor as Mr. Campbell. He was an iconoclast of the first rank. Possessing a fervent love for the truth, a giant intellect, and a moral courage that feared no opposition, coupled with studious habits and a wide range of information, the new leader threw himself into the task of reformation with all his great soul and strength. With a definite attitude now developed, the aim was not a union of warring factions, but a "restoration" of primitive Christianity as revealed in the Scriptures. From henceforth this was to be the goal and objective of the movement.

2. *Creeds and the Scriptures.*

In restoring that from which the church had departed, Mr. Campbell recognized that those things which had been substituted for the practices of apostolic days must go. Hence, in his series of articles on "The Ancient Order of Things," he waged a vigorous and unrelenting campaign against the creeds of the day which, in his opinion, stood in the way of the union which he and his father had urged and which hindered an understanding of the simple truths of the Scriptures. With him, there was to be the waging of an uncompromising war between the Scriptures and creeds. On the subject, he wrote:

> But a restoration of the ancient order of things, it appears, is all that is contemplated by the wise disciples of the Lord; as it is agreed that this is all that is wanting to the perfection, happiness, and glory of the Christian community. . . . Now, in attempting to accomplish this, it must be observed, that it belongs to every individual and to every congregation of individuals to discard from their faith and their practice every thing that is not found written in the New Testament of the Lord and Saviour, and to believe and practice whatever is

there enjoined. This done, and every thing is done which ought to be done.

But to come to the things to be discarded, we observe that, in the ancient order of things, there were no creeds or compilations of doctrine in abstract terms, nor in other terms than the terms adopted by the Holy Spirit in the New Testament. Therefore all such are to be discarded.[1]

Mr. Campbell not only condemned and renounced creeds, but his denunciation of those who would advocate creeds as contributing to any good in religious life, was with equal vigor:

. . . He that advocates the necessity of creeds of human contrivance to the unity of the church unconsciously impeaches the wisdom of God, arraigns the benevolence of the Saviour, and censures the revelation of the Spirit.[2]

With Mr. Campbell it was not a matter of subscribing to the opinions of divines, or of creeds, but Christianity rested upon the confession of faith in a fact, the fact that Jesus is the Christ; this fact, Mr. Campbell believed, is fully revealed in the New Testament, the complete constitution of the kingdom of Christ. On this point he wrote:

But the constitution of the kingdom of the Saviour is the New Testament, and this alone is adapted to the existence of his kingdom in the world. *To restore the ancient order of things* this must be recognized as the only constitution of this kingdom, and in receiving citizens they must be received into the kingdom, just as if they were received by the apostles into it, when they were in the employment of setting it up.[3]

---

[1] Alexander Campbell, "The Ancient Order of Things," *The Christian Baptist*, II, 133.

[2] *Ibid.*, p. 136.

[3] Campbell, *op. cit.*, p. 140.

Mr. Campbell never veered from this position on the futility of creeds and the all-sufficiency of the Scriptures. In writing on the "Foundation of Christian Union," published in 1835, he declared:

> Let the Bible be substituted for all human creeds; Facts, for definitions; Things, for words; Faith, for speculation; Unity of Faith, for unity of opinion; The Positive Commandments of God, for human legislation and tradition; Piety, for ceremony; Morality, for partisan zeal; The Practice of Religion, for the mere profession of it; and the work is done.[4]

In his debate with N. L. Rice, held at Lexington, Kentucky, November 15 to December 1, 1843, one of the propositions affirmed by Mr. Campbell was, "Human Creeds, as Bonds of Union and Communion, Are Necessarily Heretical and Schismatical." One of the sharpest and most caustic statements ever made by the great reformer and debater was in reply to the charge by Mr. Rice that his "Christian System" was used by Campbell's associates as a creed, when he said:

> He that does not, or cannot, appreciate the difference between making a doctrinal standard, to measure candidates for admission into Christian churches, and a book explanatory of our views of anything in the Bible, or out of it, is not to be reasoned with on any subject[5]

This unrelenting warfare against creeds continued to gain force as others turned from sectarianism to aid in the restoration of the New Testament to its proper place in the Christian religion. The creeds of men had been largely substituted for the Scriptures, confusing the minds of men and contributing to the sectarian spirit of that period.

---

[4]Campbell, *The Christian System,* p. 117.
[5]Campbell-Rice Debate, p. 783.

Today, when so few even among the denominations believe the creeds to which their churches have subscribed, it is difficult for one to appreciate fully the actual barrier they presented to the truth. The men of the new reformation recognized the necessity of their abolition before the Word of God could do its work in the hearts of men. Therefore they were unrelenting in their efforts against them.

3. *The Clergy and the Scriptures.*

At no point was Mr. Campbell more vehement in those early years than in his condemnation of what he called "the clergy." In a series of articles appearing in the early issues of *The Christian Baptist,* he conducted a withering attack against the institution as un-scriptural and anti-scriptural. When one comprehends the ignorance of the average preacher in that day, the domineering attitude they assumed toward those under their influence, and their narrowness and bigotry, he can better appreciate the things said and written by Campbell on the subject.

The first article of the series condemned the claim of the clergy to a special call from God on the ground that when God calls a man to a work, He qualifies him for that work; the men of today who claim such a special call from God are not supernaturally qualified for the work; therefore, the call is not a special call from God, he reasoned. This he claimed on the ground of New Testament teaching. Mr. Campbell contended also that a claim to a special or divine call leads men to arrogate to themselves power which God has not given them over the consciences of men.[6]

In the articles of the series following this, Mr. Campbell exposed many of the abuses by the clergy of that day, supporting his opposition to the distinction between "clergy" and "laity" on the ground that such distinctions are not only without Scriptural warrant, but that they are condemned

---

[6]Campbell, "The Clergy," *The Christian Baptist,* p. 19.

in the Scriptures. His opposition was on the ground that the Scriptures should guide in such matters and that they were wholly against the practices of the day. He contended that many of the ills in the various parties could be traced to the abuses of the clergy in arrogating to themselves authority and prestige not theirs by divine right, and that money plays too large a part in the "divine call" from one work to another, which call ministers often claimed to have received from God, when in reality the voice of additional remuneration was the real factor. Campbell further charged that forms of clerical church government were usually patterned after and according to the civil government under which they originated, rather than after the Scriptural plan. He recognized no church head or church government other than Jesus Christ as absolute monarch.[7]

"We conclude," wrote Mr. Campbell, "that one of those means used to exalt the clergy to dominion over the faith, over the consciences, and over the persons of men, by teaching the people to consider them as specially called and moved by the Holy Spirit, and sent to assume the office of ambassadors of Christ, or ministers of the Christian religion, is a scheme unwarranted by God, founded on pride, ignorance, ambition, and impiety; and, as such, ought to be opposed and exposed by all them that love our Lord Jesus Christ in sincerity."[8]

Campbell was not opposed to an educated ministry, nor did he put a premium on ignorance, as might have been charged by some because of his position on "the clergy." Many of the men associated with him were men of good education, who approached the religious problems of the

---

[7]Campbell, "The Clergy," *op. cit.,* November 3, 1823, December 1, 1823, January 5, 1824, February 2, 1824, August 3, 1823, and July 4, 1825.
[8]*Ibid.,* p. 21.

day in a scholarly manner. It was not to education that he was opposed; he was opposed to *the clergy!* In the January 5, 1824, issue of *The Christian Baptist* Mr. Campbell wrote a very satirical presentation of the education of a young clergyman, from the beginning of his preparation to his final "marriage" to a church, subject always to a call from another congregation of greater power and influence, offering greater pay. On the point that he was opposed to the education of preachers, Mr. Campbell raises the question as presented by an objector, "Must our clergy, then, be ignorant and unlettered men?" "Is ignorance the mother of devotion?" Having introduced the two questions, he entered into a warm discussion of the subject, deploring the tragedies of ignorance, to return to the question, saying:

. . . But to answer the above objector I would say, Let us have no clergy at all, learned or unlearned—let us have bishops and deacons, such as Paul appoints, such as he has described in 1 Timothy 3:1-14; Titus 1:5-9.*

One of the most satirical articles which came from the pen of the versatile editor was entitled, "The Third Epistle of Peter, to the Preachers and Rulers of Congregations—A Looking Glass for the Clergy." The article was purely a satire, written in the form of an unpublished epistle, as if it had just come to light. It contains many fine points worth the thought of "the clergy" and "gospel preachers" of today It is here given for the profit of present-day readers who may have heretofore overlooked it, and for whatever good it may do in this particular age. It definitely expresses an attitude worth keeping before preachers of each generation.

One of the best proofs that a prophecy is what it purports to be, is its exact fulfilment. If this rule be adopted in relation to the "Third Epistle of Peter,"

The Christian Baptist, p. 36.

there can be no doubt that it was written in the true spirit of prophecy. We thought it worthy of being preserved, and have therefore given it a place in this work.

How the following epistle came to be overlooked by the early saints of christendom and by all the fathers, or whether it was purposely suppressed by the Council of Nice, and why it was at last destined to be found with other old manuscripts among the ruins of an ancient city by a miserable wandering Monk, are all circumstances which my limited knowledge of these subjects does not enable me to explain.

I am answerable only for the accuracy of the translation from a French copy presented by the Monk himself. Neither can I prove the authenticity of the original, unless it be on the strict correspondence of the actual state of the church with the injunctions contained in the epistle, a correspondence which seems to hold with as much veracity as that which is found in the fulfilment of any prophecy with the prediction itself.—Translator.

CHAPTER I

THE STYLE AND MANNER OF LIVING

Now you who are called and chosen to go forth to all nations and among all people, in time present and time to come, to preach the word, see you take to yourselves marks, nay, many outward marks, whereby you shall be known by men.

Be you not called as men are called; but be you called Pope, Archbishop, Archdeacon, or Divine, or Reverend, and Right Reverend, or some like holy name; so may you show forth your honor and your calling.

And let your dwelling places be houses of splendor and edifices of cost; and let your doors be decked with plates of brass, and let your names, even your reverend titles be graven thereon; so shall it be as a sign.

Let your garments in which you minister be garments not as the garments of men, neither let them be
"seamless garments woven, throughout"; but let them
be robes of richest silk and robes of fine linen, of
curious device and of costly workmanship; and have
you robes of black and robes of white, that you may
change the one for the other; so shall you show forth
your wisdom and humility. Let your fare be sump-
tuous, not plain and frugal as the fare of the husband-
man who tills the ground; but live you on the fat of
the land, taking "good heed for the morrow and where-
withal you shall be fed."

And drink you of the vines of the vintage brought
from afar, and wines of great price; then shall the
light of your *spirits* be the light of your *countenances,*
and your faces shall be bright, even as the morning
sun shall your faces glow in brightness; thus shall you
show forth your moderation and your temperance in
all things.

Let the houses in which you preach be called
churches, and let them be built in manner of great orna-
ment without, and adorned with much cost within; with
rich pillars and paints, and with fine altars and pedes-
tals, and urns of precious stones, and cloths and velvet
of scarlet, and vessels of silver.

And let there be rooms for the changing of robes,
and places for the precious metals and mitres.

And let the houses be divided into seats for the
congregation, and let every man know his own seat;
and let the first seats in front of the altar be for the
rich that pay by thousands; and the next for the poorer
that pay by hundreds; and the last for those that pay
by tens. And let the poor man sit behind the door.

And let the seats be garnished with cushions and
crimson cloth, and with fine velvet; for if the houses
of players and vain people who deal in idle sayings and

shows of mockery, be rich and gorgeous, how much more so should be the houses that are dedicated to Him "that is meek and lowly of spirit."

Chapter II

The Choosing of Ministers

When you go out to choose holy ones to be of your brethren, and to minister at the altar, choose you from among the youth, even those whose judgments are not yet ripe, and whose hearts know not yet whether they incline to God or Mammon.

But you are wise, and you shall know the inclining of their future spirits, and you shall make them incline to the good things which the church has in store for them that are called, even those that shall be called by you.

Then shall you have taught exceeding many things. They shall not be as "ignorant fishermen," or husbandmen, or men speaking one tongue, and serving God only by the knowledge of his law. Nay, you shall make them wise in the things of your wisdom; yea, exceedingly cunning in many *mysteries*, even the *mysteries* which you teach.

Then shall they be fitted for the "laying on of hands," and when the bishop has done his office then shall they be reverend divines.

But if any man believe that he is called by God to speak to his brethren "without money and without price," though his soul be bowed to the will of the Father, and though he work all righteousness, and "speak as with the tongue of an angel"—if he be not made a divine by your rulers and by the hands of a bishop, then is he not a divine, nor shall he preach.

He that is chosen by *you* shall give *you* honor, and shall be honored by men, and honored by *women;* and verily he *expects* his reward.

Chapter III

The Performance of Preaching

When you go to the church to preach, go not by the retired way where go those that would shun the crowd, but go in the highway where go the multitude, and see that you have on the robes of black, and take heed that your pace be measured well, and that your march be stately. Then shall your "hearts be lifted up," even as the hearts of mighty men shall they be lifted up. And you shall be gazed upon by the multitude, and they shall honor you; and the men shall praise you, and the *women* shall glorify you, even by the women shall you be glorified.

And when you go in, go not as the ordained, prepared *only* with a soul to God and with a heart to men, and a spirit filled with the Holy Ghost; but go you with your pockets full of papers and full of divine words; even in your pockets shall your divinity be.

And let your sermon be full of "the enticing words of man's wisdom," and let it be beautified with just divisions, with tropes and with metaphors, and with hyperbole, and apostrophe, and with interrogation, and with exclamation, and with syllogisms, and with sophisms, and throughout let declamation be.

And take good heed to your attitudes and your gestures, knowing when to bend and when to erect, when to lift your right hand and when you left, and let your motions be graceful, even in your attitudes and in your gestures let your *grace* be. Thus shall you be pleasing in the eyes of the people and *graceful* in their sight.

Let your voice at times be smooth as the stream of the valley, and soft as the breeze that waves not the bough on its bank; and at times let it swell like the wave of the ocean, or like the whirlwind on the mountain top.

Then shall you charm the ears of your hearers and their hearts shall be softened, and their minds shall be astounded, and their souls shall incline to you; and the men shall incline to you, and likewise the women; yea, to your sayings and to your persons shall they be inclined.

And be you mindful not to offend the people; rebuke you not their sins; but when you rebuke sin, rebuke it at a *distance;* and let no man apply your sayings to his own case; so shall he not be offended.

If a brother shall raise up the manner of war against brother, and Christians against Christians, rebuke them not; but be some of you on the one side and some on the other; and tell the one host that God is on their side, and the other host that he is on their side; so make them bold to kill. And even among swords and lancets let your black robes be seen.

Preach you not "Peace on earth and good will to men," but preach you glory to the victor, and victory to the brave.

If any man go into a foreign land and seize upon his fellow man, and put irons on his feet and irons on his hands, and bring him across the great deep into bondage; nay, if he tear asunder the dearest ties of nature, the tenderest leagues of the human heart; if he tear the wife from the husband, and force the struggling infant from its mother's bleeding heart, rebuke him not!

And although he sell them in foreign slavery to toil beneath the lash all their days, tell him not that his doings are of Antichrist; for lo! he is rich and gives to the church, and is esteemed pious, so shall you not offend him, lest peradventure he withdraw himself from your flock.

Teach them to believe that you have the care of
their souls, and that the saving mysteries are for your
explaining; and when you explain your *mysteries,*
encompass them round about with words as with a
bright veil, so bright that through it no man can see.

And lo! you shall bind the judgments of men (and
more especially of women) as with a band of iron:
and you shall make them blind in the midst of light,
even as the owl is blind in the noon day sun; and behold
you shall lead them captive to your reverend wills.

CHAPTER IV

THE CLERGY'S REWARD

"In all your gettings" get money! Now, therefore,
when you go forth on your ministerial journey, go
where there are silver and gold, and where each man
will pay according to his measure. For verily I say
you must get your reward.

Go you not forth as those that have been sent,
"without two coats, without gold or silver, or brass
in their purses; without scrip for their journey, or
shoes, or staves"; but go you forth in the good things
of this world.

And when you shall hear of a church that is
vacant and has no one to preach therein, then be that
a *call* to you, and be mindful of the call, and take you
charge of the flock thereof and of the fleece thereof
even of the *golden* fleece.

And when you shall have fleeced your flock, and
shall know of another *call,* and if the flock be greater,
or rather if the fleece be greater, then greater be also
to you the call. Then shall you leave your old flock,
and of the new flock shall you take the charge.

Those who have "freely received" let them "freely
give," and let not men have your words "without money

nor without price," but bargain you for hundreds and bargain for thousands, even for thousands of silver and gold shall you bargain.

And over and above the price for which you have sold your service, take you also gifts, and be you mindful to refuse none, saying, "Lo, I have enough!" but receive gifts from them that go in chariots, and from them that earn their morsel by the sweat of their brow.

Yea, take you gifts of all, and take them in gold and in silver, and in bread; in wine and in oil; in raiment and in fine linen.

And the more that the people give you the more will they honor you; for they shall believe that "in giving to you they are giving to the Lord"; for behold their sight shall be taken from them, and they shall be blind as bats, and "shall know not what they do."

And you shall wax richer and richer, and grow greater and greater, and you shall be lifted up in your own sight, and exalted in the eyes of the multitude; and lucre shall be no longer filthy in your sight. And verily you have your reward.

In doing these things you shall never fail. And may abundance of gold and silver and bank notes, and corn, and wool, and flax, and spirits and wine, and land be multiplied to you, both now and hereafter. Amen.[10]

The influence of these early articles against the clergy continued to be felt for many years thereafter. Mr. Campbell himself never accepted salaries for his work as a preacher, but supported himself and his family by farming, teaching school, and through his publishing company. It was the general practice of the times for preachers of the movement to support themselves by their own hands, although men sent out by congregations, or engaged in meetings, sometimes received support from others in their

---

[10]*The Christian Baptist*, pp. 166-168.

work. As will be seen, the issue of "the located preacher" came up in later years, many continuing to look upon a "located preacher" as one yielding to the clergy system so bitterly opposed by Mr. Campbell in the early years of the reformation.

4. *Missionary Societies and the Scriptural Plan.*

Another matter of this particular period of the new reformation and the formation of an attitude which needs to be considered, is Mr. Campbell's attitude toward missionary societies among the denominations of that day. In these statements he was expressing his position regarding them at that time. This point is of particular importance because of the issue raised over the question in the middle of the century. In the very first article of the first issue of *The Christian Baptist* the editor launched out against the organized missionary societies of the day, on the basis that such institutions were unscriptural and that they robbed the church of glory rightfully belonging to it. Looking back to the disciples of apostolic times and to the churches of the first century for his model, he wrote of them, saying:

> . . . Their churches were not fractured into missionary societies, Bible societies, education societies; nor did they dream of organizing such in the world. The head of a believing household was not in those days a president or manager of a board of foreign missions; his wife, the president of some female education society; his eldest daughter, the corresponding secretary of a mite society; his servant maid, the vice-president of a rag society; and his little daughter, a tutoress of a Sunday school. They knew nothing of the hobbies of modern times. In their church capacity alone they moved. They neither transformed themselves into any other kind of association, nor did they fracture and sever themselves into divers societies. . . .

. . . They dare not transfer to a missionary society, or Bible society, or education society, a cent or a prayer, lest in so doing they should rob the church of its glory, and exalt the inventions of men above the wisdom of God. In their church capacity alone they moved. . . .[11]

In the second issue of his paper, under the caption, "Remarks on Missions," Mr. Campbell wrote a lengthy article on the same subject. In this article he charged the manner in which mission work was being done was grossly unscriptural, and also offered his own suggestion as to how it should be done. Introducing the call and work of Moses and Joshua under the Old Testament dispensation, he passed to the work of the twelve and the seventy under the direction of Jesus, from which he argued that these men sent out in such small numbers were endowed by God with power to confirm their preaching by the signs and miracles accompanying them. The conclusion then drawn was:

. . . The Bible, then, gives us no idea of a missionary without the power of working miracles. Miracles and missionaries are inseparably connected in the New Testament. . . . From these plain and obvious facts and considerations, it is evident that it is a capital mistake to suppose that missionaries in heathen lands, without the power of working miracles, can succeed in establishing the Christian religion. . . .[12]

Mr. Campbell's contention at that time was that a whole church should be sent to the heathen land, instead of only one or two individuals; for this he contended on the ground of the need for example, as well as instruction; a whole church could demonstrate Christianity. He continues:

[11]*The Christian Baptist*, pp. 6, 7.
[12]*The Christian Baptist*, p. 15.

The Christian religion is a social religion, and cannot be exhibited to the full conviction of the world, only when it appears in this social character. An individual or two, in a pagan land, may talk about the Christian religion, and may exhibit its morality as far as respects mankind in general; but it is impossible to give a clear, a satisfactory, a convincing exhibition of it, in any other way than by exhibiting a church, not on paper, but in actual existence and operation, as divinely appointed. . . .[13]

This he suggested as the practical way to do the work in his day, and consequently today as well:

If, in the present day, and amongst all those who talk so much of a missionary spirit, there could be found such a society, though it were composed of but twenty, willing to emigrate to some heathen land, where they would support themselves like the natives, wear the same garb, adopt the country as their own, and profess nothing like a missionary project; should such a society sit down and hold forth in word and deed the saving truth, not deriding the gods nor the religion of the natives, but allowing their own works and example to speak for their religion, and practicing as above hinted; we are persuaded that, in process of time, a more solid foundation for the conversion of the native would be laid, and more actual success resulting, than from all the missionaries employed for twenty-five years. Such a course would have some warrant from scripture; but the present has proved itself to be all human.[14]

Shortly after the appearance of these articles, Mr. Campbell inserted in his paper a letter from one who signed himself "Robert Cautious," a gentleman who commended

---

[13]*Ibid.*, p. 16.
[14]*The Christian Baptist*, pp. 16, 17.

most of the things said by Mr. Campbell, but with a few questions on some points, to which Campbell replied:

> Our objections to the missionary plan originated from the conviction that it is unauthorized in the New Testament; and that, in many instances, it is a system of iniquitous peculation and speculation. I feel perfectly able to maintain both the one and the other of these positions.[15]

> Not questioning the piety and philanthropy of many of the originators, and present abettors of the Missionary plan, we must say that the present scheme is not authorized by our King.[16]

Not only did Mr. Campbell offer his objections to missionary societies in those early days of his work, but he came eventually to voice his objection to various types of associations; especially did he object where such associations assumed dictatorial attitudes toward the churches under them. He was not opposed to members of congregations coming together for mutual fellowship and encouragement, but when the assembly assumed the form of an organization for the formation of the policies of the congregations composing it, he felt they were inexcusably imitating Romanism. In Article XXX on "The Ancient Order of Things," dealing with the "Discipline of the Church," and especially where various forms of organization were discussed, he wrote:

> . . . The Baptist system, we have always said and seen, is the most impotent of any of them. They have, in theory, sawed the horns off the Beast, and the Association is a hornless stag, with the same ferocious spirit which he had when the horns were on his head. If he is offended he makes a tremendous push with his brains, and bruises to death the obnoxious carcase which he

---

[15]*Ibid.*, p. 53.
[16]*Ibid.*, p. 54.

would have gored clear through at a single push, if he had his horns. Herodion feels the want of horns, and would have the creature furnished with at least one artificial one, which he might occasionally use. My brother of the Herald would wish to feed the stag well, but would still be sawing off the horns: perhaps I may wrong him in so saying, for indeed he is very modest about it. But, for my part, I do not love even an image of the Beast. I have no objection to congregations meeting in hundreds, at stated times, to sing God's praises, and to unite their prayers and exhortations for the social good. But whenever they form a quorum, and call for the business of the churches, they are a popish calf, or *muley,* or a hornless stag, or something akin to the old Grand Beast with seven heads and ten horns.[17]

In later years, when, among some of the younger additions to the new reformation a different attitude toward missionary societies was developed, these articles and their sentiments were used with telling effect by those who opposed the introduction of what they called "innovations" and a "departure from the ancient order of things." These quotations are numerous and lengthy, but the apology offered for inserting so many of them is that they are essential to the appreciation of the drama before us, "The Development of an Attitude."

[17]*The Christian Baptist,* p. 531.

CHAPTER V

GROWTH THROUGH EVANGELISM ON THE PLEA
OF "THE SCRIPTURES ONLY"
1830-1849

1. *A New Publication: The Millennial Harbinger.*

Before the year 1829 ended, Alexander Campbell had determined upon a new publication to take the place of *The Christian Baptist*. *The Christian Baptist* had done its work well, but there were two reasons for discontinuing its publication and introducing a new one: first, Mr. Campbell wished to enlarge the scope of his paper, and to modify its tone; and second, he feared that the name "Christian Baptist" might become associated with those who had embraced the principles of the Reformation, which he earnestly wished to avoid. Consequently, in 1830, the first issue of the *Millennial Harbinger* came from the press, destined to continue through the year 1868. The new publication was milder in its tone, although it did not cease to continue the war against the Scripture departures of the day and to promote the great principles of the new Reformation. The attitude advocated by Mr. Campbell to be followed by the preachers became the spirit of the Harbinger:

But, brethren, while we proclaim the ancient gospel, let us do it in the spirit of that gospel. Let our object be to turn sinners to God. Gravity, sincerity, mildness, and benevolence, must be the attributes of every successful proclaimer of the word. If we teach or exhort Christians, let it be with the tenderness, affection, and long-suffering of Paul and his great master—the Teacher sent from God. No witticisms, puns, jests, or satires, become him who pleads with men to be reconciled to God. A dead fly has often caused the most precious ointment of a whole discourse to send forth an unpleasant odor.[1]

The spirit herein advised for preachers was the spirit of Alexander Campbell in his own preaching and writing. He was not a polemic himself as a matter of choice, but from necessity: the very position taken with respect to the Scriptures necessitated the defense of that position as it was so completely at variance with the general position of the day. Mr. Campbell refused to print a number of articles in the *Harbinger* because of their severity; his reason for refusing to print them serves to illustrate the spirit of the new publication and the change from the spirit of the old:

> An Essay on "the middle ground" people of Kentucky is omitted because too personal, and too much in the spirit of the Opposition. *"Josephus"* also is postponed, because we have in the *Christian Baptist* done enough of that sort of work. *"Flint,"* from Virginia, has too much fire in it; and *"Martin Luther,"* from Pennsylvania, is too much in the temper of the old Reformer. These correspondents are persons of good talents and information, but their late productions are at least *seven* years after date. The time was that such philippics were necessary, but now all that can be achieved by those means is gained. . . .
>
> Our brethren will please continue their correspondence; but let it be in accordance with the progress of the reformation. Select edifying topics, and speak not so much of men and measures. Let us, brethren, reform as the reformation progresses; and if there be any flagellating or scalping to do, let it be reserved for capital offences.[2]

---

[1] *Millennial Harbinger*, 1831, p. 420.
[2] *Millennial Harbinger*, Vol. II, 1831, p. 432.

From the title of the new periodical, some expected it to advocate a theory of the millennium, many theories being extant at that time, as at all times since. However, such was not the case. In an article published ten years after its introduction, the editor declared the meaning of the "millennial" characteristic of the name, and incidentally, his conception of the "millenium":

> We have often rather jeeringly been asked, "Wherein consists the *millennial* characteristics of the *Harbinger?*"—the querists imagining that a *millennial* harbinger must be always discussing or preaching millenniary affairs. When we put to sea under this banner we had the port of Primitive Christianity, in letter and spirit, in profession and practice, in our eye; reasoning that all the Millennium we could scripturally expect was not merely the restoration of the Jerusalem church in all its moral and religious characters, but the extension of it through all nations and languages for one thousand years. To prepare the way for such a development of Christianity several things are essential—
>
> 1st. The annihilation of partyism.
> 2nd. The restoration of a pure speech.
> 3rd. The preaching of the original gospel.
> 4th. The restoration of the Christian ordinances.
> 5th. Larger measures of the Holy Spirit, as promised to those who seek for it in the appointed way.[3]

2. *Numerical Growth of the Movement.*

The movement inaugurated by the two Campbells, Barton W. Stone, Walter Scott, and others, made its most phenomenal growth throughout the years from 1830 to 1849. By 1839 there were an estimated two hundred thousand "pro-

---

[3]*Ibid.,* 1840, p. 561.

fessors of the Ancient Gospel" in the United States.[4] Garrison thinks this number too high, and offers as a probable estimate the number one hundred eighteen thousand as more nearly correct.[5] By 1844 one of the religious journals of Kentucky estimated the number of Disciples in that State to be fifty thousand; however, of this estimate Mr. Fortune says, "The number of Disciples claimed by the *Christian Journal* of 1844 was perhaps exaggerated."[6] However, as one reads the reports of meetings held throughout the country by the preachers of this period, he is impressed with the rapid spread of the movement, and the hearty reception to the Ancient Gospel as proclaimed by those zealous pioneers.

How is such a rapid growth, with no societies, no machinery, no central head or headquarters, to be accounted for? The answer is: They had a message, they believed their message to be the greatest discovery of the age and need of the world; hence, fired with the zeal of discoverers, they became propagandists of the first rank. Alexander Campbell had first ventured the proposition that baptism is for remission of sins in his debate with Walker in 1820, but by the time he met McCalla in 1823, it had become a matter of conviction with him. "It was," says Richardson, "reserved for Walter Scott, a few years later, to make a direct and practical application of the doctrine, and to secure for it the conspicuous place it has since occupied among the chief points urged in the Reformation."[7]

In 1827 Walter Scott was selected by the Mahoning Association as Evangelist upon the Western Reserve. It was while engaged in this work that he heard Jacob Osborne preach a sermon in which the speaker had remarked that no one had the promise of the Holy Spirit until after baptism.

---

[4]*Millennial Harbinger*, 1938, p. 165.
[5]Garrison, *Religion Follows the Frontier*, pp. 159-160.
[6]Alonzo Willard Fortune, *The Disciples in Kentucky*, p. 166.
[7]Richardson, *Memoirs*, Bk. II, p. 84.

"From this moment," says Richardson in writing of the incident, "Mr. Scott's mind seemed to be engrossed with the consideration of the consecutive *order* appropriate to the various items in the gospel, and being greatly given to analysis and arrangement, he proceeded to place them thus: 1, faith; 2, repentance; 3, baptism; 4, remission of sins; 5, Holy Spirit. This view relieved at once his previous perplexities, and the gospel, with its items thus regularly disposed, seemed to him almost like a new revelation."[8]

From that time Mr. Scott's preaching took on a new spirit; he was filled with the very simplicity of the process, the spirit of which was caught up by other preachers till it had swept the country.

In the October, 1828, issue of the *Christian Baptist*, Mr. Campbell, writing the ninth installment of the "Ancient Gospel," introduced the article with the statement:

In the natural order of the evangelical economy, the items stand thus: 1. Faith; 2. Reformation; 3. Immersion; 4. Remission of sins; 5. Holy Spirit; and 6. Eternal Life. We do not teach that one of these precedes the other, as cause and effect; but that they are all naturally connected, and all, in this order, embraced in the glad tidings of salvation. In the apostolic age these items were presented in this order. . . .

Those who proclaim faith in the Lord Jesus Christ and reformation in order to immersion; and immersion in order to forgiveness and the Holy Spirit, proclaim the same gospel which the Apostles proclaimed.[9]

This simple explanation of conversion not only had ample Scripture foundation, but it was easy to grasp, it was something tangible; it appealed to both the "head" and the

[8]Richardson, *op. cit.*, p. 208.
[9]*The Christian Baptist*, pp. 486, 487.

"heart." Not only was it founded on Scripture teaching, but it eliminated the old theory of agonizing at the mourner's bench seeking something which the intelligent could never find. It abolished the uncertainty of the older system based on Calvinism which often haunted the believer throughout his life. Besides all this, it was something that all could understand and teach. Fortune's observation is, "Because of their convictions, they were all evangelists. As a result of the personal work of the men and women there were responses to the invitation whenever it was given."[10] The simplicity of their message and the zeal of the new converts were the ground of their rapid growth and spread.

But let no one be deceived into thinking that it was always an easy victory, an easy thing to overcome the sectarian prejudice of the period. J. T. Johnson, writing for the *Christian Journal*, March 28, 1846, says in an essay headed, "Triumphs and Defense of the Reformation,"

We have had to battle for victory against fearful odds! We have had to contend and toil hard for every inch of ground we have gained; and we have been most unfeelingly reproached because we have gained no more. The conquest, however, has been unparalleled, except in the primitive age. Victory has crowned our efforts thus far! And many of our opponents have judged it safest to turn a deaf ear to our preaching! They have witnessed the mighty power of the ancient gospel! They have seen it sweep the land like a tornado. A community of 200,000 or more, banded together in the holiest ties of brotherhood, in less than eighteen years, furnishes unequivocal demonstration of its power; and even the locking of doors has not proved a safeguard against it. . . .

Facts are stubborn things. They are as stable as the everlasting mountains. They are as true as the needle

[10]Fortune, *op. cit.*, p. 163.

to the pole. They baffle all the skill of the religious in-triguer. They put to shame all the boasted achievements of the metaphysical hair-splitter. Is it nothing to rally and band together, within eighteen years, a respectable and intelligent party of 200,000 persons! Is it nothing to have swept from the arena everything but the Bible, as authoritative! Is it nothing to have repudiated all human names and distinctions! Is it nothing to hold up *the Church of God* as the only true Church! Is it noth-ing to restore the worship every Lord's Day to primitive simplicity! We can scarcely calculate the immense sac-rifice and expenditure of effort and means which have characterized the Reformation. And it has attained a consistency and firmness which will, in a few years, give an impetus to the cause, in evangelical effort, Bible dis-tribution and missionary enterprise, which will astonish the most sanguine of the friends.[11]

The spirit and zeal of men like Johnson, Smith, Scott and others, who believed in the all-sufficiency of the Scrip-tures to show them how to do the Lord's work and to give them a pattern to be followed in converting men, made pos-sible such marvelous results and the overcoming of the great odds that were against them in their labors.

3. *Union of Christians and Disciples.*

A consideration of the growth of this movement in Ken-tucky at this period will serve to illustrate the growth and development of the reformation in general. It will be re-membered that the labors of Barton W. Stone, from about 1800, had been confined primarily to Kentucky. Stone's labors had resulted by 1830 in some eight or ten thousand adherents.[12] They usually referred to themselves as "the

---

[11]John Rogers, *Biography of Elder J. T. Johnson*, p. 25.
[12]John Rogers, *op. cit.*, p. 25.

Christian Connection," but were often called "Stoneites" or "newlights" by the people in general.

In the year 1826 in the city of Georgetown, Stone began the publication of a paper which he called *The Christian Messenger*. About 1829 or 1830, John T. Johnson embraced the views of Alexander Campbell and leaving the Baptist Church, began to preach and organize congregations on the Word of God alone. In 1831 he joined Stone as Associate Editor of the *Messenger*, which work he continued until 1834, when Stone moved out of the state. Johnson, in connection with other preachers of this period, was instrumental in uniting the "Christians" with the "Disciples" of Kentucky.

Leaving Johnson and Stone for a moment, we turn our attention to another preacher of Kentucky whose influence was keenly felt among the "Disciples." This was John Smith, who, as a Calvinistic Baptist, began to question the doctrines of Calvinism in the early '20s and into whose hands fell a Prospectus of *The Christian Baptist* in 1823. Smith became deeply interested in the new doctrine but for some time was not convinced. He met Alexander Campbell in the spring of 1824, at which time he heard him speak. After this event, he became closely associated with the Disciple movement. Continuing an intense search of the scriptures, Smith began to devote more and more of his time to preaching, until soon he was devoting his entire time to the proclamation of the newly discovered Ancient Gospel. Passing over the many experiences through which Smith and some of the congregations with which he was associated went, it is worthy of note that the congregation at Grassy Lick, which was originally Baptist, left the Baptist Association in June, 1829, to become simply a "church of Jesus Christ." Smith, however, did not go with them at the time, but for the reason that he wished to have a voice in the next meeting of the Baptist Association; he therefore transferred his membership to the Mt. Sterling church, to leave them permanently a short time later. Under the influence of the preaching of

Smith and other men who will be introduced later, the North
District Association, which met July 23, 1831, determined to
dissolve itself as an Association, because of the lack of scriptural authority for such associations. Williams, in his *Life
of Elder John Smith,* gives the following account of the dissolution:

> But the main question, which had been held in re-
> serve, was now solemnly propounded: *"Is there any
> authority in the Word of God for this Association to
> meet at all?"* After some debate, in which nothing was
> said or done to give offense, they finally, and with much
> unanimity, resolved:
>
> No church requesting the next Association to be ap-
> pointed at any of their meeting-houses, and this body not
> having authority to force it upon any; and every church
> which appeared here by her letter and messengers unani-
> mously agreeing that the Word of God is the only rule of
> faith and practice for Christians—on motion and second,
> *that the Constitution of the North District Association
> of Baptists be dissolved*—after consultation among the
> brethren, when the question was put, it was carried in
> the affirmative; and the said Association was thereby dis-
> solved. Upon after consultation, the brethren agreed to
> attend at Sharpsburg, at the request of her messengers
> in the name of the church, on the Friday before the third
> Saturday, and the days following, in August, 1832, and
> there communicate with one another, either by letter or
> otherwise, such information respecting the progress and
> affairs of each church as they may think of sufficient im-
> portance or interest to communicate.[18]

It was only natural that those who had embraced the
reformation teaching of Barton W. Stone and those of the
reformation under Alexander Campbell should frequently
come in contact with each other. The followers of Campbell,

---

[18]J. A. Williams, *Life of Elder John Smith,* pp. 416, 417.

who called themselves "Disciples," but were generally spoken of as "Cambellites," looked with askance upon the followers of Stone who, as has been said, were generally called "new-lights" or "Stoneites." These latter were accused generally of being *Arians* or Unitarians.

Campbell insisted on refraining from speculating upon things about which the Bible had no plain, definite statement. Stone had been forced by the very circumstances of his environment to make some statements with reference to his position on matters of the Trinity and atonement in the early years of his reformation which had left some in doubt as to his soundness in these matters. Before his death, Stone lamented the fact that he had ever been induced to take such positions. In explanation of this, John Rogers says in his *Biography of John T. Johnson:*

> It is but the part of candor to admit that, in former years, we (Christians) had, by our speculations upon untaught questions (provoked, to be sure, by as improper speculations on the other side), given some ground for this odium of which we were the subjects. It is not at all strange, therefore, that our friends on the other side should have hesitated.[14]

With this difference of opinion on the matter of the Trinity and the vicarious atonement of Christ, or at least, the presumed difference, Williams says that in 1828,

> The Reformers of the North District, ignorant of the real doctrine of the *Christians,* united with their Calvinistic brethren in a resolution to withdraw from every church or Association that would commune with such a people; nor was it strange that the Calvinists of Bracken, in 1830, regarded it as evidence of the hopeless apostasy of the reformers that they could, at last, encourage these *Arians* to occupy their meeting houses.[15]

[14]John Rogers, *op cit.,* p. 30.
[15]Williams, *op. cit.,* p. 430.

However, men like John T. Johnson, John Rogers, and John Smith were determined to make an effort at uniting these two groups. Both groups had renounced all creeds but the Bible; both recognized the name Christian as a scriptural name, and both held similar views on the action and purpose of baptism. By the year 1831, efforts were being put forth, esepecially in Kentucky, to bring the two groups together. John Smith and John T. Johnson were instrumental in bringing together representatives of both parties in order to consider such a union. By the year 1831 Campbell was editing the *Millennial Harbinger,* while Stone continued *The Christian Messenger.* Both were diligently discussing these differences, as well as points of agreement. As quoted by Williams, Stone set forth in the August, 1831, issue of *The Christian Messenger,* a summary of the main differences as he conceived them, these differences being on the fellowship of immersed and unimmersed individuals, and differences respecting the name. The quotation here inserted reveals two things: first, it presents Stone's conception of the major differences, and second, it shows his spirit in the matter:

> The question is going the round of society, and is often proposed to us, Why are not you and the Reformed Baptists one people? or, Why are you not united? We have uniformly answered: In spirit we are united, and that no reason exists on our side to prevent the union in form. . . . We acknowledge a difference of opinion from them on some points. We do not object to their opinions, as terms of fellowship between us; but they seriously and honestly object to some of ours as reasons why they cannot unite. These we shall name; and let all duly consider their weight:
>
> 1. That we have fellowship and communion with unimmersed persons. They contend—so we understand them—that, according to the New Institution, none but the immersed have their sins remitted, and therefore,

they cannot commune with the unimmersed. On this point we cannot agree with them; and the reason of our disagreement is, that this sentiment, in our view, will exclude millions of the fairest characters, for many centuries back, from heaven. . . . I know our brethren say: *"We do not declare that they are excluded from heaven, but only from the kingdom on earth. We leave them in the hand of God."* But does not this sentiment lead to that conclusion? We believe and acknowledge that baptism is ordained by the King a means for the remission of sins to penitent believers, but we cannot say that immersion is the *sine qua non*, without maintaining the awful consequences above, and without contradicting our own experience. We, therefore, teach the doctrine, "Believe, repent, and be immersed for the remission of sins," and we endeavor to convince our hearers of its truth, but we exercise patience and forbearance toward such pious persons as cannot be convinced.

2. Another cause or reason why they and we are not united as one people is, that we have taken different names. They acknowledge the name Christian most appropriate; but because they think this name is disgraced by us who wear it, and that to it may be attached the idea of Unitarian or Trinitarian, they reject it, and have taken the older name Disciple. This they have done in order to be distinguished from us. Hence it is concluded that they wish to be a party distinguished from us, and have, therefore, assumed this name as a party name. This at once bars us from union in the same body; and we cannot but believe it was assumed for this purpose by some. We should rejoice to believe the contrary. Until a satisfactory explanation be given on this subject, we must view ourselves equally excluded from union with the congregations of the Disciples, as from any other sectarian establishment. We object not to the scriptural name Disciple, but to the reasons why our brethren as-

sumed it. We are ready any moment to meet and unite
with those brethren, or any others, who believe in and
obey the Savior, according to the best understanding of
his will, on the Bible, but not on opinions of its truth.
We cannot, with our present views, unite on the opinions
that unimmersed persons cannot receive the remission of
sins, and therefore, should be excluded from our fellowship and communion on earth. We cannot conscientiously give up the name Christian acknowledged by our
brethren most appropriate, for any other, as Disciple,
less appropriate, and received, or assumed, to avoid the
disgrace of being suspected to be a Unitarian or Trinitarian. We cannot thus temporize with divine truth.[16]

With Mr. Campbell it was not so much a difference of
views on baptism as of the practice of the Christians in fel-
lowshipping the unimmersed. Williams writes, "for, in their
views of this matter (the design and meaning of baptism),
they seemed generally to agree; but it was the *practice* of the
former (Christians) in receiving the unimmersed to their
communion and fellowship that seemed to present a barrier
to the union."[17] He then summarizes the position of the two
men as follows:

In fine, while both labored for the union of Christians Mr. Campbell thought that the only practicable way
to accomplish it was to propound the Ancient Gospel
and the Ancient Order of Things in the words and sentences found in the Apostolic writings; to abandon all
traditions and usages not found in the Record, and to
make no human terms of communion. Elder Stone urged,
more emphatically, but not in opposition to this sentiment, the communion of Christians in the spirit of the
Bible, rather than a formal union on that Book. He

---

[16]Williams, *op. cit.*, pp. 443-445.
[17]Williams, *op. cit.*, p. 445.

exhorted his brethren to seek for more holiness rather than trouble themselves and others with schemes and plans of union. "The love of God," said he, "shed abroad in our hearts by the Holy Ghost given unto us, will more effectually unite than all the wisdom of the world combined."[18]

In spite of these differences, it was determined by some that an effort at union should be made. Consequently, in the winter of 1831 and 1832, meetings were held at Georgetown, beginning on Christmas Day and continuing four days, and at Lexington, beginning on New Year's Day, in an effort to unite the two bodies. First, John Smith made a strong and dignified speech on behalf of the union, followed by Barton W. Stone, who warmly and fervently endorsed the things said by Smith, offering the other his hand in pledge of fellowship and union, which was readily accepted in all sincerity. It looked as if fellowship and union between the two bodies were an accomplished fact. Great joy was manifested among all the brethren, and on the following day they united to eat the Lord's Supper. Of this uniting of the groups, Williams further writes:

It was an equal and mutual pledge and resolution to meet on the Bible as on common ground, and to preach the Gospel rather than to propagate opinions. The brethren of Stone did not join Alexander Campbell as their leader, nor did the brethren of Campbell join Barton W. Stone as their leader; but each, having already taken Jesus the Christ as their only Leader, in love and liberty became one body; not Stoneites, or Campbellites; not Christians or Disciples, distinctively as such; but Christians, Disciples, saints, brethren, and children of the same Father, who is God over all, and in all.[19]

---

[18]*Ibid.*, p. 446.
[19]Williams, *op. cit.*, p. 456.

Union between the two groups prevailed over the state generally, but because of differences on the matters of preachers and elders, the two congregations in Lexington did not permanently unite until 1835. Much discussion of the issues and hard work on the part of many took place during those years to perfect union between the two. When union was finally effected, Mr. Campbell had waived his opposition to the term "Christian" as a brotherhood designation, although he had insisted that the term "Disciple" was the better of the two. Both were used and have continued to be used until the present.

As these two bodies united in Kentucky, they became known as the "Church of Christ," or the "Christian Church." Of these names by which the group was designated, Mr. Fortune observes:

> As time passed, the Christian Church became the more common designation. The members became known as Disciples, or Christians, with preference for Christians as the years passed.[20]

4. *An Effort at Union With the Sects.*

Even though the emphasis had been on the restoration of "The Ancient Order of Things" since Campbell had begun publication of *The Christian Baptist*, the Disciples never lost sight of that early phase of their life and mission. Encouraged by the success of the union of Christians and Disciples in the years 1832-35, and the growth of their labors since, J. T. Johnson, who was always hopeful of the union of Baptists and Disciples, was moved to write Campbell in January, 1841, suggesting a general meeting in Kentucky sometime that year. To this suggestion Campbell replied, "Beloved brother Johnson, your motion is an excellent one, and I will travel one hundred miles out of my way to attend such a meeting in Kentucky, on my return from Nashville the en-

---

[20]Fortune, *op. cit.*, pp. 174, 175.

suing spring. Let us have a real big meeting on the subject of union, *on Truth, and in Truth."*

After attending and settling due preliminaries, Johnson wrote and published the following notice of the meeting. It is interesting because of the attitude expressed therein:

> Union meeting, on the 2d day of April, 1841, at which all the religious parties will enjoy equal privileges.
>
> At the instance of many persons, it has been concluded to hold a union meeting at Lexington, commencing the 2d day of April, 1841.
>
> As the union of Christians is most desirable, being of eternal importance, the great object will be to ascertain the Scriptural bond of union, in order to its accomplishment. That all the talents and influence of the religious community may be enlisted and engaged in so commendable a work, the members of the different denominations, and especially their public speakers, are most pressingly and affectionately invited to attend and participate in all that may be attempted from first to last. The olive branch of peace is held out to all religious parties, and it is hoped that they will act as becomes those who have submitted to the King of peace, love and joy. J. T. Johnson, by request.[21]

The meeting was held according to announcement, but though the sectarian preachers claimed to desire union and deplore division, Rogers says, "Yet it is a matter of history, that not one participated in the meeting, outside of our own ranks, save Dr. Fishback, who was in effect with us and actually united with the church, in Lexington, shortly after the meeting."[22] Preachers from the various denominations not only absented themselves from the meeting, but were openly hostile to it throughout its continuance. This sug-

---

[21]Rogers, *op. cit.*, pp. 172, 173.

[22]*Idem.*

gests that not only was an attitude crystallizing among the Disciples during these years, but likewise there was taking shape among the sects of the day a definite attitude toward the Disciples. Speeches dealing with the desirability and basis of union were made by Johnson, Shannon, Fishback, Campbell and others during the three days' meeting. Besides the special addresses, there were discussions of the addresses. After making the following resolution, the meeting adjourned:

Resolved, That the Bible, and the Bible alone, is a sufficient foundation on which all Christians may unite and build together; and that we most affectionately invite the religious parties to the investigation of this truth.

Whatever hope some may have cherished for union between Disciples and Baptists was doomed to failure. War between these two groups has continued from then until the present.

5. *Cooperation Among the Churches.*

Rejoicing in their recently discovered New Testament church and scheme of redemption, and being strenuously opposed by the sects about them, the members of the fast-growing brotherhood were being drawn closely together by bonds of mutual love, fellowship, and a common cause. Reports appearing in the various periodicals inform us of the many cooperation meetings held throughout the country, and of the cooperation of churches in campaigns to evangelize new fields. These meetings were sectional and state meetings in which members of congregations met for mutual edification and to discuss the best possible means of furthering the work. This spirit of cooperation was contributing its share to the growth of the movement.

Strong opposition to any kind of associations that tended toward organization had existed from the very beginning. The tendency had been for congregations, as they became more deeply steeped in the Restoration plea, to withdraw from such associations. There had even been the dissolving of numerous associations in the various states, but the cooperation of congregations to preach the gospel had been encouraged by many from the start. Walter Scott had served as Evangelist for the Mahonning Association in 1827, preaching in the Western Reserve; John Rogers and John Smith had been sent out by neighboring churches in Kentucky to visit the churches, advocating and encouraging the union of Disciples and Christians, and evangelizing the northern section of that state. This work they continued through the years 1832, 1833, and 1834. Other men were being sent out by other churches, but these suffice to illustrate the spirit of cooperation in evangelistic work during the period. In his *History of the Disciples in Kentucky,* Mr. Fortune describes the meetings of the Disciples for such purposes in that state, repeatedly referring to the meetings as being held for the purpose of cooperation. Cooperation, not organization, was the desire and aim of the Christians in such meetings.

In the year 1831 there appeared in the *Millennial Harbinger* four articles on the subject of "Cooperation," in which the writer demonstrated from the Scriptures the obligation resting upon the church to evangelize the world. From the beginning it had been their plea that any work done by the church should be done through the local congregations. This principle was still recognized; this, then, was not the question. The question before them at that early date was one of *how* the work should be done. In concluding his articles on the subject, Mr. Campbell raised this as the primary question. He said:

We shall not now repeat what has been written, nor attempt again to demonstrate from scripture premises, that the Lord has left it now to the church to convert the world. He no longer employs Angels, Prophets, nor Apostles, as his agents in the work. He has fitted and furnished the church for this ministry. If they do their duty, the work of conversion goes on; if not, it stops.

The only question is, *how shall this be done to the best* advantage? The New Testament furnishes the principles which call forth our energies, but suggests no plan. The churches in every county, have from scripture and reason, all authority to bring their combined energies upon their own vicinity first, and when all is done at home they may, and ought to co-operate with their weaker neighbors in the same state, and so on increasing the circle of their cooperations, as they fill up the interior, with all light and goodness, until the knowledge of the glory of the Lord cover the whole earth.

Whether then, they shall all meet annually, semiannually, or quarterly, in one place in each county; or whether they shall appoint persons to visit all the churches in the same bounds, and to call forth all their means to enlighten and reform society at large, are questions which their own discretion must decide.

They may as rationally expect to find a law or rule on such subjects, in the New Testament, as to find a rule for the size and material of the house in which they ought to meet, and the hour of the day at which they shall commence or adjourn, and a hundred other things, purely circumstantial, which have no more faith nor morality in them than in the colors blue, black, or brown.

Some weak, but honest minds, are for converting the New Testatment into a *ritual,* and expecting to find a code of laws concerning every thing about economy, and cooperation, as if these were parts of christian faith and morals. Some have even thought it a sin to enumerate or enroll the names of members of one congregation, because David was punished for enumerating Israel and Judah; and because others have written down articles of belief, and bound them on the consciences of men, they are afraid to write down their own *names;* or to ascertain how many members compose the church of any one place. Such eccentricities of mind, resemble the conduct of a man who, because his father was drowned, would not pass a shallow ford, and of another, who, because he had been burned when a child, would never approach a fire to warm by it.[23]

As the reformation grew, the question of cooperation continued to manifest itself. John T. Johnson advocated a stronger organizing of forces than the cooperation meetings presented. Mr. Campbell thought he saw the need for some kind of combining of efforts in order to further the new cause to greatest advantage, but seemed undecided as to the best method. During the year 1839, there appeared in the *Harbinger* an article entitled "Statistics of Indiana," after which Mr. Campbell made a few "Remarks," offering the following suggestions, encouraging such general meetings for cooperation:.

. . . An annual meeting in some central point of each state in the union, conducted on similar principles, exhibiting the statistics of the churches united in the primitive faith and manners, would in many ways greatly promote the prosperity of the cause. Cooperation and combination of effort is the great secret of success. Of which matters, more in detail at a more convenient season.[24]

However, even such "cooperation" meetings were not without a few objectors. Men so recently having come out of sectarian abuses and errors, objected because of the possible dangers into which such meetings might lead. They looked not so much at the present evil of the meetings, as to the consequences. One individual in particular who opposed such meetings was Aylett Raines. Through the *Christian Teacher* Mr. Raines vigorously opposed the state meetings and the organization, which toward the end of the period, was developing. Undoubtedly he expressed the attitude of

[23]*Millennial Harbinger*, 1831, pp. 436, 437.
[24]*Millennial Harbinger*, 1839, p. 253.

many others. Fortune's remark respecting the position of Raines is in point:

> He believed there were tendencies, which, unless checked, would lead to state organizations and to a "United States organization of the congregations" which would be a dangerous consolidation of power.[25]

Time has proved the fears of Mr. Raines to have been well founded.

In the *Millennial Harbinger* for 1844, Mr. Campbell inserted the announcement of a "Cooperation Meeting, in King William County, Virginia," sent in by Thomas M. Henley.[26] In the same periodical for 1845 appears an article, "Church Organization," in which is reported a meeting held in Steubenville, Ohio, "for the purpose of a free exchange of views on the subjects of church organization, church edification, and church co-operation," of which meeting Mr. Campbell writes:

> At none of these meetings was it proposed to do anything more than to bring the subject before our brethren in a way favorable to the concentration of thought, and to the acquisition of light upon it. Our views of the Christian Institution permit nothing more than this. . . . In these matters they have just the same liberties and powers that an evangelist has in preaching the word.—He presents his views, his reasons, and his exhortations to the community to be voluntarily received or rejected by them as every one pleases.[27]

In the same article, he expresses his own views of such recommendations as were made in the meetings, saying:

> . . . While I may accord with the most of them, as did the committees which considered them,—I would not

---

[25]Fortune, *op. cit.*, p. 209.

[26]*Ibid.*, p. 92.

[27]*Millennial Harbinger*, 1845, pp. 59, 60.

bind them upon myself nor upon any one else, farther than we may voluntarily choose to be governed by them either as matters of expediency or as expressions of the divine will.[28]

The suggestions of the committee were then inserted in the above mentioned article, which suggestions consisted of three parts: 1. Organization, 2. Church Edification, 3. Co-operation. The first two dealt with the affairs of the local congregation only; the third considered the co-operation of the congregations. An excerpt from the chapter on "Co-operation" reveals the attitude of the committee at that time, which attitude was one of co-operation and not legislation:

To do this successfully (i.e., cooperate as congregations), they must either occasionally meet together, by deputies, messengers, or representatives, and consult together for the better performance of their duties. These meetings, being voluntary expedients in matters of expediency, such persons have no authority to legislate in the matter of faith or moral duty, but to attend to the ways and means of successful co-operation in all the objects of duty before them.[29]

The discussion of an attitude developed toward these meetings and for stronger organization is deferred to a later chapter. Our interest in this chapter has been the growth of the movement through evangelization, without organization, but by a simple appeal to the Scriptures as each moved only in a congregational capacity. These men believed the Scripture plan to be sufficient, and such progress without going beyond the things revealed continues to present a strong argument for their contentions. They cooperated without organizing; they carried the gospel into section after section of the country without any machinery other than individual and

---

[28]*Ibid.*, p. 61.

[29]*Ibid.*, pp. 66, 67.

personal love for the newly discovered ancient truth. What they did then can be done today, and stands a monument to the practicability of their methods. Division did not come until those scriptural methods were laid aside by some, to seek again those things from which they were so lately removing, the methods and practices of men.

CHAPTER VI

THE CRYSTALLIZATION OF AN ATTITUDE

1. *The All-Sufficiency of the Scriptures.*

It was during this period of growth and development that the doctrinal position of the movement was most clearly formulated and crystallized. Mr. Campbell felt it had been his lot to propose to the world the ground on which all the honest truth-seekers could unite. He felt that the position sustained by himself and his co-laborers presented such truths of the gospel that all men could stand thereon, and find the fullest enjoyment of religious liberty ever to be realized; for he felt the position to be that of the apostles and prophets of the New Testament.[1] All the preachers were emphatic in their denunciation of creeds, which they believed to be the fundamental causes of division, and fervent in their appeal to the Scriptures for a "thus saith the Lord" in all their contentions.

The position sustained toward the Scriptures themselves never changed, although there can be detected through the years changes in the attitude of Campbell and others in certain points of practice. Of their position toward the Scriptures, Mr. Campbell wrote in the preface to the second edition of the *Christian System*, June 13, 1839, "We take the Bible, the whole Bible, and nothing but the Bible as the foundation of all Christian union and communion. Those who do not like this will please show us a more excellent way."[2] In Chapter II under the heading, "The Bible," Mr. Campbell further says,

The Bible is to the intellectual and moral world of man what the sun is to the planets in our system,—the

---

[1]*Millennial Harbinger*, 1831, p. 418.
[2]Alexander Campbell, *Christian System*, p. 12.

113

fountain and source of light and life, spiritual and eternal. There is not a spiritual idea in the whole human race that is not drawn from the Bible. As soon will the philosopher find an independent sunbeam in nature, as the theologian a spiritual conception in man, independent of the One Best Book.[3]

Since Mr. Campbell made such a fight against creeds, it was only natural that he should be charged with writing one; in the hands of all the denominational opponents of Campbell and his co-workers, the *Christian System* became "the creed of the Campbellites." In discussing the proposition, "Human Creeds, as Bonds of Union and Communion, Are Necessarily Heretical and Schismatical," in the debate at Lexington, mention of which has been made in an earlier chapter, Mr. Rice charged that Campbell's associates in the gospel used his *Christian System* as a creed, although he admitted they had not formally adopted it as such.[4] This was the charge made generally by the sects of that day. Mr. Campbell emphatically denied that he had written a creed, or that his brethren used any of his writings as such. He paused in the midst of the discussion to raise this question:

. . . Does not the gentleman comprehend the difference between writing a book on any religious question, and making that book a creed, a test by which to try the principles of men, in order to church or ministerial fellowship?[5] . . .

After which question, he continued, saying,

We are not, then, to be impugned for writing a book; nor are our arguments against creeds to be met with the fact, that we have written a volume, or various volumes, upon the religious and moral questions that agitate and

[3]Alexander Campbell, *op. cit.*, p. 155.
[4]*Campbell-Rice Debate*, pp. 776, 777.
[5]*Ibid.*, p. 782.

disturb society. . . . He that does not, or cannot appreciate the difference between making a doctrinal standard, to measure candidates for admission into Christian churches, and a book explanatory of our views of anything in the Bible, or out of it, is not to be reasoned with on any subject.[6]

Thus far, the position of Mr. Campbell has been that discussed most generally. It must not be forgotten that there were other leaders and writers of the Reformation whose statements had great weight, if not greater in certain sections, than those of Mr. Campbell, whose statements and positions likewise contributed to the crystallization of an attitude toward the Scriptures. Among those whose words carried great influence was Walter Scott, an eloquent preacher; and probably the greatest evangelist among the earlier group. Mr. Campbell's statements quoted above have been with reference to the Scriptures and their authority. Walter Scott, in clear and unmistakable language, set forth the attitude of the Reformers toward Jesus as Messiah, and His authority as such, which became the general position of the Disciples on this point of doctrine:

In Christianity, the two great generalizations are Christ and his religion. His Messiahship rests on power, and his religion on authority. The former is, of course, the problem; the latter, the dogma. In the Scriptures, the Messiahship is never placed on authority, but on proof; and the doctrine, on the contrary, is never placed on proof, but on authority; the reason for which is this: It being there proved that Jesus is the Christ, the Son of God, it is consequently assumed that nothing he teaches can possibly be false. The strongest argument which can possibly be offered for the truth of his doctrine is, therefore, this: *Magister dixit*—Christ taught it. In Christianity, we have the faith and the doctrine—all

[6]*Ibid.*, p. 783.

things taught, and but one thing proved—the Messiahship: so much for power and authority.[7]

2. *Baptism and the "Lunnenberg Letter."*

There was no phase of the Reformers' doctrinal position more hotly contested, nor more widely misrepresented,
than that of baptism. In his first debate, that with Mr. John
Walker at Mt. Pleasant, Ohio, June 19 and 20, 1820, Mr.
Campbell had mildly suggested baptism for remission of sins
as a Bible doctrine, although it was by no means a matter of
conviction with him at that time. It was not until his second
debate, held with William McCalla in Washington, Mason
County, Kentucky, October 15 to 22, 1823, that the doctrine
was clearly announced by him. J. J. Haley says,

> The outstanding peculiarity of this discussion on
> Mr. Campbell's side was the new developments in the
> doctrine of baptism for the remission of sins. The only
> original and peculiar distinction of Mr. Campbell's re-
> formatory aspirations, thus far developed in a doctrinal
> way, was the idea of the immersion of a penitent believer,
> upon a confession of his faith, into the name of the
> Father, Son and Holy Spirit, in order to the remission
> of his past sins.[8] . . .

Since the question of baptism and its place in the Christian system was so hotly contested by the religious parties of
his day, Mr. Campbell had much to say on the subject.   As
a matter of fact, the writings of all the Reformers have
something to say about it, so instead of quoting profusely
from them, let one who has well summarized Campbell's
position speak.   Probably no one has more clearly summarized that position than has Isaac Errett, as quoted by
J. S. Lamar, who says,

---

[7]Walter Scott, *The Messiahship, or Great Demonstration*, pp.
13, 14.

[8]J. J. Haley, *Debates That Made History*, p. 52.

But Mr. Campbell taught that "baptism is a part of the process of Regeneration." Yes, he made it a part of the process of regeneration, *as defined by him;* but that he made it a part of regeneration, *as defined by the Baptists,* is not true. Just here there is need of discrimination. With the Baptists, regeneration is entirely an *internal* process, if process it can be called; the implantation of new life, or the principles of new life, in the soul. Mr. Campbell never taught that baptism was any *part* of that process. Baptismal regenerationists do; and in that respect there is a great gulf between him and them. He taught that regeneration embraced *a change of state* —a birth, a passing out of one state and one condition of life into another, and that baptism was that birth of water in which a being *already made alive to God,* passed into new conditions of life—entered into the kingdom of God.[9]

It is not to be assumed that all held to such a clear and definite conception of the doctrine, although the more enlightened of the reformers had substantially this view of the matter. That there were radical or extreme positions assumed by some, no one denies.

A discussion of the attitude toward the Scriptures gradually formulated among the Disciples and the crystallization of certain points of doctrine, would be incomplete without reference to the famous "Lunnenburg Letter," and Mr. Campbell's reply to it, which appeared in the September, 1837, issue of *The Millennial Harbinger.* A sister living in Lunnenburg, Virginia, had taken exception to some things said by Campbell in a former article in which he had made reference to one's finding Christians in all Protestant parties. The Editor's reply to the questions asked is somewhat lengthy, but because of the interest that it aroused and the light it throws on the attitudes held at that time toward certain

---

[9] J. S. Lamar, *Memoirs of Isaac Errett,* Vol. II, p. 90.

matters, both her letter and his reply are inserted entire. It will be noted that Campbell's reply contains some of the most liberal statements ever made by him, although he affirms they set forth views held by him all the time.

Lunenburg, July 8th, 1837.

Dear brother Campbell

I was much surprised to-day, while reading the *Harbinger,* to see that you recognize the Protestant parties as Christian. You say, you "find in all Protestant parties Christians."

Dear brother, my surprize and ardent desire to do what is right, prompt me to write to you at this time. I feel well assured, from the estimate you place on the female character, that you will attend to my feeble questions in search of knowledge.

Will you be so good as to let me know how any one becomes a Christian? What act of yours gave you the name of Christian? At what time had Paul the name of Christ called on him? At what time did Cornelius have Christ named on him? Is it not through this name we obtain eternal life? Does the name of Christ or Christian belong to any but those who believe the *gospel,* repent, and are buried by baptism into the death of Christ?

To this inquiry Mr. Campbell replied, as follows:

In reply to this conscientious sister, I observe, that if there be no Christians in the Protestant sects, there are certainly none among the Romanists, none among the Jews, Turks, Pagans; and therefore no Christians in the world except ourselves, or such of us as keep, or strive to keep, all the commandments of Jesus. Therefore, for many centuries there has been no church of Christ, no Christians in the world; and the promises concerning the *everlasting* kingdom of Messiah have failed, and the *gates of hell have prevailed against his church!* This cannot be; and therefore there are Christians among the sects.

But who is a Christian? I answer, Every one that believes in his heart that Jesus of Nazareth is the Messiah, the Son of God, repents of his sins, and obeys him in all things according to his measure of knowledge of his will. *A perfect man in Christ*, or a perfect Christian, is one thing; and "a babe in Christ," a stripling in the faith, or an imperfect Christian, is another. The New Testament recognizes both the perfect man and the imperfect man in Christ. The former, indeed, implies the latter. Paul commands the imperfect Christians to *"be perfect"* (2 Cor. 3:11), and says he wishes the perfection of Christians. "And this also we wish" for you *saints* in Corinth, "even your perfection": and again he says, "We speak wisdom among the perfect" (1 Cor. 2:6), and he commands them to be "perfect in understanding" (1 Cor. 14:20), and in many other places implies or speaks the same things. Now there is perfection of will, of temper, and of behaviour. There is a perfect state and a perfect character. And hence it is possible for Christians to be imperfect in some respects without an absolute forfeiture of the Christian state and character. Paul speaks of "carnal" Christians, of "weak" and "strong" Christians; and the Lord Jesus admits that some of the good and honest-hearted bring forth only thirty fold, while others bring forth sixty, and some a hundred fold increase of the fruits of righteousness.

But every one is wont to condemn others in that in which he is more intelligent than they; while, on the other hand, he is condemned for his Pharisaism or his immodesty and rash judgment of others, by those that excel in the things in which he is deficient. I cannot, therefore, make any one duty the standard of Christian state or character, not even immersion into the name of the Father, of the Son, and of the Holy Spirit, and in my heart regard all that have been sprinkled in infancy without their own knowledge and consent, as aliens from Christ and the well-grounded hope of heaven. "Salvation was of the Jews," acknowledged the Messiah; and yet he said of a foreigner, an alien from the commonwealth of Israel, a Syro-Phenician, "I have not found so great faith—no, not in Israel."

Should I find a Pedobaptist more intelligent in the Christian Scriptures, more spiritually-minded and more devoted to the Lord than a Baptist, or one immersed on a profession of the ancient faith, I could not hesitate a moment in giving the preference of my heart to him that loveth most. Did I act otherwise, I would be a pure sectarian, a Pharisee among Christians. Still I will be asked, How do I know that any one loves my Master but by his obedience to his commandments? I answer, *In no other way*. But mark, I do not substitute obedience to one commandment, for universal or even for general obedience. And should I see a sectarian Baptist or a Pedobaptist more spiritually-minded, more generally conformed to the requisitions of the Messiah, than one who precisely acquiesces with me in the theory or practice of immersion as I teach, doubtless the former rather than the latter, would have my cordial approbation and love as a Christian. So I judge, and so I feel. It is the image of Christ the Christian looks for and loves; and this does not consist in being exact in a few items, but in general devotion to the whole truth as far as known.

With me mistakes of the understanding and errors of the affections are not to be confounded. They are as distant as the poles. An angel may mistake the meaning of a commandment, but he will obey it in the sense in which he understands it. John Bunyan and John Newton were very different persons, and had very different views of baptism, and of some other things; yet they were both disposed to obey, and to the extent of their knowledge did obey the Lord in every thing.

There are mistakes with, and without depravity. There are wilful errors which all the world must condemn, and unavoidable mistakes which every one will pity. The Apostles mistook the Saviour when he said concerning John, "What if I will that John tarry till I come," but the Jews perverted his words when they alleged that Abraham had died, in proof that he spake falsely when he said, "If a man keep my word he shall never see death."

Many a good man has been mistaken. Mistakes are to be regarded as culpable and as declarative of a corrupt heart only when they proceed from a wilful neglect of the means of knowing what is commanded. Ignorance is always a crime when it is voluntary; and innocent when it is involuntary. Now, unless I could prove that all who neglect the positive institutions of Christ and have substituted for them something else of human authority, do it knowingly, or, if not knowingly, are voluntarily ignorant of what is written, I could not, I dare not say that their mistakes are such as unchristianize all their professions.

True, indeed, that it is always a misfortune to be ignorant of any thing in the Bible, and very generally it is criminal. But how many are there who cannot read; and of those who can read, how many are so deficient in education; and of those educated, how many are ruled by the authority of those whom they regard as superiors in knowledge and piety, that they never can escape out of the dust and smoke of their own chimney, where they happened to be born and educated! These all suffer many privations and many perplexities, from which the more intelligent are exempt.

The preachers of *"essentials,"* as well as the preachers of *"non-essentials"* frequently err. The Essentialist may disparage the heart, while the Non-essentialist despises the institution. The latter makes void the institutions of Heaven, while the former appreciates not the mental bias on which God looketh most. My correspondent may belong to a class who think that we detract from the authority and value of an institution the moment we admit the bare possibility of any being saved without it. But we choose rather to be associated with those who think that they do not undervalue either seeing or hearing, by affirming that neither of them, nor both of them together, are essential to life. I would not sell one of my eyes for all the gold on earth; yet I could live without it.

There is no occasion, then for making immersion, on a profession of the faith, absolutely essential to a Christian—though it may be greatly essential to his sanctification and comfort. My right hand and my right eye are greatly essential to my usefulness and happiness, but not to my life; and as I could not be a perfect man without them, so I cannot be a perfect Christian without a right understanding and a cordial reception of immersion in its true and scriptural meaning and design. But he that thence infers that none are Christians but the immersed, as greatly errs as he who affirms that none are alive but those of clear and full vision.

I do not formally answer all the queries proposed, knowing the one point to which they all aim. To that point only I direct these remarks. And while I would unhesitatingly say, that I think that every man who despises any ordinance of Christ, or who is willingly ignorant of it, cannot be a Christian; still I should sin against my own convictions, should I teach any one to think that if he mistook the meaning of any institution, while in his soul he desired to know the whole will of God, he must perish forever. But to conclude for the present —he that claims for himself license to neglect the least

of all the commandments of Jesus, because it is possible
for some to be saved, who, through insuperable ignorance or involuntary mistake, do neglect or transgress
it; or he that wilfully neglects to ascertain the will of
the Lord to the whole extent of his means and opportunities, because some who are defective in that knowledge
may be Christians, is not possessed of the spirit of Christ,
and cannot be registered among the Lord's people. So I
reason, and I think in so reasoning I am sustained by all
the Prophets and Apostles of both Testaments.[10]

This reply inspired a number of letters from subscribers
criticizing the Editor's position, suggesting a brotherhood
aroused over the article. Two lengthy articles appeared in
subsequent issues of the *Harbinger* that year, both from the
pen of Mr. Campbell, in explanation and defense of his position. In the first article written in defense of his reply to
the questions, which appeared in the November issue, the
Editor discussed what he had thought to be the real question
in the woman's mind, which was a question regarding the
condition of the unimmersed, although she had not specifically mentioned such. In the first two paragraphs of the
reply, Campbell writes:

In an article on a query from Lunenburg, which appeared in the September number, certain sentences have
been objected to by some two or three intelligent and
much esteemed correspondents. We gave it as our *opinion*
that there were Christians among the Protestant sects;
an opinion, indeed, which we have always expressed
when called upon. If I mistake not, it is distinctly avowed
in our first Extra on Remission; yet it is now supposed
by these brethren that I have conceded a point of which
I have hitherto been tenacious, and that I have misap-
plied certain portions of scripture in supporting said

Millennial Harbinger, pp. 411-414 (1837).

opinion. In the article alluded to we have said that we "cannot make any one duty the standard of Christian state or character, not even Christian immersion," etc. Again, we have said that "there is no occasion for making immersion on a profession of the faith absolutely essential to a Christian, though it may be greatly essential to his sanctification and comfort." These two sentences contain the pith and marrow of the objectionable portion of said article, to which we again refer the reader.

Much depends upon the known temper and views of a querist in shaping an answer to his questions. This was the case in this instance. We apprehended that the propounder of the queries that called for these remarks, was rather an ultraist on the subject of Christian baptism; so far, at least as not to allow that the name *Christian* is at all applicable to one unimmersed, or even to one immersed, without the true intent and meaning of baptism in his understanding previous to his burial in water. This we gathered from her epistle; and of course gave as bold an answer as we ever gave—perhaps more bold than on any former occasion, yet nothing differing from our former expressed views on that subject.[11]

After explaining his conception of who should wear the name "Christian," with a brief discussion of the "outward" and "inward" man, he continues:

Now the nice point of opinion on which some brethren differ, is this: Can a person who simply, not perversely, *mistakes* the outward baptism, have the inward? We all agree that he who wilfully or negligently perverts the outward, cannot have the inward. But can he who, through a simple mistake, involving no perversity of mind, has misapprehended the outward baptism, yet submitting to it according to his

----
[11]*Millennial Harbinger*, 1837, p. 506.

view of it, have the inward baptism which changes his state and has praise of God, though not of all men? is the precise question. To which I answer, that, in my opinion, *it is possible*. Farther than this I do not affirm.[12]

This evidently brought forth an avalanche of letters into the office of the editor protesting the liberality of his views in this matter, for the articles evidently had been construed by the enemies of the reformation as an abandonment of the position originally assumed. The use being made of the two articles was giving no little concern to disciples in certain sections, whereupon Mr. Campbell came back in the December issue with a third article, lengthy and minute, explaining more fully his position and criticizing the extreme to which, in his judgment, some of the reformers had gone. When properly understood, he felt no comfort could be found by the enemies of the reformation in what he had said. Extracts of the third article are here given, setting forth Campbell's attitude and indirectly that of some whom he felt had gone too far in the matter. After introducing the subject, which is quoted below, the writer enumerated some eight or ten instances from his former writings in support of the claim that he had held the position throughout the years, which are here omitted. He then continues:

Judging from numerous letters received at this office, my reply to the sister from Lunenburg has given some pain to our brethren, and some pleasure to our sectarian friends. The builders up of the parties tauntingly say to our brethren, "Then we are as safe as you," and "You are coming over to us, having now conceded the greatest of all points, viz., that immersion is not essential to a Christian." Some of our brethren seem to think that we have neutralized much that has been

[12]Millennial Harbinger, 1837, p. 507.

said on the importance of baptism for remission, and disarmed them of much of their artillery against the ignorance, error and indifference of the times upon the whole subject of Christian duty and Christian privilege.

My views of Opinionism forbid me to dogmatize or to labor to establish my own opinion, and therefore I hope to be excused for not publishing a hundred letters for and against said opinion. Only one point of importance would be gained by publishing such a correspondence; and I almost regret that we have not a volume to spare for it. It would indeed fully open the eyes of the community to the fact that there are but few "Campbellites" in the country. Too many of my correspondents, however, seem to me to have written rather to show that they are not "Campbellites," than to show that my opinion is false and unfounded. While, then, I have no wish to dogmatize, and feel no obligation to contend for the opinion itself, I judge myself in duty bound to attempt:

1st. To defend myself from the charge of inconsistency.

2nd. To defend the opinion from the sectarian application of it.

3rd. To offer some reasons for delivering such an opinion at this time.

I. With all despatch, then, I hasten to show that I have neither conceded nor surrendered any thing for which I ever contended; but that, on the contrary, the opinion now expressed, whether true or false, is one that I have always avowed.[13]

II. We shall now attempt to defend this opinion from the sectarian application of it:

---

[13]*Millennial Harbinger*, 1837, p. 561.

1. It affords them too much joy for the consolation which it brings; because it imparts no certainty of pardon or salvation to any particular unbaptized person whatsoever.

In reference to this opinion, all the unimmersed are to be ranged in two classes — those who neither know nor care for this opinion, and those who know it and rejoice in it. It will require but a moment's reflection to perceive that those who care nothing for this opinion will not rejoice in it nor abuse it; and that those who would, *for their own sake,* rejoice in it are not included · in it. He that rejoices in such an opinion, for his own sake, has had the subject under consideration; and it is a thousand chances to one that he is obstinately or willingly in error on the subject; and, therefore, in the very terms of the opinion, he is precluded from any interest in it. His joy, indeed, is strong presumptive evidence against him; because it is proof that he is one-sided in his feelings, which no upright mind can be—at least such a mind as is contemplated in the opinion; for it respects only those who have not had any debate with themselves on the subject, and have, without any examination or leaning, supposed themselves to have been baptized.

In no case, indeed, can there be the same certainty (all things else being equal) that he who was sprinkled, poured, or immersed on some other person's faith; or that he who was sprinkled or poured on his own faith, shall be saved, as there is that he that first believes and is then, on his own confession, immersed, shall be saved. In the former case, at best, we have only the fallible inference or opinion of man; while in the latter we have the sure and unerring promise of our Saviour and Judge. It cannot be too emphatically stated that he that rejoices *for his own sake,* that he may be accepted by the Lord on his infant or adult pouring or sprinkling, because of his dislike to, or prejudice against believer's immersion, gives unequivocal evidence of the want of that state of mind which is contemplated in the opinion expressed; and has proved himself to be a seeker of his own will and pleasure, rather than rejoicing in the will and pleasure of God; and for such persons we can have no favorable opinion.

2. But that the aforesaid opinion does not disarm us of our arguments against ignorance, error, and indifference, is evident; because it assumes that the person in question is acting up to the full measure of his knowledge upon the subject, and that he has not been negligent, according to his opportunities, to ascertain the will of his Master; for in the very terms of the opinion he is not justified, but self-condemned, *who only doubts,* or is not fully persuaded that his baptism is apostolic and divine.

3. To admit that there may be Christians among the sects, does not derogate from the value or importance of baptism for the remission of sins, any more than it derogates from the superior value and excellency of the Christian Institution to admit that salvation was possible to the Jews and Patriarchs without the knowledge and experience of all the developments of the New Testament. For besides the Christian disposition, state, and character, there are the Christian privileges. Now, in our judgment, there is not on earth a person who can have as full an assurance of justification or of remission of sins, as the person who has believed, confessed his faith, and been intelligently buried and raised with the Lord; and therefore the present salvation never can be so fully enjoyed, all things else being equal, by the unimmersed as by the immersed.

4. Again, as every sect agrees, that a person immersed on a confession of his faith is truly baptized, and only a part of Christendom admits the possibility of any other action as baptism: for the sake of union among Christians, it may be easily shown to be the duty of all believers to be immersed, if for no other reason than that of honoring the divine institution and opening a way for the union and co-operation of all Christians. Besides, immersion gives a constitutional right of citizenship in the universal kingdom of Jesus; whereas with our opponents, themselves being judges, their "baptism" gives the rights of citizenship only in some provinces of that kingdom. For as far as baptism is concerned, the Greek, the Roman, the English, the Lutheran, the Calvinian, the Arminian, the Baptist communities will receive the immersed; while only a part of Christendom will acknowledge the sprinkled or the poured. Therefore, our opinion militates not against the value of baptism in any sense.

5. In the last place, to be satisfied with any thing that will just do in religion, is neither the Christian disposition nor character; and not to desire to know and do the whole will of God, places the individual out of the latitude and longitude of the opinion which we have advanced. These things being so, then we ask, wherein does the avowal of such an opinion disarm us of arguments for professor or profane, on the value of the baptism in the Christian Institution; or the importance and necessity of separating one's self from all that will not keep the commandments of Jesus; and of submitting without delay to the requisitions of the illustrious Prophet whom the Almighty Father has commanded all men to obey?

III. In the third and last place, we offer some reasons for delivering such an opinion at this time:

1. We were solicited by a sister to explain a saying quoted from the current volume of this work, concerning finding "Christians in all Protestant parties." She proposed a list of questions, involving, as she supposed, either insuperable difficulties or strong objections to that saying; and because she well knew what answers I would have given to all her queries, I answered them not: but attended to the difficulty which I imagined she felt in the aforesaid saying.

2. But we had still more urgent reasons than the difficulties of this sister to express such an opinion: Some of our brethren were too much addicted to denouncing the sects and representing them *en masse* as wholly aliens from the possibility of salvation—as wholly antichristian and corrupt. Now as the Lord says of Babylon, "come out of her, *my people*," I felt constrained to rebuke them over the shoulders of this inquisitive lady. These very zealous brethren gave countenance to the popular clamor that we make baptism a saviour, or a passport to heaven, disparaging all the private and social virtues of the professing public. Now as they were propounding opinions to others, I intended to bring them to the proper medium by propounding an opinion to them in terms as strong and as pungent as their own.

The case is this: When I see a person who would die for Christ; whose brotherly kindness, sympathy, and active benevolence know no bounds but his circumstances; whose seat in the Christian assembly is never empty; whose inward piety and devotion are attested by punctual obedience to every known duty; whose family is educated in the fear of the Lord; whose constant companion is the Bible: I say, when I see such a one ranked amongst heathen men and publicans, because he never happened to inquire, but always took it for granted that he had been scripturally baptized; and that, too, by one greatly destitute of all these public and private virtues, whose chief or exclusive recommendation is that he has been immersed, and that he holds a scriptural theory of the gospel: I feel no disposition to flatter such a one; but rather to disabuse him of his error. And while I would not lead the most excellent professor in any sect to disparage the least of all the commandments of Jesus, I would say to my immersed brother as Paul said to his Jewish brother who gloried in a system which he did not adorn: "Sir, will not his uncircumcision, or unbaptism, be counted to him for baptism? and will he not condemn you, who, though having the literal and true baptism, yet dost transgress or neglect the statutes of your King?"

3. We have a third reason: We have been always accused of aspiring to build up and head a party, while in truth we have always been forced to occupy the ground on which we now stand. I have for one or two years past labored to annul this impression, which I know is more secretly and generally bandied about than one in a hundred of our brethren may suspect. On this account I consented the more readily to defend Protestantism; and I have, in ways more than I shall now state, endeavored to show the Protestant public that it is with the greatest reluctance we are compelled to stand aloof from them—that they are the cause of this great "schism," as they call it, and not we.[14]

The correspondence speaks for itself. While it not only reveals Mr. Campbell's position on baptism and his attitude toward the pious among denominations, it also reveals, indirectly, an insight into the attitude developed among many of the members of the church toward the same two subjects.

---

[14]*Millennial Harbinger*, 1837, pp. 563-565.

3. *Debates and the Crystallizing of Attitudes.*

It was impossible that a movement spreading with such sweeping force, and constantly gaining momentum, should escape the field of polemics. It is usually thought that Mr. Campbell was disputatious by nature, constantly seeking debates with his opponents on religious questions; such is not the truth, but contrary to it. Mr. Campbell held but five oral debates throughout the entire period of his public career. Nor did he favor debates as the best method of settling differences; or propagating truth, in the early part of his work. Notwithstanding the fact that he held such a position in his early years, and then held only five debates in his lifetime, it is doubtful if there have been held upon the American continent religious discussions of such far-reaching influence as those in which Mr. Campbell participated. Of his early attitude toward debates, he wrote in the *Christian Baptist:*

In the year 1820, when solicited to meet Mr. Walker on the subject of baptism, I hesitated for about six months whether it were lawful thus to defend the truth. I was written to three times before I gained my own consent. I did not like controversy so well as many have since thought I did; and I was doubtful of the effects it might have upon society. These difficulties were, however, overcome, and we met. It was not until after I discovered the effects of that discussion that I began to hope that something might be done to rouse this generation from its supineness and spiritual lethargy.[15]

Of his attitude toward public discussions, Haley says:

He did not regard debating and fighting as equivalent terms. On the contrary a debate from his point of view was a friendly and brotherly exchange of ideas

---

[15]*Christian Baptist,* p. 661.

with a single end in view, viz.: the elicitation, exposition, and vindication of truth and righteousness. His aim was to speak the truth in love, and to bring before a distracted world and a divided church, the regenerating and unifying principles of the more excellent way so plainly and urgently revealed in the word of God.[16]

Haley quotes Bishop Purcell as having said, after the debate between himself and Mr. Campbell:

Campbell was decidedly the fairest man in debate I ever saw, as fair as you can possibly conceive. He never fought for victory, like Dr. Johnson. He seemed to be always fighting for the truth, or what he believed to be the truth. In this he differed from other men. He never misrepresented his case nor that of his opponent; never tried to hide a weak point; never quibbled. . . . Like his great friend, Henry Clay, he excelled in the clear statement of the case at issue. No dodging with him. He came right out fairly and squarely.[17]

Although Mr. Campbell may have changed his attitude toward religious discussions after his debate with Walker in 1820, considering them conducive of good under proper circumstances, his fellow-reformer, Barton W. Stone, regarded them with disfavor throughout his entire ministry. He felt that they were not in keeping with the Christian spirit and were unworthy of Christian preachers; consequently he never participated in such discussions. However, this was not characteristic of the reformers in general, as most of them were always ready to defend their newly discovered position, and at some time in their career were called upon to do so.

The three debates of Mr. Campbell that made the greatest impression upon the generation of his day, and

---

[16]Haley, *op. cit.*, p. 21.
[17]Haley, *op. cit.*, p. 14.

did as much as anything other than his publications to put him before the public, were those with Robert Owen, Bishop John Purcell, and N. L. Rice. On these a brief word will have to suffice.

The first of these last three debates was held with Mr. Robert Owen, of New Lanark, Scotland, in Cincinnati, Ohio, April 13 to 21, 1829. Mr. Owen had challenged the whole American clergy to meet him in a discussion of his sociological ideology. In the challenge Owen charged all religions with having originated in error, and being responsible for the sociological confusion of the times. He was an idealist who believed his ideology, and who was willing to put thousands of dollars into his experiments. The clergy of the nation failed to accept the challenge, but Mr. Campbell, although denying himself to be of the "clergy," met him as a gospel preacher and simple defender of the Christian religion. Of the general spirit which pervaded throughout the discussion, J. J. Haley writes:

> It may be doubted if any debate on theological and social issues in the whole history of human differences, was ever characterized by such gentlemanly and friendly conduct between the disputants as this one in Cincinnati between Robert Owen and Alexander Campbell, skeptic and heretic as they were.[18]

The two men became intimate friends, each possessing a high regard for the other as a gentleman and citizen. Mr. Owen visited in the home of Mr. Campbell, where many pleasant moments were spent together, and although it was the desire of Campbell to see his friend reject his atheistic theory and embrace Christianity, he was denied that pleasure. It was later reported in the *Millennial Harbinger* that a son of Robert Owen had embraced the Christian religion, thus rejecting the ideology of his father.

----

[18]Haley, *op. cit.*, p. 70.

The next debate was with Bishop John Purcell, Roman Catholic of the Cincinnati Diocese. This debate, on the Roman Catholic religion, was held in the Sycamore Street Meeting House, Cincinnati, Ohio, from the thirteenth to the twenty-first of January, 1837. The debate was the result of things said in the city by Bishop Purcell prior to some lectures delivered in the same city by Mr. Campbell, who, in the course of his lectures, referred to the things formerly acclaimed by the Bishop. The citizens of Cincinnati presented a warm and urgent request to Mr. Campbell, asking that he remain in the city or return at his convenience, and engage the Catholic Bishop in a public discussion of the issues involved. This Mr. Campbell did. It is said of this debate:

> . . . There has been but one debate on the Roman Catholic religion. The priestly method of meeting an opponent from Martin Luther on, has been to put the enginery of persecution in motion against him, or to stir up a mob to deal with him by "direct action." The Cincinnati Bishop has had no polemic successors, and no disciples nor imitators.[19]

In describing the ability of Bishop Purcell in comparison with the other opponents of Mr. Campbell, the same author writes:

> In personality, culture, scholarship, argumentative ingenuity, and controversial ability, the Catholic Bishop is the greatest of Mr. Campbell's opponents. He was weak in logic, but powerful in rhetoric.[20]

The last debate ever held by Mr. Campbell was with N. L. Rice, Presbyterian, in Lexington, Kentucky; the debate continued from November 15 through December 1, 1843. The discussion fills nine hundred twelve closely

---

[19]Haley, *op. cit.*, p. 128.
[20]*Idem.*

printed pages. Henry Clay, statesman and a warm friend of Mr. Campbell's, presided as chairman over all sessions of the discussion. The propositions discussed pertained to the questions of the action of baptism, infant baptism, the purpose of baptism, the administrator of baptism, the operation of the Holy Spirit in conversion, and the heretical and schismatical character of creeds. Campbell affirmed four of the six propositions while Rice affirmed the other two. The reading of the debate led many to turn to the reformation position.

It was only natural that many debates other than these should have been held by the disciples; some on an equally high ethical plane; others were little more than mere wrangles. But whether ethical or unethical in their nature, they contributed much toward the crystallizing of an attitude, and toward getting the principles of the reformation before the people.

4. Societies.

a. Cooperation and Evangelism.

Unity of opinion on the subject of cooperation in doing evangelistic work was never realized completely by the disciples, either in this period or in the period which followed. Out of the questions arising, two attitudes were taking shape. Among some, there was a gradual leaning toward organization for doing certain work, among others, a growing fear of any kind of organization, even of cooperation, when it began to assume the shape of an organization in embryo. Consequently, the question of cooperation and organization presented a continuous problem to the restorers. Cooperation meetings and cooperation in evangelism have been discussed already, but the attitude now crystallizing toward such meetings and efforts among the members demands a brief notice.

The article written by Mr. Campbell on behalf of cooperation so early as 1831, drew fire from some of the disciples, who believed the step was one in the wrong direction. One who signed himself "A. B. G." wrote, "I see by the last *Harbinger* an association in embryo. It was from exactly such a beginning that the many-headed monster grew."[21] This sentiment expressed the jealousy, not only of the individual but of many, for their newly discovered freedom in Christ, freedom from the ecclesiasticism out of which they were just emerging. In 1835, a Mr. Winans wrote the Editor of the *Harbinger*, ·reporting the meeting of churches in Ohio for the purpose of selecting one or more evangelists and raising his support by mutual cooperation. He was forced to conclude the report, however, by saying, "But I regret to add that some of the brethren are opposed to the measure. They so much fear that we will fall into some of the old sectarian tracks, that they would prefer idleness to the doing of anything.[22]

From the earliest years of his work, Mr. Campbell had favored cooperation, even when condemning societies in his articles written for *The Christian Baptist*. Tyler says he opposed the dissolving of the Mahoning Association in 1827.[23] His reply to the attitude of those who opposed the co-operation of congregations manifests some impatience at the failure of brethren to realize that in some things God left it to the wisdom of men to carry out the specific charges which He had given them. In Campbell's opinion, the co-operation of the churches was the expediency for carrying out the things which God specifically commanded, namely, the preaching of the gospel. He said:

There is too much squeamishness about the *manner* of cooperation. Some are looking for a model similar to that which Moses gave for building the tabernacle. These seem not to understand that this is as impossible

[21]*Millennial Harbinger*, 1832, p. 201.
[22]*Millennial Harbinger*, 1835, p. 119.
[23]B. B. Tyler, *History of the Disciples of Christ*, p. 71.

as it would be incompatible with the genius of the gospel. A model for translating the Scriptures from Greek into Latin, and from Latin into the English, French, and Spanish tongues; a model for making types, paper, ink, and for printing the Bible, might be as rationally expected, as a model for the cooperation of churches on the banks of the Ohio for republishing the gospel in the valley of the Mississippi.

The only model that could be given, is, that the first churches in Judea, Samaria, Galatia, etc., etc., did all they could in the way of sending out and supporting those who labored in the gospel among the heathen, and that they did it in the best manner they could. For them they prayed, and for them they contributed all carnal or temporal things, according to their several ability and the demands of society. Let us, then, go and do likewise, and not spend our days in talking about the ways and means, and in doing nothing.[24]

More and more, men were coming to find it difficult to devote their time to preaching while supporting themselves at secular work. Earning a living at secular work required so much time that gradually the preachers entered the field of secular labor to the neglect of preaching. This condition was bringing some to see the need for greater cooperation among the congregations if the evangelistic work was to continue with any degree of success. However, with opinion divided, some fearing any kind of organization while others advocated more organization, the problem was fraught with added difficulties. Realizing the need and sensing the objection, Mr. Campbell wrote in 1838:

We want cooperation. Some of our brethren are afraid of its power; others complain of its inefficiency. Still we go for cooperation; but it is the cooperation of

---

[24]*Millennial Harbinger*, 1835, p. 119.

Christians; not the cooperation of Sceptics, Deists, Jews
and Christians, but the cooperation of Christians—practical whole-hearted Christians: not even a cooperation of
churches; for in this sense of cooperation Christ has
but one church. We go for the cooperation of all the
members of that one church in whatever communities
they may happen to be dispersed, and for their cooperation in heart and soul, in prayers, in contributions, in
efforts, in toils, in struggles for the salvation of their
fellow-men at home and abroad.[25]

b. *Societies Among the Denominations.*

The change in attitude toward organized work is expressed in an article written by Mr. Campbell in 1843, in
which he highly commended the "Protestant Association"
being organized at that time.[26] Not only did he commend
the Association, but in subsequent issues he reported in
full the Address of the Association.[27] Some in the church
found difficulty in harmonizing this new position with that
taken by him earlier in the eighteen-and-twenties. While commending the Association, Campbell nevertheless declared himself as bitterly opposed to any unscripturalness of Protestantism as to the unscripturalness of Catholicism:

. . . We are all Protestants—Protestants in body,
soul, and spirit—Protestants against Protestants themselves whenever they show any affection for the contra-
band wares and merchandise of the mystic city, Babylon
the Great, and the great mother of all manner of abominations.[28]
. . . I believe much in protesting even against Protestants themselves when they gulp down unbroken tra-

[25]*Millennial Harbinger*, 1838.
[26]*Millennial Harbinger*, 1843, pp. 182, 183.
[27]*Ibid.*, pp. 205-209, 318-322, 340-346.
[28]*Ibid.*, p. 183.

ditions and dogmas of the self-ycleped successor of "The Prince of the Apostles."[29]

Although not advocating a missionary society among the disciples, Mr. Campbell did not hesitate to commend the work of the Baptist Missionary Society, inserting in his paper "The Report on Foreign Missions, made to the North Carolina Baptist State Conventions." Not only did he commend the work they were doing, but also he encouraged congregations to make contributions to it. In his commendation of the society, he said:

> . . . No one who is unacquainted with the difficulties which lie in the way of a successful prosecution of an enterprize of foreign missions, can at all appreciate the labor and zeal which it has required on the part of our Baptist friends to get under way their society, nor realize the obligations under which all true Christians are placed to lend them a helping hand in their benevolent labors. . . .

> From these facts and others which we copy below, from the Report, we think no real friend of the extension of the reign of Christ and the universal diffusion of the blessings of Christianity, can hesitate to throw in his mite into the treasury of the Baptist Missionary Society, and thus speed the cause so nobly and successfully begun. When the work is good, and well and scripturally done, we will not stop to dispute about instrumentalities, unless indeed we forget the glory of God, and aim only to build up and perpetuate the land-marks of sectarianism. . . . Every congregation should resolve itself into an auxiliary society, and thus raise, to the extent of their means, a fund for the encouragement of missions and the circulation of the scriptures.[30]

---

[29]*Ibid.*, p. 352.
[30]*Millennial Harbinger*, 1845, pp. 186, 187.

From these statements of Mr. Campbell, written over a period of years, it appears that he was changing his attitude toward organized missionary work from what it had been in the earlier days of his reformatory labors. Because of his influence in the movement, it is only natural that the attitude of many should have been influenced by his opinions, while others, holding to the earlier position, would find themselves influenced by the Alexander Campbell of the decade prior to 1830. But let it again be said, however they may have developed in later years, that the meetings of the congregations prior to 1849 were always toward "cooperation," and not for the purpose of "organization."

Mr. Campbell's attitude toward the Sunday school during this period is interesting, inasmuch as he had included it in his vigorous and iconoclastic writings of earlier years. In 1847 Mr. W. W. Corey of the Sunday School Union wrote Mr. Campbell for his position and sentiment toward the Union, as he had met with opposition and cooperation toward his work among Campbell's brethren. To this request for his position, Mr. Campbell replied most warmly and cordially in favor of the Sunday school:

. . . Next to the Bible Society the Sunday School institution stands pre-eminently deserving the attention and cooperation of all good men; for without the people can read the Bible, of what use is the multiplication and diffusion of the Divine Volume! I never had but one objection to the *administration* of the system— never one to the system itself. That objection was simply to the sectarian abuse whenever any bias was given either the Sunday School itself or in the tracts or little volumes presented as premiums, by which it seems to me that there was an unfair advantage taken in making an institution peculiarly catholic, sectarian and partial.[81]

[81]*Millennial Harbinger*, 1847, p. 200.

c. *The Attitude Toward Bible Societies.*

To complete this period of the development of an attitude among the disciples, a word needs to be said about "Bible Societies." In the August, 1845, issue of the *Millennial Harbinger,* there appeared a notice from Aylett Raines of the organization by the Disciples of the American Christian Bible Society, in Cincinnati, Ohio. This was followed by another article, taken from the *Christian Intelligencer,* setting forth the principles and policies of the organization.[32] On these two notices Mr. Campbell made some "Remarks," in which he voiced his objection to the society, not on the ground of Scripture, but on the basis of "expediency and practicability." He reasoned that since the Baptists had a Bible Society doing the same work, in which all the disciples could cooperate, there was no need for another, inasmuch as the Baptists were doing no more through their society than issuing the pure Scriptures.[33]

D. S. Burnet, the father of the society newly born among the disciples, was vexed at Mr. Campbell's attitude toward the new institution, and in the following issue (September) of the *Harbinger* severely rebuked him for his position and indifference.[34] To this Mr. Campbell made a calm and dignified reply, but continued to sustain his position relative to the inexpediency of the move at that time.[35]

The following year (1846) the March issue of the *Harbinger* carried a notice of the annual meeting of the American Christian Bible Society, signed by D. S. Burnet, in which only the auxiliary societies and auxiliary church were invited. To this announcement Mr. Campbell added another "Remark," stating his objection to the invitation, on the ground that it did not include all the members of the church,

---

[32]*Millennial Harbinger,* 1847, pp. 366, 367.

[33]*Millennial Harbinger,* 1845, pp. 372, 373.

[34]*Ibid.,* pp. 452-455.

[35]*Ibid.,* pp. 455-460.

which he contended should have been included, instead of a specified group only.[36]

That Mr. Campbell never felt any enthusiasm for the society founded in Cincinnati is evident from other articles which appeared later, in which he highly commended the American and Foreign Bible Society, urging the congregations everywhere to cooperate with it. In reply to a letter from William H. Wyckoff, Corresponding Secretary of the American and Foreign Bible Society, he said:

> . . . Of all the benevolent operations of this remarkable age, I regard the Bible Society and the Missionary Association as the greatest and best. These, indeed, are but two branches of the same great enterprise to enlighten and save the world. . . . I am, indeed, a friend and an humble contributor to the American Bible Society, as well as one of its life directors. Still I am much more interested in your Society (i.e., the American and Foreign Bible Society).[37]

But of the Christian Bible Society of Cincinnati, organized by the disciples, he said in the same article:

> . . . I can neither approve the way of getting it up, nor see any necessity for it. To create an institution of this sort merely as a denominational affair, is on our premises, in my judgment, wholly inexpedient.

Mr. Campbell manifested his friendliness toward Bible societies, not only in his article, but in a concrete way as well. He was both a contributor to, and a life director of, the American Bible Society and the American and Foreign Bible Society.[38] He arranged that his share of the proceeds from the sale of the published debate with Bishop Purcell

---

[36]*Ibid.,* p. 176.
[37]*Millennial Harbinger,* 1846, p. 564.
[38]Robert Richardson, *op. cit.,* Vol II, p. 497.

be directed to the two societies in equal proportion;[39] and he had a joint agreement with N. L. Rice that the whole of the proceeds from their published debate should go to the two societies.[40] He was a friend to these societies set up for the distribution of the Bible; but he was not the friend of any of them when they manifested a sectarian spirit, even though it be one organized by his own brethren.

A definite attitude toward the Scriptures, and definite doctrinal positions as the result of such an attitude, were now crystallized among the disciples. Through the press, through debates, through preaching in the highways and by-ways of the times, this definite attitude had been formulated. The "Restoration" movement was making rapid strides, and on the whole, harmony and unity prevailed throughout the brotherhood as the end of this particular period is reached. Would that it should have continued! But this unity, alas, was to be short-lived, for the next must be discussed as a period of strife and division among those who, in the beginning of their work, had so nobly contended for Christian unity, and whose plea was such that if ever unity be possible, it should have been possible upon the platform presented to the world by those earnest seekers after truth.

[39]Robert Richardson, *op. cit.*, p. 433.
[40]*Ibid.*, p. 503.

PART TWO

THE MIDDLE PERIOD: ORGANIZATION, CONTROVERSY, DIVISION
1849-1875

Chapter VII

THE FIRST MISSIONARY SOCIETY—THE
BEGINNING OF CONTROVERSY

1. *The American Christian Missionary Society.*

The year 1849 is the pivotal year in Disciple history; not because of any cataclysmic upheaval that year, but because of the organization of a society against which there was widespread opposition, and which eventually led to division. The church had been taught to believe that all work done by the church should be done through the local congregations. The introduction of a society through which to do the work became a testing ground of the movement originating to unite the religious bodies; and at the same time, it challenged the practicability of the Restoration slogan, "Where the Scriptures speak, we speak, and where the Scriptures are silent, we are silent."

During the year 1849, Alexander Campbell had five articles in the *Millennial Harbinger,* entitled "Church Organization."[1] In these articles he discussed the subject of local church organization and some kind of general church organization for the furtherance of the work by the church collectively. Evidently Mr. Campbell expected opposition to the latter, for in the fourth article he wrote:

> . . . If our brethren will, in moderate size, forward their objections, approval or emendation by letter, we will despatch the matter with all speed and concur with them in the call of a general meeting in Cincinnati, Lexington, Louisville, or Pittsburgh.[2]

Later in the same year, before the convention met in October, Mr. Campbell had another article in the *Harbinger,*

---

[1] *Millennial Harbinger,* 1849, pp. 90-93, 220-224, 269-271, 271-273, 459-463.

[2] *Millennial Harbinger,* 1849, p. 273.

endorsing such a meeting and expressing his personal wish that such should be held; nevertheless he betrayed in the article some apprehension of danger in such conventions, for he says:

> I am of opinion that a convention, or general meeting, of the churches of the Reformation, is a very great desideratum. Nay, I will further say, that it is all important to the cause of reformation. I am also of opinion that Cincinnati is the proper place for holding such convention. But the questions are—*How shall such convention be obtained, when shall it be held, and for what purposes?* These I cannot more than *moot*, or propound. . . . It is not to be composed of a few self-appointed messengers, or of messengers from one, two, or three districts, or States, but a *general* convention. I know that neither wisdom nor piety are rated by numbers; still in the multitude of counsellors there is more general safety; and more confidence than in a few.[3]

The convention met in Cincinnati, Ohio, October 24-28, 1849, at which time the *American Christian Missioinary Society* was organized. The following resolution was proposed by John T. Johnson, of Kentucky, and passed by the group:

> *Resolved,* That the "Missionary Society," as a means to concentrate and dispense the wealth and benevolence of the brethren of this Reformation in an effort to convert the world, is both scriptural and expedient.
>
> *Resolved,* That a committee of seven be appointed to prepare a constitution for such a society.[4]

After full discussion of the matter, a constitution was adopted, the first five articles of which were as follows:

---

[3]*Millennial Harbinger,* 1849, p. 476.
[4]*Millennial Harbinger,* 1849, p. 690.

Article 1st. This Society shall be called the American Christian Missionary Society.

Article 2d. The object of this Society shall be to promote the spread of the Gospel in destitute places of our own and foreign lands.

Article 3d. The Society shall be composed of annual delegates, Life Members and Life Directors. Any church may appoint a delegate for an annual contribution of ten dollars. Twenty dollars paid at one time shall be requisite to constitute a member for life, and one hundred dollars paid at one time, or a sum which in addition to any previous contribution shall amount to one hundred dollars, shall be required to constitute a director for life.

Article 4th. The officers of the Society shall consist of a President, 20 Vice Presidents, a Treasurer, a Corresponding Secretary, and a Recording Secretary, who shall be elected by the members of the Society at its annual meeting.

Article 5th. The Society shall also annually elect 25 managers, who together with the officers and life directors of this Society, shall constitute an executive board, to conduct the business of the Society, and shall continue in office until their successors are elected, seven of whom shall constitute a quorum for the transaction of business.[5]

Alexander Campbell was elected President, although he was absent from the meeting because of illness;[6] David S.

---

[5]*Millennial Harbinger*, 1849, p. 690.

[6]Joseph Franklin says, "Alexander Campbell approved, and was for years nominally president, although so advanced in years and feeble in strength that he never presided over its sessions. He was present a number of times, and read an address at the opening of its sessions." Franklin and Headington, *The Life and Times of Benjamin Franklin*, p. 340.

Burnet was elected First Vice-President, with nineteen
others to the same office.[7] Following the report of the
organization of the Society, as made by W. K. Pendleton
in the *Harbinger*, Mr. Campbell adds a statement of regret
at having been forced to miss the meeting, but commending
the work done. Because of the influence of Mr. Campbell
among the churches, and positions formerly taken on matters of this kind, his commendation is worthy of note:

> Our expectations from the convention have more
> than been realized. We are much pleased with the result,
> and regard it as a very happy pledge of good things
> to come. The unanimity, cordiality, and generous con-
> currence of the brethren in all the important subjects
> before them, was worthy of themselves and the great
> cause in which they are all enlisted. Enough was done
> at one session, and enough to occupy our best energies
> for some time to come. Bible distribution, and evan-
> gelical labor — two transcendent objects of Christian
> effort most essential to the conversion of the world—
> deserve at our hand a very cordial and generous sup-
> port. . . .
>
> Denied the pleasure of having been present on
> this interesting occasion by an unusually severe indis-
> position, I am peculiarly gratified with the great issues
> of deliberation. The Christian Bible Society, cooperat-
> ing with the American and Foreign Bible Society—now
> approved by all the churches present, and commended
> by them to all the brethren, removes all my objections
> to it in its former attitude, and will, no doubt, now
> be cordially sustained in its claims for a liberal patron-
> age from all our communities. The Christian Mission-
> ary Society, too, on its own independent footing, will be
> a grand auxiliary to the churches in destitute regions,
> at home as well as abroad, in dispensing the blessings of

[7]*Millennial Harbinger*, 1849, pp. 689-694.

the gospel amongst many that otherwise would never
have heard it. These Societies we cannot but hail as
greatly contributing to the advancement of the cause
we have been so long pleading before God and the people. There is, indeed, nothing new in these matters,
but simply the organized and general cooperation in all
the ways and means of more energetically and systematically preaching the gospel and edifying the church.
We have always been, more or less, commending and
sending abroad the Bible, and sustaining evangelists in
their missions to the world. But we have never before
formally, and by a generous cooperation, systematically
assumed the work. Union is strength, and essential to
extensive and protracted success. Hence, our horizon,
and with it our expectations, are greatly enlarged.[8]

F. M. Green,[9] historian of missions among the disciples,
and Archibald McLean,[10] president of the *Foreign Christian
Missionary Society* from 1900 to 1920, ascribe to David S.
Burnet the credit for organizing the first general missionary
society among them. Burnet at that time was forty-two
years of age, in the very prime of his life, and considered
by many "the silver-tongued orator of the Restoration."
Of Burnett's resolution to foster such a movement, Green
says:

In a letter written February 28, 1867, he (Burnet)
says: "I consider the inauguration of our society system which I vowed to urge upon the brethren, if God
raised me from my protracted illness of 1845, as one of
the most important acts of my career.[11]

[8]*Millennial Harbinger*, 1849, pp. 694, 695.

[9]F. M. Green, *Christian Missions and Historical Sketches*, p. 172.

[10]Archibald McLean, *The Foreign Christian Missionary Society*,
p. 20.

[11]Green, *op. cit.*, p. 172.

Commenting on the statement of Burnet that the idea had originated in a sickroom, John T. Lewis says, "You know sprinkling for baptism also came from a *sick room*."[12]

At this first meeting there were one hundred fifty-five delegates, representing one hundred twenty-one churches, from ten States.[13] Many illustrious names are to be found among the group, such as Walter Scott, J. T. Johnson, Elijah Goodwin, Benjamin Franklin, L. L. Pinkerton, W. K. Pendleton, C. L. Loos, and C. Kendrick. The original co-operation meetings of the disciples, held for the purpose of mutual fellowship and encouragement, as well as to stimulate greater evangelistic efforts among the congregations, had now become a full-fledged organization; and that among a people who had bitterly opposed organization of any kind other than the local congregation, and who claimed a "thus saith the Lord" for all they did.

2. *Opposition—from the Beginning.*

No sooner was the information circulated among the disciples that such an organization had been effected than opposition began to arise. Gates says, "The first serious internal controversy arose on account of the organization of the first missionary society."[14] In his *History of the Foreign Christian Missionary Society*, President McLean writes:

> From the first there were those who opposed the American Society. They assailed it in season and out of season, and refused to be conciliated by any conces-

---

[12]John T. Lewis, *The Voice of The Pioneers on Instrumental Music and Societies*, p. 50.

[13]*Green, op. cit.*, pp. 100, 101. W. E. Garrison differs slightly from this report; he says, "There were 156 delegates from 100 churches." *Religion Follows the Frontier*, p. 186.

[14]Gates, *The Disciples of Christ*, p. 240.

sions. Because opposition abounded, the love of many grew cold. . . .[15]

Mr. McLean gives four primary grounds for the opposition as follows:

The grounds of opposition were these: First, the Constitution provided for life directorships, life memberships, and delegates from churches. . . . It was said that the Society was built on a money basis and that a money basis was essentially wrong in principle, inasmuch as all believers are equal. . . .

Secondly, another objection was urged even more strenuously than this, if that were possible. . . . It was said that the Book of God knows nothing of a confederation of churches in an ecclesiastical system, culminating in an earthly head, for government or for any other purpose. . . . It was a dangerous precedent, a departure from the principles for which we have always contended. . . .

Third, fears were expressed that the Society would grow into an oppressive ecclesiasticism. . . .

Fourth, it was believed that work abroad hindered the work at home. Let us confine ourselves, it was said, to home missions, where there is enough to be done, to enlist all our means and efforts in fields that will yield a good harvest, until our work here is done; and then we will turn our attention to some other part of the world.[16]

Gates says, "The first leader of the anti-missionary element was Jacob Creath, Jr."[17] Creath objected to the organization primarily on the ground of its departure from the plea which had characterized the disciples from the begin-

---

[15]McLean, *op. cit.*, p. 22.
[16]McLean, *op. cit.*, pp. 24-26.
[17]Gates, *op. cit.*, p. 242.

ning; he also charged Mr. Campbell with inconsistency then as compared with his position in the days of *The Christian Baptist*. A lengthy quotation from two of his letters written to Mr. Campbell suffice to illustrate the general tone of the arguments made by the opposition at that time:

In the first place, it will be seen that, in this discussion, the advocates of conventions have *totally abandoned* the rule on which we and all Protestants set out—that the Bible alone is the religion of Protestants. They have not produced one passage of scripture, to countenance these assemblies, from the New Testament. Is not the Protestant rule of faith, then, imperfect? Is it not too short to accomplish all that the Protestants desire to do? If this rule of ours is fit only for Protestants to use against Catholics, and for us to use against sects, and is not fit for us to work by, ought we not to throw it aside? Ought we not to acknowledge, publicly, that we have been hitherto mistaken; that this rule, when applied to our own practice, fails. . . . While we have a rule of our own choosing, I am for working by it, or else throw it away and get another, or add more to it, until we can get one that will answer our purpose; and let us tell mankind in words, as we have already told them in acts, that our former rule will not answer. The Catholics have three infallible rules of faith and practice—to wit: the Bible, the church or their clergy, and tradition. Are they not more consistent than we are? We have the Bible alone. Our rule of apostolic precept or example, for all religious acts, does not authorize these conventions. Who called them? Our clergy or church? Then we have two rules. From whence did we derive the knowledge of these conventions? From the Catholics and Protestants? Then we have three rules of faith, as well as the Catholics and sects—the Bible, our clergy or church, and tradition. If our brethren will publish that our rule is not a good one, and will lay it aside, or add another to it, they will be more consistent than they now are. I desire to see this point now *settled forever*. I hope you and they will bring all your great powers to bear upon it. . . .

Because God our Father *divinely commissioned* his Son to our world, and his Son sent the apostles as missionaries to the world, and they *divinely organized* individual congregations all over the Roman empire, in the first century, does it, therefore, follow, that we in the nineteenth century, without any *divine warrant* and contrary to our own rule of faith, have the right to call conventions, form Bible, missionary, and tract societies, elect popes, and do all other things we wish? My logic does not run that way. They had divine credentials for what they did. We have none for what we are doing. That is the difference between them and us. We are bound, as well as the early Christians, to spread the gospel. They did it without conventions; so can we do it without them, and have done it. The Apostles and early Christians were condemned by Jewish conventions—clerical organizations; Christians were condemned after 325 by Catholic and Protestant organizations.

As an attempt has been made to weaken the force of my essays by denying that the meeting in Cincinnati, in October, 1849, was a clerical meeting, it behooves those who deny this, to test what sort of an organization it was. Was it a clerical or a laical meeting; or a mixture of the two? Was it a human or an angelical organization; or a mixture of the two? What proportion of the two ingredients were in it? Have we not denominated such assemblies clerical organizations or meetings? Our meetings were composed of our leading men—men in the flesh —not disembodied spirits, as similar meetings were among Jews, Catholics, and Protestants. Why, then, object to calling things by their appropriate names? If I could be convinced that our men had not the same passions that other men have had who have sat in conventions, and that it was impossible for them to do the same evil deeds that others have done in conventions, then I might believe there is no evil in our having clerical organizations.—J. Creath, Jr.

In the Methodistic Conference, held in St. Louis, in May, 1850, a proposition was warmly debated (I do not know whether it was carried), to have a legislature —an upper and lower house; one for the laity, the upper one for the clergy—to finish the imperfect laws of Jesus Christ. They were as *humble and modest* in their first conventions as we are; but ambition makes ladders, with rounds in it to go up higher. Tall oaks from little acorns grow.—J. C.[18]

In reply to this, Mr. Campbell had only a brief note, in which he said,

The conventions, combinations, councils and decrees, of which he speaks, are not plead, not adopted, nor favored, by any one known to me in our ranks. Our associated meetings are wholly *executive*—neither *legislative* nor *judicial.*

We are perfectly agreed on all the premises and arguments of Brother Creath, as they apply to such institutions and assumptions. But a building committee, a school committee, a missionary committee, or a Bible manufacturing or Bible distributing committee or convention, is neither a pope, nor a sanhedrim, nor an ecclesiastical council, any more than it is not an inquisition, or a conclave of Cardinals or Lord Bishops. It is neither a General Assembly nor a Methodist Conference. And therefore, we ask, what does this essay and its predecessors reprove?[19]

---

[18]*Millennial Harbinger*, 1850, pp. 615, 616.

[19]*Millennial Harbinger*, 1850, p. 616.

Creath's last article in the series sought to set Alexander
Campbell of *The Christian Baptist* against Alexander Campbell of the *Millennial Harbinger.* Said Creath:

... Now permit me, my dear brother (Campbell),
to say to you in all kindness and candor, that your brethren who now oppose conventions, and who have opposed
them since they entered this Reformation, are equally
sorry to find you and others opposing conventions in the
great platform you laid down for us in the Christian
Baptist, and now to find you and them advocating conventions as zealously as you then opposed them. If you
were right in the Christian Baptist, you are wrong now.
If you are right now, you were wrong then. If you were
right in the Christian Baptist, we are right now, in opposing conventions. We follow the first lessons you gave
us on this subject. If we are wrong, Bro. Campbell
taught us wrong. Instead of denying this fact, and endeavoring to conceal it, and to throw the blame upon us,
we believe it would be more *just* and Christian to confess
the charge, and to acknowledge that the arguments you
offered in the Christian Baptist, against conventions, are
much more unanswerable than any that have been offered
for them since that time. It is the desire of many
brethren, who sincerely love and admire you, that you
will reconcile the arguments in the Christian Baptist,
offered against conventions, with those you now offer
for them. We are unable to do this, and, therefore, we
ask it as a favor of you to do it. You have condemned
them by the *wholesale* and *retail.* For proof of this fact,
as well as to correct the following mistake you made in
the September number, when you "speak of those assumptions which have, unfortunately, presented themselves to the imagination of our own affrighted brother,
who saw in a vision, in the Elkhorn Association in Kentucky, some five and twenty years ago, a young Pope,
with two heads and four horns, rising out of the earth

under the moderator's chair," to make the following citations from the Christian Baptist. I quote from the third essay against ecclesiastical characters, *councils*, creeds and sects, July 5, 1824. Vol. i., p. 212, first and original edition, you say:

"In the two preceding essays under this head, we partially adverted to the causes that concurred in ushering into existence that *monstrum horrendum informe ingens cui lumen ademptum;* that monster, horrific, shapeless, huge, whose light is extinct, called an ecclesiastical court. By an ecclesiastical court we mean those meetings of the clergy, either stated or occasional, for the purpose either of enacting new ecclesiastical canons or of executing old ones. Whether they admit into their confederacy a lay representation, or whether they appropriate every function to themselves, to the exclusion of the laity, is, with us, no conscientious scruple; whether the assembly is composed of none but Priests and Levites, or of one-half, one-third, or one-tenth laymen, it is alike anti-scriptural, anti-christian, and dangerous to the community, civil and religious. Nor does it materially affect the character of such a combination, whether it be called Presbyterian, Episcopalian or Congregational; whether such an alliance of the priests and the kirk be called a session, a presbytery, a synod, a general assembly, a *convention,* a conference, an association, or an annual meeting, its tendency and results are the same. Whenever and wherever such a meeting either legislates, decrees, rules, directs, or controls, or assumes the character of a representative body, in religious concerns, it essentially becomes the man of sin and son of perdition. An individual church or congregation of Christ's disciples, is the *only* ecclesiastical body recognized in the New Testament. Such a society is the *highest court of Christ* on earth. Furious controversies have been carried on, and bloody wars have been waged, on the subject of church government. These, in their origin, progress, and termination, have resembled the vigorous efforts made to obtain the Saviour's tomb; or like the fruitless endeavors of the Jews to find the body of Moses. We intend to pay considerable attention to this subject, and to give details of the proceedings of ecclesiastical courts," etc.

You then cite a long piece from Dr. Alexander Carson, on the words church and government, and his piece corroborates yours; and his piece is in the following strain: "There is not the least intimation in the New Testament of a representative government." You endorse all this piece of Dr. Carson. Dr. Carson, and Bro. Alexander Campbell, of the Christian Baptist, are both at war with Dr. Alexander Campbell, of the Millennial Harbinger.[20]

In his reply to Jacob Creath, Mr. Campbell denied any departure from his former attitude, but endeavored to harmonize the two statements as follows:

This objection, and all this alleged antagonism between the Christian Baptist and the Millennial Harbinger, are disposed of, or, rather, annihilated, by one remark, viz.: *convention* indicates merely a coming together for any purpose. Such is its established meaning. Hence, a convention may be either scriptural or unscriptural, consistent or inconsistent with Christian law and precedent, good or evil, just as the end or object for which it is constituted, or for which it assembles. Paul and James have been, with as much reason and divine authority, arrayed against each other, as the Christian Baptist and Millennial Harbinger, on the subject of justification. The former affirms that a man is justified by faith; the latter, that a man is justified by works. Bro. Creath can reconcile Paul and James. The same amount of perspicacity of mind and candor will, no doubt, enable him to see that

---

[20]*Millennial Harbinger*, 1850, pp. 637, 638.

in contrasting the Christian Baptist and the Millennial
Harbinger, he is warring against a chimera. A convention, authoritatively to decide matters of faith and Christian doctrine, and a convention to deliberate on the ways
and means of printing the Bible, of supplying waste and
desolate places with the Book of Life, or for sending
out evangelists and providing for their maintenance, are
just as different as a lion and a lamb, though both are
quadrupeds.[21]

It has been difficult for modern students to harmonize
Campbell's two positions, that of earlier days and of 1850.
One of two things must be admitted: either he never realized
fully the nature of the new society, continuing to think only
of cooperation of churches, or he changed his mind and position from that formerly held. So far as can be detected
from his writings, he never admitted changing his mind.

An interesting sidelight to this whole affair is the view
taken of it by two Baptist preachers. Mr. Inglis, a Baptist
minister friendly to the Reformation, wrote Mr. Campbell
commending many things of the Reformation, saying, "I
do not judge the extent of your success by the numbers who
have joined the body known distinctively as Disciples, but
by what meets me everywhere, even where it would be most
indignantly disclaimed—the modification of the teaching of
almost every sect by the influence of the Reformation, in
which it has been your mission to lead."[22] Mr. Inglis proceeded by anticipating and predicting certain successes of
the future, adding, however,

. . . But, amidst these anticipations, the movement
excites my apprehensions, too. The body of Disciples is
now influential in point of numbers and resources. They
have advanced, through a severe conflict, to their present

[21]*Millennial Harbinger,* 1850, pp. 638, 639.
[22]*Millennial Harbinger,* 1850, p. 202.

prosperity, and now is the time when a denominational spirit will be apt to spring up. The selfish canto of "our denomination," may steal in under a mere change of phraseology, the critical period in this respect, is in the outset of your associated efforts and organization.

My apprehensions on this score are quickened by some features of the constitutions of the several societies formed by the Convention at Cincinnati, and by some corresponding features in the proceedings of the Convention itself. To these let me invite your attention.

The evangelization of the world is the inalienable mission of the churches. . . . It (the Society) appeals to the vanity of the human heart, and consecrates it by enlisting it in a holy cause; it is the open introduction of carnal principles and policy into this sacred business, which says, "By all means, and from all motives, give us money."[23]

Several points in Mr. Campbell's reply to Inglis are not only highly interesting, but throw light on the attitude and fears of Campbell, as well as the effort he was making to harmonize his former and latter views, and to justify the new Society. His lack of defense for what had been done appears out of harmony with his endorsement in the matter. Said he:

The subject to which you more especially call my attention, is one, I am glad to say, in which I fully accord with you. In my early writings on the missionary and other benevolent schemes of this progressive age, I had much to object to the manner of conducting these operations. Always believing the Christian religion to be designed for the whole world, and by its Divine Founder commanded to be preached to the human race, I have ever regarded the missionary spirit as the spirit of the

---

[23]*Ibid.,* p. 203.

gospel, and the missionary enterprize as the proper enterprize of the Christian church.

Bible and tract, and all other auxiliary societies for diffusing Christian knowledge, are but means for carrying out more effectually, and more successfully, this grand intention of converting the world by evangelical missionaries or evangelists. In my first essay in the first volume of the Christian Baptist, I took the ground that *the church,* in her own capacity, was the only scriptural missionary institution known to the primitive church and to christianity, as propounded by "its Founder and his prime ministers," and that no separate or distinct association, composed of other persons than its members, could be regarded as of divine authority, or in harmony with the genius and spirit of the gospel and the church. To this view I am as much devoted to-day as I then was; and while consenting to a missionary society as a distinct object of contemplation, and as a means of diffusing the gospel, I now regard it as I then regarded it, as the church of any given district, in council assembled by her messengers, to devise ways and means for accomplishing this object with more concentrated power and efficiency.

It is no more nor less than a synod, a convention, or a cooperation meeting, properly organized, with such agents or officers as may most expeditiously and advantageously conduct and consummate such object. The more simply, the more promptly and the more effectually to accomplish this, is purely a matter of Christian expediency, and must vary according to times and circumstances. Whether you have a secretary, a treasurer, or any other agent, he is, in scripture style, a deacon or a messenger of the Christian community or communities so represented and so co-operating.

And as to life-membership, it belongs to all the members of the Christian church so agreeing to act in con-

cert, and is not a mere honorary or purchased membership for one, or twenty, or any definite number of years.
But it may be expedient for a great community, owing
to an innumerable variety of circumstances, to organize
a portion of its members statedly to act for it, subject
to its own agreement or direction.

That places of honor and of influence in Christ's
Kingdom should be purchased by money, never did suit
my religious taste or feelings, any more than my conscience. There is no spiritual aristocracy of wealth in
the kingdom of Christ, and no place of Christian honor
or power to be secured by any donation or offerings,
however munificent or liberal. As you justly state, a
widow's mite may be more liberal and evangelical than
a nobleman's talents of gold.

I am as fully with you in the sale of life-mem-
berships and life-directorships. This way of giving to
an individual frequently more influence and power than
to a whole church, is of the most questionable policy,
and is wholly destitute of any New Testament authority.

But for these aberrations from evangelical propriety
and principle, our apology is, that our infant society,
when entering into life, took hold of Esau's heel, not so
much for supplanting him as for ushering itself into life.
It followed the example of other Baptist and Paedobap-
tist institutions, and did not inquire into the bearing and
tendency of such precedents. But for doing this, I confess my inability to offer a more satisfactory defence.[24]

The other Baptist preacher was Jeremiah B. Jeter, a
man not so kindly disposed toward Mr. Campbell as was Mr.
Inglis. In his book, *Cambellism Examined,* a book caustic
and bitter in its attack against the reformation, Mr. Jeter
devoted considerable space to the discussion of Campbell's
position on mission societies in the early years of his work,

---

[24]*Millennial Harbinger,* 1850, pp. 207, 208, 209.

quoting copiously from *The Christian Baptist* where Campbell had severely criticised such institutions. When he comes to mention the newly organized society among the Disciples, he says:

The reader has already been informed, through the extracts transferred from the writings of Mr. Campbell to these pages, of his views on the subject of Christian missions; and will, doubtless, be surprised to learn that the Reformers, with Mr. Campbell at their head, have engaged in the missionary enterprise. Soon after their separate organization, they sent out, not *missionaries,* but *evangelists—paid* preachers—to proclaim the "ancient Gospel." For the appointment of *missionaries,* not endowed with miraculous power, there could, at that time, be found in the Scriptures, neither precept, example, or inferential authority; but the appointment and support of *evangelists* to itinerate and proclaim the "ancient Gospel," was plainly sanctioned by the "Living Oracles." But recently they have organized a *Foreign Mission Board*—and have sent forth, not a church, according to the original Bethany plan for evangelizing the world, but individual missionaries, "without the power of working miracles," of which, said Mr. Campbell, "the Bible gives us no idea." Chn. Bap., p. 15.

The above facts will suffice to show the favorable changes which have taken place among the Reformers. The Reformation has been gradually and greatly reformed. The present Millennial Harbinger is a far more respectable and dignified monthly than the old Christian Baptist. Though, it must be conceded, that its pages occasionally furnish proof that its veteran editor has not forgotten the art of vituperation. The Disciples generally are less opinionated, less eager for battle, and far more courteous and conciliatory, in their intercourse with other Christians, than they formerly were. In short, they seem to have taken the road back to Babylon, and have nearly completed their journey.[25]

Opposition to the Society from the very beginning was not limited to individuals; congregations as a body took action against it. Among those that raised their voice in opposition, refusing to have fellowship with it in any way, was the church at Connelsville. Pennsylvania. A letter was sent from the church to four of the leading papers of the Disciples, including the *Millennial Harbinger,* asking that it be printed in each paper. In the letter were ten resolutions made by the church, which are here inserted, stating the grounds upon which that congregation objected to such an organization; these objections are the expression of an attitude:

The Church of Christ at Connelsville, Pennsylvania, having received from the "Christian Missionary Society" a circular enclosing its constitution, held a meeting to take into consideration the propriety of becoming an auxiliary society; and after an impartial investigation of the scriptures in reference to this subject, the following resolutions were unanimously adopted:

1st. That we deem it the duty of every Christian, to do all within his power for the advancement of the cause of Christ, by holding forth the Word of Life to lost and ruined man.

2d. That we consider the Church of Jesus Christ, in virtue of the commission given her by our blessed Lord, the only scriptural organization on earth for the conversion of sinners and sanctification of believers.

3d. That we, as members of the body of Christ, are desirous of contributing, according to our ability, for the promulgation of the gospel in foreign lands; but,

4th. That, conscientiously, we can neither aid nor sanction any society, for this or other purposes, apart

---

[25]Jeremiah B. Jeter, *Campbellism Examined,* pp. 347, 348.

from the church, much less one which would exclude from its membership many of our brethren, and all of the apostles, if now upon the earth, because silver and gold they had not.

5th. That we consider the introduction of all such societies a dangerous precedent—a departure from the principles for which we have always contended as sanctioning the chapter of expediency—the evil and pernicious effects of which the past history of the church fully proves.

6th. That we also consider them necessarily heretical and schismatical, as much so as human creeds and confessions of faith, when made the bonds of union and communion.

7th. That for missions, both foreign and domestic, we approve of a plan similar to that adopted by the brethren of Tennessee, for evangelizing that State. (See Chris. Mag., Vol. ii., No. vi, p. 228.)

8th. That we consider it the duty of all the churches to cooperate in home missions, and that we are *willing* and *ready* to unite with those of Western Pennsylvania, in sustaining evangelists to proclaim the gospel in destitute places.

9th. That we highly approve of a new and pure translation of the Holy Scriptures, both for home and foreign uses.

10th. That a copy of these resolutions be sent, for publication, to the "Millennial Harbinger," "Christian Age," "Christian Magazine," and the "Proclamation and Reformer."

The above resolutions are not the offspring of an overheated imagination—not the result of wild enthusiasm—neither are they dictated by a spirit of covetousness. We have no desire to appear peculiar; no disposition to divide or distract the body of Christ; no longings for rule or pre-eminence; but they are the result of mature deliberation, calm, dispassionate reflection, and a thorough investigation of the Word of God; are dictated by a spirit of love, and a determination to be guided by the Holy Scriptures, though they should fail to furnish us a king like those of the surrounding nations, and to sanction nothing for which we cannot find a "thus saith the Lord."

The 1st, 3d, 7th, 8th, 9th and 10th, need no comment: we commence, then, with the 2d. That the Church of Jesus Christ, is, in its constitution and design, essentially missionary, we conceive to be an axiomatic truth. Not *a* missionary society, but emphatically and pre-eminently *the* missionary society—the only one authorized by Jesus Christ or sanctioned by the Apostles. Her President is Jesus Christ; her constitution the Holy Scriptures; the end for which she was established, the conversion and sanctification of the world. For this purpose she is fully commissioned by her great Head, and fully qualified to fulfil that commission. To affirm that she is not competent, is to charge her all-wise Founder with the inconsistency of assigning her a duty which she is unable to perform. If, then, she is authorized and competent, all other societies for this purpose are not only unscriptural, but they are unnecessary and uncalled for. Unscriptural, because they appropriate to themselves the duty and honor which rightfully belong to the church; unnecessary, because the end for which they are instituted the church is fully able to accomplish. But we are told that the church has not done her duty, and, therefore, they are necessary. Then may we, with equal propriety, have Odd Fellows, Free Masons, and Temperance Societies, for this is the very argument urged by their advocates; and if it is sufficient to introduce Bible, Missionary and Tract Societies, it will also introduce benevolent societies to such an extent as to make the church an useless organization. But grant that she has not done her duty. What then? Must we organize other societies to do that which she has failed to do? Or must we set about reforming her, in order that she may do it? Certainly the latter.

But here we are asked, How can the church, without these societies, send the Bible to the heathen, the missionary to foreign lands, and the glad tidings of salvation to the uttermost corners of the earth? Then we ask, If she cannot, what society upon earth can? If Jesus Christ has not qualified her for the work, can uninspired men institute any thing better? If she did it in her infancy, can she not do it now? If other societies were *unnecessary then,* why are they *necessary now?* But the document referred to in the seventh resolution, will, we think, show how it can be done. This brings us to the fourth resolution.

We know it is thought by some, that these societies are not separate and apart from the church, but part and parcel of her. But by a little reflection, it will be seen, that although they may be entirely composed of members of the church, (which is not often the case), yet they are separate and distinct from her; as much so as any Free Mason or Temperance Society composed of church members. Her president is not the president of any of them; her constitution is not the constitution of any of them; her laws are not their laws; *she* has an initiatory *rite—they* have initiatory *fees;* and but comparatively few of her members are members of any or all of them. Hence, it follows that they are distinct organizations, separate and apart from the church.

But we also object to them because they require a *property qualification* of voters, officers, etc. For instance, no person can become a life-member of the so-called Christian Missionary Society, without first paying $20; nor a life-director, however competent, for

less than $100. But if a brother, "in good standing,"
be so fortunate as to have that amount, he may become
a *director for life,* though an ignoramus, and unfit to
be a director of one of our common schools. The same
principle obtains in all similar societies.

But few words will be necessary to explain the
sense of the fifth resolution. We have always professed
to show a "thus saith the Lord" for every measure we
have adopted; but the introduction of these societies
is a flagrant departure from that *safe rule.* It sanctions
the principle of expediency, and places in the hands of
our opponents a weapon which has already begun to
be wielded with no little skill, and the effects of which
we will soon begin to feel. Had it not been for this
chapter of expediency (which we cannot find in the
Bible) who would ever have heard of infant church
membership; infant sprinkling; human creeds; a Pope
of Rome, and a thousand other evils, which have been
sown broadcast in the church? Let us, then, beware
of taking the first step in the dangerous path of expediency.

The sixth resolution declares that they are "necessarily heretical and schismatical," which will appear from
the fact that they *invariably* divide the body of Christ,
by including a part and excluding a much larger portion
of its members. What more have human creeds ever
done? What more can they do? The only difference
is that human creeds first create division in views, which
is followed by division in action; whereas, these societies first cause division in action, the inevitable consequence of which is diversity of views, sentiments and
feelings.

With this we close, praying the Heavenly Father to
strengthen us all with might by his Holy Spirit; that
we may walk worthy of the vocation wherewith we are
called, with all lowliness and meekness, with long suf-

fering, forbearing one another in love, endeavoring to
keep the unity of the spirit by the bond of peace. And
hoping that the time is not far distant when all sectarianism, and every thing which tends to create division,
shall be buried in oblivion, and the saints of God shall
unite, with one heart and voice, in ascriptions of praise
to Him who loved us and washed us in His blood; to
whom be glory, honor and dominion, now and forever.
Amen.

> A. Shollenberger,
> L. L. Norton,
> E. Haliday,
> *Comm'ee.*

These objections to the new society offered by the
church at Connelsville led Alexander Campbell to make
some comments on the position taken by the congregation,
under the heading "Remarks." These "remarks" throw
additional light upon the two attitudes now developing.
He said:

That differences in judgment, as to the ways and
means of evangelizing the world, by the circulation of
the scriptures in different languages, and by sending
our evangelists to labor in the gospel, were to be encountered, was anticipated by all who had thought much
and long upon the subject. Differences on this subject
occurred even in the age of the apostles, and gave occasion to some sharp words and dissentions amongst the
chief men, all of one faith, one hope, and one grand
aim and purpose in all that pertained to the constitution, laws, doctrine, and usages of the apostolic church.
We only ask and entreat our brethren to hasten leisurely
in finding fault with such things as may, to them,
appear not exactly to coincide with their best judgment
and conclusions, especially in any of those matters which
are more or less left to human judgment and expediency,
as some things are, and, of necessity, must ever be. . . .

Their second resolution is the basis of all their objections, and yet it is, in the main, such a one as we all approve. The only question is, whether Christ's church is one community, or all the communities, founded upon a belief of his divine person, office and mission. A church of Christ at Connelsville, Philadelphia, Cincinnati or New York, is not *the church* of Christ. The church of Christ is a very large and widely extended community, and possesses a large field, even the habitable earth. The church for which Christ died, and for which he lives and intercedes, is not the church at Connelsville, Rome, Ephesus or Jerusalem, but is composed of all who have been baptized into his gospel, and continue to walk in him.

Now, it is competent to *"the church of Christ"* to consult and co-operate with all the individual communities called churches of Christ, which enter into her own constituency, in whatever state, nation or empire, they may be found, in each and every matter beyond their own individual duties to themselves and their localities. These are matters which we regard as conceded by all our brethren, and, therefore, we offer no argument in support of them. . . .

But, notwithstanding all this, and much more yet to be affirmed, on this subject, we do not make one a pattern or type of the other; nor do we justify the convention, in all respects, from the allegation of the church at Connelsville. We only make these prefatory remarks to prepare all concerned for a more candid and scriptural examination of the subject of co-operation in all things pertaining to the spread and progress of the Messiah's Kingdom.[20]

Among the men who strongly favored the organization of the Society, but later changed their position relative to it,

---

[20]*Millennial Harbinger,* 1850, pp. 282-287.

Benjamin Franklin was one of the most outstanding. Franklin, associated with C. L. Loos, served the Society as corresponding secretary in 1857; having been enthusiastic for it from its beginning. In his report to the board that year, he says of the opposition which had existed, "But there has been strong prejudice against the missionary society. This we have labored to counteract and, I think, to a considerable extent it has abated."[27]

In this Mr. Franklin was mistaken, as events which followed demonstrated. At that time Franklin was editor of the *American Christian Review,* a very influential paper among the Disciples, through which he was giving his' vigorous support to the Society in every way. As time went on, however, the editor's zeal for the Society seemed to cool. Yet when the Louisville Plan was introduced, of which mention will be made later, Mr. Franklin even then endorsed the plan and put his strength behind it in an effort to make it succeed. His biographer, Joseph Franklin, tells us, "Finally, Mr. Franklin turned against the new arrangement and pronounced it a failure."[28] In an editorial appearing in his paper January 11, 1876, Mr. Franklin explained his reason for making the change; he concluded the entire missionary program a failure and that the Disciples had made a mistake in departing from the original system of doing evangelistic work.[29] One quotation from the editorial will suffice to show his conception of its failure and unscripturalness:

In the past six years we have paid to one man for salary, traveling expenses, stamps, stationery, etc., some $15,000 to $18,000, and to half a dozen State Secretaries a little less each. We have had agents in the field that did not raise money enough to pay their salaries. We

[27]F. M. Green, *op. cit.,* p. 124.
[28]Franklin and Headington, *op. cit.,* p. 345.
[29]The editorial is found complete in *The Life of Elder Benjamin Franklin,* by Franklin and Headington, pp. 346-351.

have had schemes for building meeting-houses by societies, and men out raising money for these enterprises, and money has been paid, but houses not built. We do not condemn the good men that have been in these schemes and advocated them. We did the same. But must we shut our eyes on matters of *fact,* and not only believe without evidence, but against evidence; against the stern logic of events; without a precept or an example in the Bible that these schemes are good, wise and scriptural? We can go for them no further nor longer, without going against light and knowledge, the clearest convictions of our inmost soul. With what face can we come before the people, with all these matters before us, and ask for more money to go into any of these schemes?[30]

Of Franklin's change in position, Garrison says:

To do him justice it must be understood that his opposition was not to missionary work, nor to cooperation in itself, but to the existence of a society to do the work of the churches. Let the churches cooperate . . . but without all this machinery. . . .[31]

A short-lived but powerfully influential paper of the period was *Lard's Quarterly,* first issued in the fall of 1863, but forced to discontinue publication in 1868. Although of short duration, it was able to wield a strong influence among the brotherhood because of the recognized power and influence of its editor, Moses E. Lard. Numerous articles appear in the *Quarterly* during these years, discussing the "society" problem. Lard himself was a strong supporter of the society in the earlier period of its existence. His opposition which finally developed was not opposition to missionary societies

[30]Joseph Franklin, *The Life and Times of Benjamin Franklin,* pp. 349, 350.
[31]W. E. Garrison, *Religion Follows the Frontier,* p. 240.

on the ground of their unscripturalness; but he came to oppose the one founded by the Disciples on the ground that it left the sphere of service for which it had been organized. Having discussed the attention Mission Societies had held in the ranks of the Disciples for several years, Lard drew several conclusions from the discussions pro and con and from the general utility of the American Christian Missionary Society specifically. He concludes, "That Missionary Societies are not in themselves wrong. To my mind, I confess, this proposition seems incapable of being seriously debated." But he also concludes "That they are not absolutely necessary. This proposition we think as obviously true as the preceding." On this point he says further, "As to a showing by actual facts, we strongly incline to the opinion, that of all the modes in which the church can cause the truth to be proclaimed, the agency of the Missionary Society is the most unwieldly, the most dangerous, and the one which yields the smallest results for the amount of funds consumed, of any in use." He continues in his conclusions, "That Missionary Societies may be rendered useful to an extent which fully warrants the use of them." But also concludes, "Since no Christian man is to be proscribed because he can not, in conscience, consent to the creation of these societies, so neither is he to be proscribed when, in his discretion, he decides that they should be dissolved. They are in no sense or view to be made a test of soundness in the faith or of fellowship. The moment they are so, in my opinion, the wrath of God settles down upon them, and upon those who make them tests."

His final conclusion was at that time the ground on which Lard based his strongest opposition to the Society. He says:

> Missionary Societies are dangerous institutions. Not in themselves, of course, or when doing right, or acting within their own proper bounds; but dangerous

because of their extreme liability to usurp power which does not belong to them, and to perform acts hurtful and oppressive to the feelings of God's children, which they can not lawfully perform. . . . But their most dangerous features lie, not in their efforts to preserve themselves, but in their usurpation and use of unwarrantable power. As a mournful and humiliating illustration of what is here said, we have only to refer to the action of our own general Missionary Society, within the two years preceding the past, in turning aside to pass resolutions expressive of the political feelings of a majority of those then present, to the pain and grief of remonstrating and dissenting brethren.[32]

In 1864 the copyright of *The Christian Hymn Book* was transferred by Mr. Campbell, who had owned it until that time, to the *American Christian Missionary Society,* profits from the sale of which were to be used by the Society.[33] To this Mr. Lard objected, believing that the Society was departing from its original purpose and that such departure would lead to a political and ecclesiastical organization, dangerous to the independence of the congregations. His most scathing denunciation of the Society was over this matter. He wrote:

Again; Brother Campbell is now a venerable old man, with memory gone, and wholly unfit for any kind of business. From him in his declining years the right to the Hymn Book has been obtained. Could it have been obtained fifteen years ago? No more would that sagacious brain have done then what it has now done, than would it have burnt the nails from the fingers which compiled those hymns. We are ashamed of the cunning which preys upon the infirmities of old age, and induces

Lard's Quarterly, II, pp. 135-138.
Garrison, op. cit., p. 240.

it to do what that very cunning knows it could not have effected when memory was good and judgment clear.[34]

By 1868 articles were appearing in the *Quarterly* openly opposing the *American Christian Missionary Society*. To be sure, many of the strong and influential men of the church were for the Society, but they were not without opposition from men equally as strong in their power and influence. The Society was able to do some work of a constructive nature, but it was so nearly dead by 1869 that it was realized something must be done; this realization resulted in the dissolving of the older society, now twenty years of age, and the introduction of a new organization, the proposal of which was known as the "Louisville Plan."

3. *An Attempt at Compromise.*

Because of opposition to certain aspects of the *American Christian Missionary Society*, especially that of raising money by selling life memberships and life directorships, a committee of twenty men was appointed at the semi-annual meeting in St. Louis, May, 1869, to work out some kind of plan whereby the Society could be financed, and more of the members and churches interested in mission work. This committee was to report to the general convention at Louisville that fall. In October the convention met at Louisville, with over six hundred delegates present. A compromise plan was adopted, but it had no power to function. Among the many changes made, the name was changed to the *General Christian Missionary Convention*.[35] F. M. Green says of the plan:

The "Louisville Plan" was mainly an attempt to reach general "church co-operation," and an honest effort was made for ten successive years to realize something from it. It was a failure; and whoever reads and care-

---

[34]Lard's *Quarterly*, II, p. 142.
[35]F. M. Green, *op. cit.*, pp. 155-159.

fully studies the history of the Church of Christ from the beginning, may well doubt whether "church co-operation" was ever realized except in very limited circles.[36]

. . . As a theory of church co-operation it was a success, but as a practical business plan for missionary work, it was a ghastly failure.[37]

The "Louisville Plan" lived a little less than twelve years. It pleased neither group after a short time. It was succeeded by another constitution accepted by a convention meeting in Indianapolis, in the year 1881.

In 1866 Isaac Errett began the publication of a new weekly, the *Christian Standard*. Mr. Errett was a strong supporter of the missionary society efforts of the Disciples, and also an advocate of a more liberal interpretation of the old principle of "speaking where the Scriptures speak." To him is given the credit for having saved "the principle of church co-operation through societies for the Disciples of Christ."[38]

Expressing his personal estimate of Isaac Errett, Mr. Garrison says:

He was the most important influence in promoting more liberal attitudes among the Disciples during their middle period and in preventing them from going the way of all other innumerable groups which had arisen to "restore primitive Christianity" in all its details and had ended by tithing ecclesiastical mint, anise, and cummin.[39]

As has been said already, the controversy was not one of doing missionary work; both groups agreed that the work

---

[36]*Ibid.*, p. 148.

[37]*Ibid.*, p. 157.

[38]Alfred Thomas DeGroot, *The Grounds of Divisions Among the Disciples of Christ*, pp. 117, 118.

[39]W. E. Garrison, *op. cit.*, p. 193.

should be done. It was a question, fundamentally, of an attitude toward the Scriptures. Do the Scriptures furnish authority and pattern for the organization of societies, or should the work be done through the local congregations? As Mr. Garrison has well stated,

> . . . the crux of it was a difference of opinion as to the extent to which the church of today and of all time is limited by the pattern of the primitive church.[40] . . .

Among the conservatives, i.e., the churches of Christ, the matter of missionary societies is still a question of authority and of New Testament teaching. The question of Missionary Societies began the breach among the Disciples, into which the question of Instrumental Music in the worship was driven as the wedge which finally divided the body into two groups. It was the result of two attitudes toward the Scriptures developed over a period of half a century.

---

[40]*Ibid.*, p. 238.

CHAPTER VIII

MISCELLANEOUS PROBLEMS OF THE MIDDLE PERIOD

Other questions arose during this period over which there was much discussion, but no rupture, even though the times were tense and nerves were taut. The questions are unrelated except in the matter of time and in the expression of an attitude. Since these came during the same period, we consider them in the same chapter. The questions of slavery and the Civil War, of "open" and "close" communion, and the "pastor system," or located preachers, are of special interest. There was also a rather interesting gesture at union with the Protestant Episcopal Church during the period which merits a brief consideration.

1. *The Question of Slavery.*

Throughout the year 1845, Alexander Campbell published a series of articles in the *Millennial Harbinger* on the subject of "Slavery." In the main, these articles present the general views of the Disciples, although there were radicals on both sides of the issue who differed widely from him on the question. Mr. Campbell was desirous of two things: first, arriving at the truth and imparting it to others, and second, holding together the body of Reformers without a breach in those trying times in which Civil War threatened the nation. He was not an advocate of abolition or of slavery; he sought to show what the relation of a Christian should be to the existing situation. A quotation from his third article of the series states clearly his position:

As an American citizen, I have my opinion upon the policy and honor of the institution; but these can neither sanction, nor annul, nor modify my Christian obligations. I neither assume to be an apologist for American slavery, a reformer, nor an abolitionist of slavery. The laws sustain it; and so long as the laws sustain it, abstractly right or wrong, it is the duty of every Christian man to respect it and to offer it no violence whatever. A Christian may, indeed, seek by his vote to have it annihilated or modified; but he cannot, as a law-abiding citizen or a Christian, violate or tempt others to violate existing laws without offending his Lord and becoming obnoxious to his displeasure.[1]

In a later article Mr. Campbell set forth the ground on which the question should be settled and upon which the body of Christians should be preserved as a unit. The question of slavery, as he argued, is a matter of *opinion*, being neither authorized nor condemned by the Scriptures; while the attitude of the individual Christian as a master or a slave toward the other, since that is regulated by Scripture, is a matter of *faith:*

Now as our tenets are the apostolic writings, which, while they inculcate a strict adherence to the *faith,* the *precepts,* and ordinances of Christ, allow to every man the right of private opinion and judgment in all other matters, we never can, without a renunciation of our tenets, make any man's opinions about the expediency or inexpediency of the continuance, or of the existence of such an institution, on the part of the State, a term of Christian fellowship. Amongst the peculiarities of our profession there is a prominent one—that *we are not allowed to make our own private judgment, interpretation, or opinion, a ground of admission into, or of exclusion from, the Christian church.* The faith, the precepts, the ordinances, and the promises of the gospel are public property; while our own reasonings, inferences, and opinions are private property, and are so to be regarded by all. . . . Opinions as to the policy or impolicy, the

---

[1] *Millennial Harbinger,* 1845, pp. 108, 109.

prudence or the imprudence of any set of measures, or of what other persons ought to do in certain circumstances, whether similar or dissimilar to our own, not being matters of revelation, or of express precept, are not to be causes of alienation and schism among the members of the household of faith.[2]

Through the editorial column of the *American Christian Review*, Benjamin Franklin likewise was seeking to keep the question of slavery out of the church. He considered the fact of Christianity's non-interfering spirit with secular institutions one of the most sublime evidences that the Christian religion is from God. He considered the mission of the church to be that of preaching the Gospel of Christ, at the same time keeping itself disentangled from the world and its political questions. In answer to the question, "Where is the Safe Ground?" he concluded by saying, "In one word, having been born, brought up, and having lived in a free State, without ever having any interest in a slave, and intending never to have any, we have no commission from Jesus Christ to upturn the civil institutions of slave States, whether good or bad, much less authority for making the Church of God a political engine for such a purpose."[3] His biographer assures us he was not a pro-slavery man, nor was he considered as such by his friends of the South. "He was simply fixed in the belief, common to nine-tenths of the leading men of the Reformation prior to the organization of the Republican party, that it was purely a question of politics, and not of religion."

At the outbreak of the war, the question, "Shall Christians go to War?" became a practical question. The *Review* stood on the negative. In April, 1861, J. W. McGarvey introduced the subject in an article, in which he said,

---

[2]*Millennial Harbinger*, 1845, p. 233.
[3]Franklin & Headington, *op. cit.*, pp. 283, 284.

I know not what course other preachers are going to pursue, for they have not spoken; but my own duty is now clear, and my policy is fixed. I shall vote, when called upon, according to my views of political policy, and, whether I remain a citizen of this Union, or become a citizen of a Southern Confederacy, my feelings toward my brethren everywhere shall know no change. In the meantime, if the demon of war is let loose in the land, I shall proclaim to my brethren the peaceable commandments of my Saviour, and strain every nerve to prevent them from joining any sort of military company, or making any warlike preparations at all. I know that this course will be unpopular with men of the world, and especially with political and military leaders; and there are some who might style it treason. But I would rather, ten thousand times, be killed for refusing to fight, than to fall in battle, or to come home victorious with the blood of my brethren on my hands.[4]

Mr. Franklin concurred heartily in the sentiments expressed by McGarvey, and in commenting on the article expressed his own attitude in the matter by saying:

We cannot always tell what we *will*, or *will not do*. There is one thing, however things may turn, or whatever may come, that *we will not do*, and that is, *we will not take up arms against, fight and kill the brethren we have labored for twenty-years to bring into the kingdom of God*. Property may be destroyed, and safety may be endangered, or life lost; but we are under Christ, and we will not kill or encourage others to kill, or fight the brethren.[5]

Both editors refused the columns of their papers to a bitter discussion of the issue; in this their wisdom was well

[4]Franklin & Headington, *Life and Times of Benjamin Franklin*, pp. 286, 287.

[5]Franklin & Headington, *op. cit.*, p. 287.

displayed. With the issue stated, there was no cause for wrangling over it.

Only one or two incidents of importance tended to mar the serenity of sectional relations throughout the period. At the annual meeting of the Missionary Society in October, 1861, a resolution was offered by Dr. J. P. Robinson, of Ohio, urging brethren to be loyal to the United States.[6] The resolution failed to pass that year. Two years later, however, a rather mild and inoffensive resolution was passed, expressing allegiance to the government of the country and sympathy for those on the field of battle.[7] The Southern Christians paid little attention to the resolution; they simply recognized it as the natural thing that would be done under prevailing circumstances. Summarizing the whole experience, W. T. Moore, in his great history of the period, writes:

Notwithstanding all the trying influences to which the Disciples were subjected, during the war period, they never lost faith in their great plea for Christian union, nor did they fail to practice this union among themselves wherever it was possible for them to do so. . . . Of one thing they may be justly proud, viz., the prediction of their enemies, that their union would not hold in a crisis, was clearly proved to be a false prophecy.[8]

Of the Disciples in Kentucky, one of the border States in the great conflict, Professor Fortune says,

In spite of this bitter controversy the Disciples remained as one body. After the war was over they met in one convention and planned their work together. In a short time the sectional feeling was forgotten and no permanent cleavage remained.[9]

[6]William Thomas Moore, *A Comprehensive History of the Disciples of Christ*, p. 492.

[7]*Ibid.*, p. 493..

[8]*Ibid.*, p. 495.

[9]Alonzo Willard Fortune, *The Disciples in Kentucky*, p. 367.

Such was the joy over their ability to remain congenial, without sectional strife over the question of slavery and the war, that some were led enthusiastically to declare division impossible! In the year 1863, under the caption, "Can We Divide?" Moses E. Lard wrote,

> . . . Suppose fifty of our churches were to combine to produce a creed, to introduce organs, and to encourage dancing. As a people, we certainly have no power to prevent it; still we are not without a remedy . . . if they persisted in standing apart on these grounds they would have to be rejected. . . . Indeed, a division of the body of Christ, except in the sense of causing a faction, is impossible. What divine authority makes one it is difficult for man to make two.[10]

That such should not happen, he advises in the same article,

> . . . Let no sectional conventions be called, no sectional papers be printed, no sectional preachers be sustained; in a word, let the very notion of sectionalism perish from our memories and our hearts.[11] . . .

But alas for the prediction! Without a breach anywhere because of sectional strife, the Disciples weathered the great tragedy which separated other religious bodies, the only American religious body to emerge from the disaster of the Civil War not torn by sectional strife, only to be plunged into controversy over the question of instrumental music in the worship.

2. The Question of Communion.

As observed above, there is no connection between the controversy of slavery and the communion; the two simply came in the same period. The latter is here noticed because

---

[10] *Lard's Quarterly*, Vol. III, April, 1863, p. 333.
[11] *Ibid.*, p. 336.

of its relation to the general theme, "The Development of an Attitude."

A letter from R. Hawley to W. K. Pendleton, then editor of the *Millennial Harbinger,* dated October 16, 1861, introduced the subject of communion with what he termed "the sects." Should an un-immersed person be invited, or even permitted, to eat the Lord's supper in the services of the immersed? To this inquiry replies were made by Isaac Errett, Robert Richardson, and W. K. Pendleton, all influential men, associated with Bethany College and the *Millennial Harbinger.* Since these replies opened the subject to general discussion, excerpts from the replies of the three are here given:

. . . Our practice, therefore, is, *neither to invite nor reject* particular classes of persons, but to spread the table in the name of the Lord, for the Lord's people, and allow all to come who will, each on his own responsibility. . . .[12]

. . . We neither discuss nor determine this question. We simply leave it to each individual to determine for himself. It is really, as the brethren you refer to say, an "untaught question."[13]

. . . We have ever most cordially approved the general, I may say almost universal, custom of the churches, in disclaiming all authority to exclude from the Lord's supper any who, by their walk and conversation, and in their own hearts, approve themselves as the Lord's people. . . .[14]

These statements were replied to by George W. Elley in an early issue of the *Harbinger* in 1862; throughout the year numerous articles appeared by Elley and others discussing the matter. John Rogers and Benjamin Franklin entered

---

[12]Isaac Errett, in *Millennial Harbinger,* 1861, p. 711.
[13]Robert Richardson, *Ibid.,* p. 712.
[14]W. K. Pendleton, *Ibid.,* p. 713.

the discussion through the pages of the *American Christian Review*. In 1863 Moses E. Lard began publication of his *Quarterly*, in which he had an article from his own pen on the subject in the first issue, then later carried on a lengthy discussion of the matter by several brethren under pen names.

A quotation from Elly in his reply to Errett, Richardson, and Pinkerton, serves to illustrate the general trend of argument made by the "Close Communionists."

> . . . I will state my position in a few words: 1. That the church of God is composed only of those who are avowedly "born again." 2. That none are thus born who have not been immersed in water, upon their public avowal of their faith and repentance. 3. That such, and such only, are citizens of Christ's kingdom; and such are (all other things being equal) lawfully entitled to the ordinances of God's house. Fellowship with all the pious people among any of our neighbor parties who have been immersed upon their faith, we do not recognize as partaking of "open communion," but regard it simply as communion with that class of God's children who are improperly associated. . . .
>
> In refusing the bread or wine to unimmersed persons, we act consistently with all our pleadings. To open the door for "all to come," upon their own responsibility, is, in my judgment, going to Rome, and not Jerusalem. . . .[16]

Probably no writer of the period was capable of wielding a sharper pen, characterized by a severer logic or more lucid expressions, than Moses E. Lard. His conclusions on the subject are worth considering. Writing under the caption, "Do the Unimmersed Commune?" he said:

> The present discussion, be it remembered, is one confined entirely to our brotherhood. We are not conducting it with others, but strictly amongst ourselves.

---

[16]*Millennial Harbinger*, 1862, pp. 41, 42.

This being so, the following particulars may be assumed:

1. That belief in Christ, a fixed purpose to forsake sin, and the immersion of the body in water, are necessary to constitute a man a Christian—always and everywhere necessary. . . .

2. That the Kingdom or Church is something wholly distinct from the world; that between them exists a line deep, legible, and ineffaceable; that from the world into the kingdom a man cannot pass except by a birth of water and spirit, and that without this birth he is not a Christian. . . .

That the institution called the Lord's Supper exists wholly within the kingdom; and in no sense nor in any part out of it. . . .

. . . When out of the kingdom, but one thing can alter his (any individual's) relation to it; namely, a birth of water and spirit. This alone, therefore, can entitle him to commune. . . .

. . . It is high time that the world understood us on the present point; and that we understood ourselves. If we mean to teach without mincing the matter, that immersion, for this is the only difficulty in the way, is necessary always and everywhere, since the founding of the kingdom, to constitute a Christian, let it be unqualifiedly said and then let it stand forever as the unalterable expression of our faith. Or if we do not mean to teach thus, let us avow what we do mean to teach.

. . . If a man can be a Christian without immersion, let the fact be shown; or if a man can or may commune without being a Christian, let the fact be shown. I deny both. Immovably I stand here. . . .

. . . True, the Bible does not expressly prohibit the unimmersed to commune; but then no one will contend that a man may do the things which the Bible does not prohibit, merely because it does not prohibit them. We infer duties, not from what the Bible does not say, but from what it does say.[16]

The matter is of interest to us because of its bearing upon the development of an attitude toward the Scriptures. There was growing up within the movement a group with ultra-conservative views, and alongside it another with much more liberal views. In the process of the development of these views, it is only natural that in the heat of controversy men should swing to the side of one extreme in order to meet their opponents, who likewise would be swinging to an extreme in their position. This particular discussion contributed nothing within itself toward the division that came later, so far as can be determined, except to crystallize more intensely the attitudes of the two parties.

An interesting sidelight to the controversy is found in a comment made upon it by the *Western Recorder* (Baptist), in an article entitled, "The Reformation in Trouble on the Communion Question," inserted in the *Harbinger*. After ridiculing Alexander Campbell for not having settled this question conclusively in the earlier stages of the Reformation, that the "smaller luminaries" might have been spared the correction then taking place, the writer continues:

> But there is no accounting for these 'war times.' We are living in a day pregnant with great events. And not the least of the events now portentous, is, that a *schism* is imminent in the *Christian* or Campbellite church, and that, too, on the *Communion question*.
>
> We had been looking for a rupture in that Babel for some time, but never dreamed that it would be on the communion of the Lord's supper.[17]

---

[16]*Lard's Quarterly*, Vol. I, 1864, pp. 43-45.
[17]*Millennial Harbinger*, 1862, p. 459.

The spirit of this Baptist writer toward the Reformation is well expressed toward the close of his article, which sentiment still characterizes certain denominations toward the churches of Christ in many localities: "For next to the abominations of Catholicism, we know of no patent of error or false religion more seductive and dangerous than the heresy of the 'Reformation.' "[18]

The controversy did much to clear the atmosphere among the Disciples. It was conducted on a high plane by men of ability whose interest was that of truth. There were the extreme liberals who would invite all, the extreme radicals, who carried their position of exclusion to an opposite pole. The position generally taken by churches of Christ and Christian Churches is that of the middle of the road group of that period. They let those present decide for themselves.

3. *The Located Preacher.*

The early practice among the Disciples was for the men who preached to earn their living in secular work, generally by farming. They would work all week, then preach, usually at different places, each Sunday. Many of them would devote several months during the summer to holding meetings throughout the country. Those who devoted all of their time to preaching usually divided their time among numerous congregations and in evangelistic meetings.

Alexander Campbell's position toward located preachers in the early days of the Reformation has already been alluded to and quotations made from *The Christian Baptist.* In an early issue of the *Millennial Harbinger,* he had this to say of employing a full-time preacher in one congregation:

---

[18]*Ibid.*, p. 460.

To employ men to preach the gospel in a Christian congregation is a satire upon that congregation which employs them. But if it be the duty of every Christian, in his individual character and capacity, to proclaim the word to those ignorant of it, and to publish the excellencies of Him who has called him out of darkness into His marvelous light, it is the duty of the whole congregation, as circumstances may require, and their opportunities permit, to put forth all their talents and enterprize for the conversion of those without, or for the reformation and salvation of the world.[19]

Since Mr. Campbell wielded such an influence through his two publications, it is only natural that the sentiment expressed therein should, in a large measure, have dominated the attitude of most preachers and congregations. However, as the churches grew in number and size, there developed a demand by the congregations for men to locate with them and preach regularly. Likewise, it was only natural that there should have been opposition to this from the beginning. There was the general fear that these "located preachers" would become like the "clergy" about them. Mr. Campbell had been very bitter in his opposition to the "clergy." There was also opposition to the use of the titles "reverend" and "pastor," as applied to preachers. This opposition was based on an appeal to the Scriptures, it being affirmed that the term "reverend" distinguished the preacher from the rest of the congregation, which was contrary to the genius of Christianity. Also, some opposed it on the ground that the term "reverend" is found only one time in the English Bible, and then it applies to Jehovah (Psalm 111:9). Opposition to the term "pastor" was on the ground that the pastor is an elder or bishop of the church and that there is a difference between the overseers of a congregation and the gospel preacher.

---

[19]*Millennial Harbinger*, Vol. 2, 1931, p. 237.

Gradually, the opposition to a preacher's devoting all his time to preaching in one community and being supported by the congregation was overcome. Furthermore, as division finally came over instrumental music, those preachers who endorsed the instrument and the body known as the Christian Church, accepted the title of "reverend" and spoke of their preachers as "pastors." Among the conservatives, who came to be known as churches of Christ, the title "reverend" is still rejected and opposed, and the preachers speak of themselves as "evangelists" or "ministers." Although the major wedge which divided the body, as we shall show in the next chapter, was instrumental music, the controversy over the "located preacher" and the titles "reverend" and "pastor" contributed its share to the division.

At times the controversy over these issues waxed from warm to hot. Beneath the surface, an attitude of greater liberalism was gradually coming to be manifested more and more among preachers in the great movement. This has been mentioned several times already. Among some there was still the zeal and fervor of discoverers—men who continued to insist that the New Testament pattern must be restored and adhered to in all matters. Others, who were not so zealous for this spirit, were becoming satisfied to assume a place among the religious bodies simply as "another denomination." In discussing the attitude of some of the preachers, as early as 1867, Moses E. Lard made some very severe criticisms of and accusations against some preachers of that day. Several of his statements are worth repeating today with the same emphasis which he gave them in his day. He said:

. . . A falling away will occur, and the iniquity which will induce it is at this moment at work. The sturdy love for the primitive faith which characterized the early preachers in the reformation is cooling in men who still linger in our ranks and call us brethren. . . .

In the first place, they are intensely sentimental; rather, they are intensely transcendental. They are very clerical in bearing, soft in speech, and languid and effeminate in spirit. They are poets and ladies' men, exquisites in parlors, and never condemn anything except their brethren. . . . They are "beautiful" men, and preach "beautiful" sermons. Their prayers are "beautiful" things, their songs "beautiful" songs. Moreover, they are very abstract men, and the aesthetic, the moral, the true, the beautiful, and the good are very fond phrases in their bloodless and virtuous lips. . . .

In the second place, they have an enormous fondness for sects and sectarians; and scowl on no one so indignantly as on the brother who dares to speak against them. With them sectarians are all Christians; and it is a favorite saying among them that "we are as sectarian as any other people." They seldom speak of their brethren except to disparage them; and never of "the other" parties of the day except to laud them. In plain English, these men see nothing good in the great brotherhood to whom they are an offense, nor anything bad in the sects with whom their affinities really are. . . .

Another circumstance, very significant to my mind, marks the career of these men. With hardly an exception they indorse and admire Ecce Homo. And it must be confessed that no book has appeared within the last twenty-five years which embodies so much of their faith or expresses it so well as that book. The man who indorses Ecce Homo is the enemy of Jesus Christ and of the cause He died to establish. With me nothing is more certain than this. . . .

To the brethren everywhere I say, see to it that your preachers are kept to the Book. Allow no departure from it; and all will be well.[20]

---

[20]*Lard's Quarterly*, Vol. 4, October, 1867, pp. 347, 348.

Although the book *Ecce Homo* may seldom be read today, and even unknown to most preachers, it was among the early books in the modernistic movement to make of Jesus a mere man. What Mr. Lard said with regard to the readers of the book in that day can be said of men today who become too deeply infatuated with the sentimental vapories of modern writers who deny the deity of Jesus Christ. No reading will so equip a preacher of today to proclaim the gospel of Christ as to become saturated with the Bible itself and the writings of the pioneers of the great Restoration movement.

4. *Flurries at Union.*

It will be remembered that the Restoration Movement had its beginning in a desire for union among the warring denominations of the early part of the century, but as progress continued to be made and animosities were excited among the sects of the country, the element of union was gradually largely lost from view. However, the Disciples never forgot completely that which in early days they had considered their special mission. In 1866 the Baptists and Disciples of Virginia met in conference at Richmond to consider grounds upon which the two bodies could unite. The meeting was conducted behind closed doors, it being decided that more careful and sober deliberation could thereby be had. In the conference it was agreed that the minutes should not be printed at the time, but Jeremiah B. Jeter, an editor of the Baptist paper, *Religious Herald,* gave a brief account of it, in which he said in speaking of the differences between the groups, "The most serious of which perhaps concerns the design of Baptist."[21] On this difference Baptists and Christians have never been able to agree.

The conference did not effect union, but Mr. Moore says of it, "Its influence was salutary in creating a better

---

[21]William T. Moore, *History of the Disciples of Christ*, p. 591.

spirit than had prevailed between the Baptists and Disciples."[22]

In 1871 overtures were received from the Free Baptists, inviting the Disciples to confer with them on grounds of union. William Thomas Moore was sent by the Disciples' Convention to represent them at a conference with the Free Baptists, held that year in Providence, Rhode Island. Mr. Moore made an address to the group assembled, and later there was some exchange of pulpits among the preachers of the two groups, but beyond this, nothing came of this effort.[23]

Another consideration of union was with the Protestant Episcopal Church in the decade 1880-1890. Tyler, in his *History of the Disciples,* devotes considerable attention to this consideration of union between the two groups. As early as 1853 the bishops of the Episcopal Church had appointed a commission to confer with the religious bodies in the United States. In 1887 this commission sent its declaration, which had been published to the world, to the convention of Disciples of Christ at its annual meeting held at Indianapolis that year. The declaration contained what the Protestant Episcopal Church considered a fair statement of the basis upon which it and other bodies could unite. Among other things, it stated:

Furthermore, deeply grieved by the sad divisions which afflict the Christian church in our land, we hereby declare our desire and readiness, so soon as there shall be any authorized response to this declaration, to enter into brotherly conference with all or any Christian bodies seeking the restoration of the organic unity of the church, with a view to the earnest study of the conditions under which so priceless a blessing might happily be brought to pass.[24]

[22]*Ibid.,* p. 597.
[23]William T. Moore, *op. cit.,* p. 607.
[24]Benjamin B. Tyler, *American Church History Series,* Vol. 12, p. 82.

The matter was taken under consideration by a committee appointed in the Disciples' Convention, which communicated a rather lengthy reply to the invitation of the bishops. In keeping with its attitude toward creeds, the committee said, "But a basis of union involving anything as essential other than what is contained in the revealed Word of God we regard as utterly impracticable."[25] Summarizing its statements on the principles of unity, the committee further said:

It will be seen that this is *catholic* ground. 'The Holy Scriptures of the Old and New Testaments as the revealed Word of God' is catholic. This cannot be said of any creed of human compilation.

Faith in Jesus as the Christ, the Son of God, is catholic. It is the faith of all who accept the Old and New Testaments as the revealed Word of God.

The immersion of believers into the name of the Father, and of the Son, and of the Holy Spirit is catholic. No one disputes that the believer is a proper subject of baptism, while there is serious and widespread controversy over the admission of infants to that ordinance. All admit that the immersion of a proper subject is valid baptism, while there is endless controversy over sprinkling and pouring.[26]

The report was signed by a committee of men outstanding among the Disciples for leadership and scholarship. The names appended thereto were: Isaac Errett, J. W. McGarvey, D. R. Dungan, J. H. Garrison, B. J. Radford, C. L. Loos, and A. R. Benton. A standing committee on Christian Union was appointed by the General Convention in 1890. These made a lengthy report the following year, but nothing seems to have come from the

Ibid., p. 87.
Ibid., p. 90.

gesture at union between the two groups. The whole movement had by this time reached the point that it was no longer a matter of uniting specific denominations entire by the Disciples. By this time it was recognized that the Scripture plan is one of converting individuals to Christ and His authority and the salvation offered in Him as revealed in the New Testament, and that these thus converted became one in Him, and in the church.

CHAPTER IX

INSTRUMENTAL MUSIC—THE DIVIDING WEDGE

1. *Two Attitudes, an Inevitable Development.*

The whole of the new Reformation movement, which the pioneers were pleased to call "The Restoration" (for to them it was a restoration of those primitive principles upon which the church of apostolic days had stood), came into existence and grew because of an attitude toward the Scriptures. It had been the firm conviction of the Reformers that the Scriptures provided a complete blue-print for the church of all ages; not only in the matter of salvation from sin, but also in church organization, in worship, and in the moral life of the individual. With so many coming into the movement from current denominations, it would have been impossible for some not to bring with them more liberal views than others; nor must the general social changes taking place over the country be overlooked. Consequently, there developed gradually two distinct attitudes: one, that the Scriptures provided the all-sufficient guide in matters of doctrine, worship, and morality; the other, that where the Scriptures did not specifically forbid a thing, the worshipper was at liberty to use his own judgment and wisdom in the matter of its introduction.

There had been opposition to the missionary societies, but no definite split had resulted in the decade following the organization of the first one in 1849. But as the year 1860 approached, a new cloud appeared on the horizon, destined to break into a storm which would result in complete division. Gates has well said of the music controversy, "The organ controversy was the missionary controversy in a new form, for both grew out of the opposition to human innovations in the work and worship of the church. . . .[1]

[1]Errett Gates, *The Disciples of Christ*, p. 250.

197

Of the two interpretations of, or attitudes toward, authority developed, Alonzo W. Fortune, a historian of the liberal Disciples, correctly summarized the matter when he wrote:

> There were two different interpretations of the church which inevitably came into conflict. There were those who believed the church should move on with the rest of the world and adapt the spirit of the New Testament to conditions that were ever changing. They held that, when not forbidden by the New Testament, they were free to adapt their program to changing needs. On the other hand, there were those who believed the matter of the church was fixed for all time, and the fact that certain things were not sanctioned was sufficient ground for rejecting them. The men on both sides were equally honest, but they had a different approach to these issues that were raised.[2]

It should be said of those who opposed the introduction of mechanical instruments into the worship that they were not "anti-progressive," but they were "anti-digressive"; they were opposed to any digression from what they understood to be the divinely instituted worship of God. W. E. Garrison accurately stated their position when he wrote:

> . . . The anti-organ side did not argue that there must be explicit authority for every accessory of worship—pulpits, pews, glass in the windows, stoves in the meeting house, printed Bibles and hymn-books—but only that every *element* of worship must be scripturally authorized. We have precept or precedent for sermon, song, prayer, scripture-reading and the Lord's Supper, but none for instrumental music. The position is consistent enough, granted the premise that "the elements

---

[2]A W. Fortune, *The Disciples in Kentucky*, pp. 364, 365.

of public worship are prescribed, inclusively and exclusively."[3]

That this premise mentioned is valid is affirmed by the latter group to be the truth in the matter.

2. *Introduction of the First Instrument Into the Worship.*

Controversy over the introduction of musical instruments into the worship broke in 1860. Prior to that time, few, if any, of the churches of the Reformation had used instruments of any kind, at least this is true of the Middle West and West. As early as 1827 a resolution forbidding the use of instrumental music in worship had been passed by the "United States General Conference," a conference made up of "Christian" groups in New England and North Carolina, of which Barton W. Stone was one of the leaders. In speaking of some activities of the conference, Garrison says, "In 1827 it passed resolutions condemning the use of the title "reverend" and the employment of instrumental music in public worship."[4]

The question of instruments in worship had bobbed up a time or two prior to 1860, but was of no portentous magnitude until that year. All historians among the Disciples credit Dr. L. L. Pinkerton, of Lexington, Kentucky, with introducing the first instrument into the worship among the Disciples. For a number of years Dr. Pinkerton had served the church in Midway, Kentucky, as its minister; in 1858 or 1859 he introduced a melodeon into the congregation at that place.

In January, 1860, Benjamin Franklin published in the *Review* an article against instrumental music in worship; his biographer says of the article and its result:

. . . He did not, at that time, foresee the dreadful strife which was to grow out of it (i.e., out of

---

[3]W. E. Garrison, *Religion Follows the Frontier*, p. 236.
[4]*Ibid.*, p. 150.

instrumental music), and supposing that only here and there could ever be found a church which would use an instrument, he suggested, ironically, some cases where the use of an instrument might prove to be an advantage; for instance, "Where the church never had, or have lost the spirit of Christ," or, "If the church only intends being a fashionable society, a mere place of amusement." The church in Midway, Kentucky, under Dr. L. L. Pinkerton, were using a melodeon, and Dr. Pinkerton therefore felt called on to reply. We quote the opening and closing paragraphs: "So far as known to me, or, I presume, to you, I am the only 'preacher' in Kentucky of our brotherhood who has publicly advocated the propriety of employing instrumental music in *some* churches, and that the church of God in Midway is the only church that has yet made a decided effort to introduce it.[5]

In commenting upon Dr. Pinkerton's reply, which Mr. Franklin published straight-way, he said, "We heard that the church in Midway had an instrument in it probably a year ago, but heard again that it had been taken out, and supposed it to be still out."[6] Since Franklin had heard that the church at Midway was using an instrument in its worship a year prior to that time, January, 1860, it would mean that the instrument had been introduced at Midway in the year 1858 or in 1859; 1859 is the date generally accepted.

Dr. A. T. DeGroot says that L. L. Pinkerton served the church at Midway for sixteen years as its pastor, where he achieved the unique distinction of being the first Disciple in the Mid-West to introduce a melodeon into church wor-

---

[5]Franklin and Headington, *The Life and Times of Benjamin Franklin*, pp. 409-411.
[6]*Ibid.*

ship. In a footnote the writer says of the particular melodeon used by the church at the time:

. . . The instrument in question has recently been found by Edgar C. Riley, Business Director of the Kentucky Female Orphan School, at Midway, where it is now preserved. A brief account of the discovery of the historic melodeon, given to this writer by Mr. Riley, is worthy of recording here.

HISTORIC MELODEON FOUND

In the home of the Nugent sisters at the crossroads on Shadylane between Versailles and Midway, Kentucky, was found recently the first musical instrument used by the Christian Church in the world. . . . Dr. L. L. Pinkerton, one of the founders of the Kentucky Female Orphan School, was the pastor of the little church at Midway. He introduced a melodeon into the worship service.[7]

It appears safe to conclude that the first instrument of music introduced by the Disciples into their worship, was at Midway, Kentucky, by Dr. L. L. Pinkerton, about the year 1859. Dr. Pinkerton's name is linked also by historians with the first liberal movement among the Reformers, which will be considered later.

3. *The Controversy, Warm and Bitter.*

The storm did not break in all its fury until 1864; but in the years following, until 1870 especially, the instrumental music question held first place among topics discussed in the *Millennial Harbinger* and *Lard's Quarterly*. Of the discussion in Kentucky, A. W. Fortune says:

---

[7]A. T. DeGroot, *The Grounds of Divisions Among the Disciples of Christ,* pp. 117-118.

202 ATTITUDES AND CONSEQUENCES

> . . . The controversy became very keen in Kentucky because many of the strongest antagonists of the use of instrumental music were in that state. Among these were Moses E. Lard, J. W. McGarvey, and I. B. Grubbs.[8] . . .

In writing of the controversy raised by the question of instrumental music, Joseph Franklin says in the biography of his father,

> . . . The periodical literature was filled to overflowing with controversial articles on these subjects, until readers sickened of the discussion and demanded a cessation of hostilities. Editors were compelled to close their columns against it.[9]

By the time the question had become an issue, Mr. Campbell was too old to enter into the discussion; but as early as 1851 an article from his pen appeared in the *Harbinger*, setting forth his views on the use of instrumental music in the worship. John Rogers, a noted preacher of the period, wrote Mr. Campbell, asking him a number of questions, manifesting a greatly disturbed spirit over dancing, theatre going, and instrumental music, placing all of them in the same class.[10] Mr. Campbell replied to the letter in the next issue of the paper, with the exception of the question on instrumental music; he made no allusion to it. Later that year (October), however, he replied to an article signed "G," in which he expressed himself fully and clearly on the subject; his language being characteristic of the vigorous manner of his writings:

> The argument drawn from the Psalms in favor of instrumental music is exceedingly apposite to the Roman Catholic, English Protestant, and Scotch Presbyterian

---

[8] A. W. Fortune, *op. cit.*, p. 374.
[9] Franklin and Headington, *op. cit.*, p. 267.
[10] *Millennial Harbinger*, 1851, p. 468.

churches, and even the Methodist communities. Their churches having all the world in them—that is, all the fleshly progeny of all the communicants, and being founded on the Jewish pattern of things—baptism being given to all born into the world of these politico-ecclesiastic communities—I wonder not, then, that an organ, a fiddle, or a Jews-harp, should be requisite to stir up their carnal hearts, and work into ecstasy their animal souls, else "hosannahs languish on their tongues, and their devotions die." And that all persons who have no spiritual discernment, sympathies of renewed hearts, should call for such aid, is but natural. Pure water from the flinty rock has no attractions for the mere toper or wine-bibber. A little alcohol, or genuine Cogniac brandy, or good old Madeira, is essential to the beverage to make it truly refreshing. So to those who have no real devotion or spirituality in them, and whose animal nature flags under the oppressions of church service, I think with Mr. G., that instrumental music would be not only a desideratum, but an essential prerequisite to fire up their souls to even animal devotion. But I presume, to all spiritually-minded Christians, such aids would be as a cow bell in a concert.[11]

It is impossible in a work of this nature to trace all the ramifications of the controversy or to discuss the various articles written, arguments made, and debates held on the subject. It will be sufficient to observe the positions of a few outstanding leaders of the period, with brief excerpts from some, and more lengthy ones from others, where their statements are pertinent to our theme.

One of the strongest arguments offered by its advocates for instrumental music in worship was that the singing in the churches was inferior, and the instrument would tend to improve it. While emphasizing preaching and teaching in their

---

[11]*Millennial Harbinger,* 1851, pp. 581, 582.

assemblies, the churches had failed to cultivate good congregational singing. As early as 1861, Isaac Errett, mentioned above as one of the most brilliant among the younger men of the day, wrote a lengthy article for the *Harbinger* on the subject of "Church Music," tracing its history from early days to the present, pleading for better singing in the worship among the Disciples, deploring the poor singing too often found, and stating the question confronting the congregations at that time. Of the issue involved, he said,

> . . . To a sense of this great imperfection the churches are waking up. But, *What shall be done?* is the question. Some are for seeking a remedy in choir singing. Others are urging the necessity of instrumental music, alike to guide and elevate the taste of our churches. Many, on the other hand, are in favor of going back to the old tunes: and we presume a large majority of the brethren tenaciously cling to the practice of congregational singing—preferring even poor music where all may join, to the most attractive performances, where this delightful part of worship is surrendered to a few.
>
> It is urged, on one hand, that the New Testament knows nothing of choir singing and instrumental music —that it is contrary to the social and spiritual nature of Christianity—that it is born of pride, begets pride, and tends to formalism—that it will surrender fervent piety at the shrine of fashion, and rob the church of her power over the world.
>
> It is replied, that the New Testament knows as little of congregational singing as of choir singing; that the same course of argument would abolish note-books, and even metrical compositions; that in all these matters where the Scriptures do not decide, we must decide under the general rule—"Let all things be done to edifying"; that pride is not in the notes, the choir, nor the organ, but in the *heart,* and may steal into any form of worship; that discordant and uncultured singing is offen-

sive to good taste and detrimental to piety; and that as *educated mind* is desirable to advance the interests of the cause of salvation, so *educated voices* and *educated tastes,* if found promotive of the best interests if the church, should be religiously and diligently encouraged, as auxiliary to the great work of saving the world from sin and death.

We do not intend here to enter into this rising controversy. We prefer to forestall the discussion by a full statement of facts bearing on the question, and a calm and unprejudiced utterance of the conclusions which we think legitimately flow from the premises submitted. We think the following are lessons clearly taught in the facts which we have presented:[12]

Of the "lessons" pointed out, three bear directly upon this subject. In these three he said,

4. That the genius of this reformatory movement, like that of previous reformations, is not favorable to choir singing and instrumental music. Its sympathies are with the bewildered and sin-oppressed masses, and it wants "music for the million." Its original power will be largely lost when the stirring melodies of its early days shall have been supplanted by stately artistic *performances.*

5. As the church of Christ is the common home of all his people—"Barbarian, Scythian, bond and free," who are "all one in Christ Jesus"; and as singing is the only part of worship in which the great mass of Christians can personally participate; no choir singing or instrumental music should ever be allowed to interfere for a moment with this privilege and right of the saints. If such appliances can be made to *assist* rather than *hinder* this great object of uniting the whole congregation in the worship, the most serious objection to them is removed.

---

[12]*Millenniail Harbinger,* 1861, p. 558.

6. The innovation of choirs and instruments will not be checked by captious objections. The only way to put a stop to it, is *to set to work diligently to train the churches in vocal music.* Take away the cause of complaint. We forewarn the brethren, especially in the cities and large towns, that if they wish to block up the way against the introduction of choirs and organs, and the formalism resulting therefrom, they must employ suitable teachers of vocal music, and spend a portion of every year in training all the voices in the churches in the knowledge of musical science and the practice of suitable tunes—so that the present partial, discordant and unedifying music of our churches may be abandoned and forgotten.[18]

J. W. McGarvey is recognized by many as the greatest scholar among the Disciples of his day; probably more books have been left to us from his pen than from any other writer of the period. At the time of the controversy he was in the prime of life, having been born March 1, 1829, near Hopkinsville, Kentucky. He began preaching at the Main Street Church in Lexington, in the year 1862, and teaching in the "College of the Bible of Kentucky University" in 1865. He continued to teach in the College of the Bible until 1895, when he became its president; he continued in this position until his death in 1912.

McGarvey opposed instrumental music in the church worship from the beginning of the controversy until his death. He left the Broadway church in Lexington in 1902, when, as an elder in the congregation, the instrument was introduced over his protest, by popular vote of the congregation. Throughout the years of his busy life he wrote much on the subject. As early as 1864 there appeared from him an article in the *Harbinger* in which he stated the position from which, so far as is known, he never retreated. In this he declared

---

[18]*Millennial Harbinger*, 1861, p. 559.

the position taken by the men of the Reformation, when he said, "In the earlier years of the present Reformation, there was entire unanimity in the rejection of instrumental music from our public worship. It was declared unscriptural, inharmonious with the Christian institution, and a source of corruption."[14]

Several statements from the article are worthy of consideration, since they state the issue clearly:

> By what standard shall we judge of this question? If there is any Scripture authority upon the subject, then, of course, we must hear that first; if not, then expediency must supply the test. . . . But if the Scriptures do not leave us at liberty, then we have no right to appeal to expediency, except for the purpose of vindicating the decision of the Scriptures. . . . Now it must be admitted that the New Testament is silent upon this subject, and that this argument is at least plausible. . . .
>
> . . . We cannot, therefore, by any possibility, know that a certain element of worship is acceptable to God in the Christian dispensation, when the Scriptures which speak of that dispensation are silent in reference to it. To introduce any such element is unscriptural and presumptuous. It is will worship, if any such thing as will worship can exist. On this ground we condemn the burning of incense, the lighting of candles, the wearing of priestly robes, and the reading of printed prayers. On the same ground we condemn instrumental music.
>
> If, now, any man can mention an act or an element of worship known to be acceptable to God, but not authorized by the New Testament, he will prove this argument against instrumental music in the church invalid. I know not how it can be done in any other way.[15]

---

[14]*Millennial Harbinger*, 1864, p. 510.
[15]*Millennial Harbinger*, 1864, pp. 511-513.

The article brought forth a reply from A. S. Hayden; there followed an interesting but lengthy discussion of the issues involved between McGarvey and Hayden, in which the former summed his argument in the form of a syllogism, clearly stating what he considered to be the real issue:

The fact that any part of the Jewish worship was discontinued by those who organized the Christian church, is a direct condemnation of it by the spirit of God, as unsuited to the new institution.

The use of instrumental music is an element of Jewish worship which was thus discontinued.

Therefore, the use of instrumental music in worship is condemned by the spirit of God, as unsuited to the new institution.[16]

This argument cannot be appreciated by one of "modernistic" inclinations who has no interest in "covenants" and a "divine pattern," and no respect for the authority of Jesus Christ; but to all who recognize the difference between the Old and New Testaments, the New as revealing a divine pattern of organization and worship, backed by the authority of Christ and not Moses, it carried and continues to carry great weight.

No outstanding student affirmed the use of instrumental music in the worship to be authorized by Scripture. It was generally contended for by those favoring its use on the ground of liberty and expediency. W. K. Pendleton, twice the son-in-law of Alexander Campbell, and the successor of Mr. Campbell as editor of the *Millennial Harbinger*, and as President of Bethany College, wrote in the *Harbinger* of 1864, setting forth his views of the organ in worship and his reasons for the position assumed at that time. He did not object at that time to the instrument on the same grounds as others objected, although he admitted there was no Scrip-

---

[16]*Millennial Harbinger*, 1865, p. 91.

tural authority for it. His objections voiced in that article were based primarily on the fact that it would interfere with congregational singing, which is "the *prime privilege of the' church.*" Of Scriptural authority for the practice, Mr. Pendleton says, "With respect to instrumental music, I presume that no one at all acquainted with ecclesiastical history will pretend to claim for its introduction in the church any pretense of primitive authority or warrant.[17] . . .

Four years later this same writer came out much stronger in his denunciation of instrumental music in the worship. Although the following quotation is lengthy, the position of respect and influence held by Mr. Pendleton in the church after Alexander Campbell's death coupled with its definiteness of statement, justify its insertion:

> No thoughtful observer of the state and expression of religious feeling in America can have failed to see that the vague and delightful, but semi-sensuous emotions excited by the grand and sublime power of music, are becoming the fashionable substitute for the simple and genuine worship of the apostolic church. . . .

Continuing, speaking of the influence of such as a "delusion that it is worship," the writer then quotes the following from the New York *Herald:*

> . . . "In public worship New York now absolutely wrecks its religion on music. . . . It will be also impossible to expunge the excess of music from religious worship at present. Presbyterians doctrinally orthodox, have fallen into it; Methodists exhort in musical notes and semibreves; Episcopalians cantillate everything, even prayers and responses; and Catholics, always grand and copious in this respect, are becoming more and more so, in consonance with the general spirit of religious worship in the metropolis. The Baptists, only, as a great body, have held

---

[17]*Millennial Harbinger,* 1864, p. 126.

aloof and kept to the letter of their original simplicity;
and these will no doubt gradually soften and mingle with
the general pulp. . . .

Mr. Pendleton then made the following comments to the
sentiments expressed in the article from the *Herald:*

It is a high compliment to the "Baptists" to say that
"They only, as a great body, have held aloof and kept the
letter of their original simplicity." We trust that the
prophecy will not prove true, "that they will no doubt
gradually soften and mingle with the general pulp."
Nothing can save them or any people from this all-en-
gulfing tendency of the human heart, but to fill its yearn-
ings, its aspirations and its enthusiasm with the great
truths, the precepts and the promises of the Bible. Men
must worship something, and they will find modes of expressing this human instinct. God has made provision
for this propensity of our nature in the revelation of his
word. But when this is not put into the minds of the
people, their hearts run astray after inventions of man,
and spend their zeal in forms, which are not according
to knowledge. It is still true, "Where there is no vision,
the people perish." The people are without "the knowledge of God and of Christ, whom to know is life eternal."
This knowledge is revealed only in the Bible. It is no out-
gush of the religious instinct,—no form, which the struggling religious sentiment shapes for itself, and to which
it then bows down in worship. *All conditions originating in this way are idols.* Let these words be written in
letters of fire upon the walls of all our temples, that man
may know,—he is not to make his own religion. God
has revealed it and written it in a book, and to that book
we must go for it. What is the reason of this tendency
of the religious feeling of the American people, of which
the Herald speaks? Why do the people seek to "music as
the organ of a certain vague, boundless aspiration and

enthusiasm, which must be wreaked upon something," if
not because, the true objects of this aspiration and enthusiasm are not discovered to them? Paul found the
Athenians in this condition. With their *thirty thousand*
idols, they were still unsatisfied, and seeking to wreak
their vague and boundless feeling upon something, they
knew not what—"the idol of the Unknown." Had he
imitated our modern Priests, he would have wheeled a
huge Berlin organ into their midst, and cried, "Behold
the object of your devotions! Hear its thundering
bravuras; let your souls rise on its majestic waves of
harmony and float away into the fathomless abysses of
the infinite. 'Whom you ignorantly worship, him declare
I unto you.'" But Paul had not reached this sublime
height, to which the development of the religious feeling
is fast lifting the free, progressive American mind; and
he was content to preach to them Christ, and him crucified. He could not leap over sin, to worship;—he could
not stifle the religious conscience with the vague and be-
wildering cantatas of religious music. Hence he directed
this vague, boundless aspiration and enthusiasm, not to
music, but to "Jesus and the resurrection."

We must keep the people to the Bible, if we would
save them,—fill their hearts with the sure words of eternal life; inspire them, not with the love of music, but the
love of God and their fellow man,—and lead them by
paths of virtue and charity into ways of righteousness
and peace.

If the people will have an idol, music is perhaps as
respectable a one as the religious development of the nineteenth century can invent. We are not arguing the relative merit of human inventions. We are denying that the
Christian Religion is, in any part,—jot or tittle,—a human
invention at all. "Development" has nothing to do with it.
It came from its divine author perfect and complete, and
the great work of the church is to hold the people to it;

to protest, to remonstrate, to anathematize against anything that sets itself up beside it,—till every imagination
of man is crushed under its feet and withered by the
breath of its nostrils. "Pure religion and undefiled"—
sublimated into music! the sweet charities, that fall like
heavenly dew upon its arid places of human woe—ex-
pired in screaming ecstasies of sound! 'Tis too impious.
Better for the people, that some stern iconoclast should
rise in the holy indignation of the old prophets, and break
to pieces all the senseless organs and scatter all the god-
less choirs that desecrate our fashionable cathedrals, than
that this fatal tendency to substitute a musical senti-
mentalism for a living Christianity, should be allowed to
go unrebuked until it has fixed itself, with the power of
a fatal delusion, upon the habits and the credulity of
the age.

. . . . .

It has been said, that nothing is so absurd but that
someone will be found foolish enough to embrace it. It
would seem especially true, in matters of religion. This
folly of elevating organ-grinding and accompaniments
into the place of apostolic worship, illustrates it. Who
could have thought that with the Bible in their hands, the
American people could ever have drifted into such idol-
atry! Is it true that the Baptists are breasting the current? Then honor to the Baptists! Let us hold up their
hands in this work. They are with the Savior and the
apostles, and there is where we profess and desire to
stand. Let us keep music in its place, as the expression of
the melody of the heart, the instrument and aid, not the
essence and end of our worship.[18]

Moses E. Lard, who possessed one of the keenest and
most penetrating minds of the day, threw the weight of his
influence and that of the *Quarterly* with the opposition to the

---

[18]*Millennial Harbinger*, 1868, pp. 39-42.

introduction of instruments into the worship. Lard appealed to the Restoration plea of the Scriptures and their authorization for all acts of worship and matters of doctrine. The old attitude found one of its strongest advocates in this keen and trenchant writer. In an article appearing in 1864, warning the churches of the ultimate apostasy which would be occasioned by forsaking the old position on authority, he said:

> . . . Now that we as a people have agreed to accept the New Testament as that standard is a fact too notorious to admit of question. To this we have consented to bring the smallest point of doctrine, and the most trivial feature in practice. And furthermore, we have solemnly covenanted that whatever cannot be clearly shown to have the *sanction* of this standard shall be held as not doctrine, and shall not be practiced. . . . As a people we have from the first and continually to the present proclaimed that the New Testament and that alone is our only full and perfect rule of faith and practice. . . .

> . . . In what light then must we view him who attempts to introduce it into the churches of Christ of the present day? I answer, as an insulter of the authority of Christ, and as a defiant and impious innovator of the simplicity and purity of the ancient worship. . . .

> . . . The day on which a church sets up an organ in its house, is the day on which it reaches the first station on the road to apostasy. From this it will soon proceed to other innovations; and the work of innovating once fairly commenced, no stop can be put to it till ruin ensues.[19] . . .

After writing at much length on the subject, opposing it on the ground of its unscripturalness, he closed one of his articles with these words, expressing his own personal attitude toward the introduction of such innovations:

---

[19]*Lard's Quarterly,* Vol. 1, 1864, pp. 330-332.

. . . Thus these organ-grinding churches will in the lapse of time be broken down, or wholly apostatize, and the sooner they are in fragments the better for the cause of Christ. I have no sympathy with them, no fellowship for them, and so help me God never intend knowingly to put my foot into one of them. As a people we claim to be engaged in an effort to return to the purity, simplicity, freedom from ostentation and pride, of the ancient apostolic churches. Let us, then, neither wink at anything standing in the way, nor compromise aught essential to this end. The moment we do so our unity is at an end, and our hopes are in the dust.[20]

The attitude toward the whole question was summed up by the same writer a few years later, when writing under the caption, "The True Worship of God," he declared:

. . . Every man among us must stand nobly up for the following position: *In all acts of worship we must do only what is prescribed in the New Testament, or was done with divine sanction by the primitive Christians.* Not the semblance of innovation must be allowed on this sacred principle.[21]

About that time the church in St. Louis bought from the Episcopal Church a building containing a very fine organ which many of the members wanted to retain in the building, using it in the church services. This desire on the part of the church brought forth an address from Dr. Christopher in 1867 opposing those wishing to retain it. Dr. Christopher had written much on the subject prior to that time. C. L. Loos, associated with Mr. Pendleton as a professor in Bethany College and as assistant editor of the *Harbinger*, wrote an article commenting upon and commending the address delivered by Dr. Christopher. Loos summed up his own position in a few words, saying:

---

[20]*Ibid.*, p. 333.
[21]*Lard's Quarterly*, Vol. I, 1867, p. 395.

... Every new experience in this matter strengthens the conviction that the *participation and edification of the congregation in the solemn and joyful service of praise to God, is hindered and often destroyed by instrumental music.* All the pleadings of the defenders of this practice seem to fail to cure the evil, and to convince men against the testimony of their own eyes and ears. So far as the *argument* is concerned, not the persons nor the place, it is an exact parallel to the question of theaters. Strong pleadings are perpetually repeated of what they ought to be, can be, and might be made;—but unfortunately all the meantime, they *are*, and continue uninterruptedly to be, bad. Don't wonder then, good brethren, that we fail to be convinced, when there is so much against and very little for it.[22]

Commenting upon the same address by Dr. Christopher, Moses E. Lard said,

The question of instrumental music in the churches of Christ involves a great and sacred principle. . . . That principle is the right of men to introduce innovations into the prescribed worship of God. This right we utterly deny. The advocates of instrumental music affirm it. This makes the issue. As sure as the Bible is a divine book, we are right and they are wrong. Time and facts will prove the truth of this. The churches of Christ will be wrecked the day the adverse side triumphs; and I live in fear 'that it will do it. Our brethren are now freely introducing melodeons into their Sunday schools. This is but the first step in the act, I fear.[23]

In 1869 there was an article by Professor Robert Richardson published in the *American Christian Review*, which was endorsed and commended by the editor, and considered

---

[22]*Millennial Harbinger*, 1867, pp. 476, 477.
[23]*Lard's Quarterly*, 1867, p. 368.

by Mr. Franklin to have been unanswerable. Mr. Richardson
practiced medicine for a number of years. In 1835 he moved
to Bethany where for many years he was associated with Mr.
Campbell as co-laborer on the *Millennial Harbinger* and professor of chemistry in Bethany College. Mr. Richardson was
also a preacher and lecturer of no mean ability. His greatest
work, no doubt, is his "Memoirs of Alexander Campbell."
In his *History of the Disciples of Christ*, W. T. Moore ranks
him (Richardson) among the "Big Four of the Nineteenth
Century, Reformation." Because of Mr. Richardson's importance in the movement under discussion, the article from
his pen on the subject of instrumental music in the worship
is especially interesting.

As it regards the use of musical instruments in
church worship, the case is wholly different. This can
never be a question of expediency, for the simple reason
that there is no law prescribing or authorizing it. If it
were anywhere said in the New Testament that Christians
should use instruments, then it would become a question
of expediency what kind of instrument was to be used,
whether an organ or a melodeon, the "loud-sounding cym-
bals" or the "light guitar"; whether it should cost $50,
or $500, or $1,000; and what circumstances should regu-
late the performance. It happens, however, that this is
nowhere said; and, consequently, no such questions of
expediency can ever arise in a church that is truly and
really governed by the law of the Lord.

A writer in the Standard, indeed, attempted some
time ago to show that musical instruments were actually
commanded, because implied in the word "psalms." This
effort was altogether in the right direction, and afforded
quite a contrast to the far-fetched sophistries of others,
who have sought to justify the use of instruments by
something else than the law of Christ. For the proper
question is not, Is it expedient? nor, Does it assist the
singing? nor, Is it not as lawful to use a musical instru-

ment in the church as in the social circle? (the implied principle of which question, if decided in the affirmative, would authorize equally the introduction into the church of blind man's buff, or a game of hot-cockles) ; but, Is there any law for it? Have we a "thus saith the Lord" for it? Have we an approved precedent for it among the primitive churches? Nay; it is perfectly well known that there is not a shadow of authority in the Christian Scriptures for it, and that instrumental music was not practiced by the primitive Christians—the organ having been introduced for the first time into the church served by Maranus Sanutus, in the year 1290. This delay is not attributable to the absence of suitable instruments at an earlier period; or, as some allege, to the poverty of the early Christians—an assertion disproved by the apostolic exhortation to the rich; but simply because a progressive musical refinement had not previously demanded this additional corruption of primitive order as a concession to "itching ears."

I think I showed, in noticing the argument based upon the word *psalms,* that the law authorizing the exercise of singing not only does not imply the use of musical instruments, but in its very terms prohibits this, as incapable of fulfilling any of the requirements of the law. I have seen no attempt to set aside these arguments, though, as sophists practice, something of the sort was promised to be forthcoming "at another time." The introduction of a musical instrument into a church is a triumph of the sensual over the spiritual. The innovation once effected, the sensual mind seeks to justify the act by plausibilities, as any error may be sustained, and to trust to the Christian forbearance of those who are unconvinced, until the habit of hearing the instrument shall at length silence their scruples. There will be no joy, however, I fancy, at the great day, in a triumph thus gained over conscientious conviction, where the soothing

strains of music are employed, not to "admonish" or to
enlighten, but to put to sleep the guardian of the soul.
The humble, law-abiding Christian will not thus introduce anything that wounds the consciences of his brethren. His inquiry is: what hath the Lord answered? and,
what hath the Lord spoken? He must first find the law
before he can render the obedience, and before he can
admit of any questions of expediency, as to the manner
in which, or the circumstances under which, he is to ful-
fill the duties enjoined upon him.[24]

It is not to be thought that none were to be found who
favored the introduction of the instruments into the worship,
for that side had its champions as well as the opponents to
instrumental music. Isaac Errett became the champion of a
more liberal attitude among the Disciples, the greatest defender of the Missionary Society, and a supporter of the
introduction of instruments into church services. In 1866
the *Christian Standard* was founded with Mr. Errett as editor.
The first issue appeared just after the death of Mr. Campbell,
carrying an announcement of the death of the great leader.
Many now began to look to Mr. Errett for leadership, especially from among the more liberal group, which was only
natural as he was a forceful preacher and popular writer. In
an article appearing in the *Standard* in 1870, Mr. Errett
stated the position of his paper, saying:

The Review and the Standard can agree to oppose
the introduction of instrumental music in our churches,
but they are not likely to agree in the style of their opposition, for they differ radically in the grounds of their
opposition.

The Review regards the use of instruments as an
attempt to introduce a new element of worship, and de-
claims against it as utterly wanting in divine authority.

*F. M. Green, *Life and Times of John Franklin Rowe*, pp. 117,
118.

The Standard regards it as an expedient, proposed to aid the church to perform, in an edifying way, the duty of singing; and advises against it as not necessary to that end, and as tending to create strife in many of our churches. The conclusions reached are as different as the premises. On the ground of the Review, it must be condemned and rejected as a corruption of the worship—a daring attempt to invade the authority of the Head of the Church, and those who have anything to do with it must be dealt with as violators of the laws of the kingdom. From our point of view it must be treated simply as a question of expediency, and decided according to its real merits as an expedient, not as a matter of positive law.

The Review admits expedients—means of obeying the divine precept to sing—such as hymn-books, note books, tuning forks, etc., and notwithstanding all the brave talk in its former article against inferences, is compelled to infer the propriety of these and many other arrangements for promoting the edification of the church. Why, then, raise such a clamor about instruments? Why may they not be treated as expedients, and a decision reached for or against them as such? Because, says the Review, "The instrument, when introduced, is made an integral part of, and an element in, the worship." That is just where we fail to agree. We do not so understand the friends of instrumental music. A few, it is true, have attempted to advocate it as of divine authority, but these are the exceptions, and these attempts we have uniformly condemned. But the advocates of instrumental music generally, so far as our brethren are concerned, urge it simply as a means of promoting congregational singing, and a false issue is made with them when they are represented as seeking to alter or amend the worship instituted by the Lord.

We must be allowed, therefore, to treat this question from the point of view which those who favor instru-

mental music occupy; and we are sure we can do more
with them in this way than the Review can possibly do
in attempting to compel an issue which they will not
accept.[25]

A. S. Hayden, J. S. Lamar, and others wrote rather ex-
tensively on the subject, not so much in favor of instrumental
music in worship, as in objection to the positions taken by
those who opposed it. Here is suggested a sample of Mr.
Lamar's reasoning:

I must still contend, therefore, that "within the Word
is authority—all beyond is liberty." This statement may
be expanded so as to read: What the Scriptures declare,
or necessarily imply, is law; anything not inconsistent
with law, belongs to the domain of freedom.[26]

Mr. Lamar contended that instrumental music in worship was not inconsistent with "law"; therefore it belonged
to the domain of freedom. With him, here was the issue.

Many other articles, for and against, splendid and timely,
appeared in the periodicals of the period, but these suffice.
To find such men as Alexander Campbell, W. K. Pendleton,
J. W. McGarvey, Moses E. Lard, Isaac Errett, I. B. Grubbs,
Benjamin Franklin, and a host of others equally as vigorous
and influential, opposing the introduction of the new practice, seems proof that no scriptural authority could be produced for its introduction. Its introduction became the result
of a disposition to get away from the early position of the
reformers. The new tendency within the body appears to
have been the consequence of the development of an attitude
different from that which had characterized the pioneers.
But a rather large group continued to adhere to the old position, although they constituted a minority of the brotherhood.
Besides the men mentioned above, Tolbert Fanning and David

[25]Green, *op. cit.*, pp. 107, 108.
[26]*Millennial Harbinger*, 1868, p. 666.

Lipscomb in Tennessee were staunch opposers to the introduction of the instruments, who wielded a great influence against it in the South, where the "anti-organ" group has always been its strongest. Of the arguments pro and con, Garrison says, "The pro-organ arguments, then and later, did not always do full justice to the logic of the anti-organ position,"[27] which is an admission worthy of reflection.

4. Division and the Fundamental Issue.

Division came, not all at once, but gradually and surely. By 1875 the cleavage was a reality, although not fully recognized by all. It was not until 1906 that two separate groups were listed in the United States Census of Religious Bodies.[28] Since that time the body of Disciples using instrumental music in the worship, and supporting the missionary societies, have been known generally as the "Christian Church" and "Disciples," while those who do not are known as "churches of Christ" and the individuals as "Christians." This, however, is not always true, for many congregations using the instrument are known in certain sections as "Churches of Christ," while the more liberal wing speak of themselves as the "Disciples Church."

Beginning with the organization of the first missionary society and culminating with the introduction of mechanical instruments of music in the worship, a new attitude was growing up beside the older one, which could not but eventually lead to division. "Shall two walk together except they have agreed?" asked the prophet.[29] Hard feelings resulted, harsh things were said, each party blaming the other for the division. A statement from Jacob Creath, an opponent to missionary societies and instrumental music, written when he was an old man, is to the point just here. Said he:

---

[27] W. E. Garrison, op. cit., p. 236.

[28] A. T. DeGroot, op. cit., p. 127-134.

[29] Amos 3:3, American Standard Version.

The tendency of all such things (modern music in churches, prizes, fairs, etc.) is to promote two parties or divisions among us,—and then ultimately to throw the blame of the split upon those who have strictly *adhered* to our Rule."[30]

The fundamental issue was one of an attitude toward the Scriptures and the extent of their authority in prescribing the faith, worship, and life of the church. We may not be sufficiently far away from the division, or far enough into the new period, to fully determine the place of the two bodies in the religious world just now. It remains for us in this work to consider a few of the problems which later arose among each group, the new problems being the fruits of attitudes slowly but definitely formulated.

Millennial Harbinger, 1867, p. 346.

PART THREE

RE-ORGANIZATION OF TWO GROUPS
1890–Present

CHAPTER X

"THE PROGRESSIVES"

In its beginning, the work of Thomas and Alexander Campbell had been that of union among the existing religious bodies; which crusade for union never lost its appeal for many of the leading spirits in the movement. However, as Alexander Campbell come to realize that the union of existing denominations could not be effected, and as he better understood the teaching of the New Testament, he and those associated with him recognized the direction of the whole movement as one contending for a restoration of the church after the New Testament pattern. In looking to the New Testament for the pattern of doctrine, worship, church government, and moral life, there could but develop in the minds of a large group a fixed attitude for a "one and only" church, which group refused to be diverted from the New Testament in its religious functions. Simultaneous with such an attitude, there began to develop among others a disposition toward more liberal interpretations of the original position, assuming that where the Scriptures did not forbid a thing, they were at liberty to introduce it. Too, the desire for union of the various religious bodies led many of the more liberal minded to feel that such union should be effected even at the sacrifice of a rigid adherence to the policy of "restoration."

With the division which came finally over the instrumental music as the immediate factor in the controversy, but over an attitude as the real cause, two groups were in the field: the "Progressives" and the "Non-progressives," as each was called by the other, oftentimes in derision. Each group was motivated by an attitude toward the Scriptures developed during the two previous decades. It shall be our purpose to follow briefly these two groups, considering some of the problems that arose among each, the result of the attitude developed in that particular body.

In the period from 1875 to the present, among the "progressive" group, who are called "Disciples" or the "Christian Church," three main issues have been raised: Biblical criticism, open church membership, and the centralizing of power in a united organization of all Boards. These questions have aroused no little discussion and concern among them, since there remained in the group many who were conservative on most points, except for the introduction of instrumental music. The entire group ranged from the conservative element just mentioned, to those extremely liberal in their views. Although there has been no open break among them, the Disciples are divided into three camps: the conservative group, represented by the *Christian Standard;* the "middle-of-the-road" group, represented by the *Christian Evangelist* and the *Christian Board of Publication,* both being owned by the brotherhood; and the ultra-liberal group, represented by such men as E. Scribner Ames, Herbert Willett, and Charles Clayton Morrison. The *Christian Century* grew out of this last named group, representing for some time their views; however, it has since become an interdenominational paper, no longer representing the brotherhood in any way. Of this last named group more shall be said presently.

1. *Liberalism and Criticism.*

As many of the younger preachers went East to complete their education in the liberal universities of that section, they became indoctrinated with the attitude toward the Bible introduced by German rationalism, called "higher" criticism. This became a severe test to the Disciples, as J. H. Garrison says:

> . . . It can readily be understood that a people who stand so thoroughly committed to the authority of the Scriptures as the Disciples of Christ would not regard

lightly any movement whose object and effect were
thought to undermine the Bible.[1] . . .

The first instance of concern about "modernism" among
the Disciples seems to have been over R. L. Cave, pastor of
the Central Christian Church, St. Louis, in 1889, of whom
W. E. Garrison writes:

> . . . he preached a sermon, and later sponsored a
> series of resolutions, in which he asserted that Abraham
> and Moses were grossly ignorant of the true character of
> God, denied the virgin birth and the bodily resurrection
> of Jesus, described the Bible as an evolution and not a
> revelation, declared that there is no such thing as a
> divinely given "conditions of salvation," and held that
> there is no water-baptism in the commission (St. Louis
> Republic, December 8, 1889).[2]

The *Christian Evangelist,* which later became a liberal
paper, led in the fight against Mr. Cave, whereupon he and a
group pulled off from the Christian Church and started wor-
shiping separately. He was soon lost to the Disciples, however.

Dr. L. L. Pinkerton, previously mentioned as the first to
introduce the musical instrument into the worship, was also
the first to publicly declare himself against the generally accepted views of the Scriptures. He and John Shackleford
published a magazine, the *Independent Monthly,* whose purpose was the reverse of *Lard's Quarterly.* Of Pinkerton's
position, A. W. Fortune writes:

> In this magazine Dr. Pinkerton published an article
> on "Bible Inspiration," in which he denied "the old theory
> of the plenary inspiration of the Scriptures." He criti-
> cized Milligan's "Reason and Revelation" and expressed
> the conviction that young ministers who were taught to

---

[1] J. H. Garrison, *The Story of a Century,* p. 235.
[2] W. E. Garrison, *Religion Follows the Frontier,* p. 267.

accept the ninth verse of the one hundred and thirty-seventh psalm as inspired by the Lord would "perpetuate a great many follies in his name."[3]

J. W. McGarvey led in the fight against the rationalistic tendencies of the period. Much splendid material from the pen of this scholarly saint has been preserved for the present generation. The controversy proper had its beginning in a series of articles written by Mr. McGarvey against Liberalism which began to be published in the *Christian Standard* in 1890, continuing for nearly twenty years. This series of articles did much to bring before the Disciples the real issues involved in the controversy. Of McGarvey and this phase of controversy among them, Errett Gates has said: "He has been the centre and brain of the opposition to higher criticism among the Disciples."[4]

The period was one in which rationalism from Germany was being introduced into the various religious bodies of America; and it was impossible that it should not find its way into the thinking of some preachers among the Disciples. In 1894 the Disciples House was established in connection with the University of Chicago, out of which grew an organization known as the "Campbell Institute." E. Scribner Ames was one of the leading figures in the organization of this group, the organ of which is *The Scroll*. In the fly-leaf of an occasional copy is briefly set forth the history and aim of the "Institute"; it reads as follows:

The Campbell Institute is an organization of ministers, teachers, and laymen among the Disciples of Christ. It was organized in 1896 with fourteen charter members. There are now six hundred members. The purpose of the Institute is to promote scholarship, fellowship, and the religious life.[5]

---

[3]A. W. Fortune, *The Disciples in Kentucky*, p. 377.
[4]Errett Gates, *The Disciples of Christ*, pp. 312, 313.
[5]*The Scroll*, March, 1944, fly-leaf.

From its birth, this organization has stood for the ultra-liberal movement among the Disciples. The *Christian Standard* has been unrelenting in its fight against the Campbell Institute, indicting it upon such charges as the following:

> . . . the leaders had in mind all the time a propaganda to swing the Restoration movement out of its historical course.[6]

> . . . This organization has been a source of strife for twenty years; it has, either directly or indirectly, contributed to the majority of our brotherhood troubles.[7]

This organization and its publication, *The Scroll*, have led, not only in the ultra-liberal and rationalistic view of the Scriptures, but also in the practice and encouragement of open membership. The attitude of those constituting the Campbell Institute may be seen at a glance by briefly considering a few positions advocated in *The Scroll*. One writer advocates that all the two hundred larger churches come out in favor of open membership, boasting that he had been practicing it for some time;[8] another writer urges that until the people of the denomination recognize that "baptism was a custom-demanded and not a Christ-demanded" practice of the early Christians they would not get very far handling the matter;[9] another, in sketching a funeral sermon preached in one of the Disciples' meeting-houses, says of the former articles of faith held by believers, "These questions, tormenting as they might be, are of no concern to us today, for we know beyond a doubt that the commands, the rites, the public confessions which profess to lead one into heaven and which in times past we thought to be the commands of God are but commands of men, are interpretations of what men believed to be the will of God;"[10]

---

[6]*Christian Standard*, October 5, 1918, p. 4.
[7]*Ibid.*, p. 91.
[8]*The Scroll*, June, 1934, pp. 167-170.
[9]*The Scroll*, May, 1935, p. 135.
[10]*Ibid.*, February, 1935, p. 56.

while yet another compares the present conception of the Resurrection of Jesus to the conceptions our grandfathers had concerning ghosts.[11] These reveal the distance some have gone from the original position held by the pioneers of the Reformation, only a few generations past.

Not only through his writings, but as Professor of Bible and later as President of the College of the Bible, Lexington, Kentucky, J. W. McGarvey made a strenuous fight against the invasion of liberalism into the ranks of the Disciples. However, upon his death the liberals gained control over the school and have controlled it for a quarter of a century.

In 1912 A. W. Fortune and W. C. Bower were added to the faculty of the school, to be joined by E. E. Snoddy in 1914. Professor Fortune says of the three men, they "introduced new methods of teaching in their classes, assigned new textbooks and reference books in their courses, and endeavored to bring their work to a graduate basis."[12] Soon these men were charged with liberalism, and trouble followed. In such a position Mr. Fortune should be able to represent acceptably the attitude of the liberal wing. In a series of addresses delivered in Fort Forth, Texas, in 1942, before a meeting of preachers of the Christian Church, Mr. Fortune said:

> There is no fixed doctrine in the New Testament which one is to accept and believe in order to be a Christian. . . . In the second place, there is no fixed New Testament church which can be regarded as a norm for all time. When we talk about restoring the New Testament church we should be clear in our minds as to what we mean.
>
> The New Testament was not intended to be a constitution for the church, outlining in detail its organization, its worship, and its doctrine. Instead of the New

---

[11]*Ibid.*, January, 1938, pp. 468-474.
[12]A. W. Fortune, *The Disciples in Kentucky*, p. 282.

Testament indicating a plan according to which the church was constituted, it is a document that came out of the life of the church. Instead of the New Testament producing the church, the church produced the New Testament.

The New Testament is a record of the experience of the church under the leadership of the apostles. Instead of regarding that church as a model, according to which the church of all time must be patterned, we are to try to catch their spirit, and in the light of their experience try to adapt the church to the needs of our own time. We have previously noted the difficulties encountered by Alexander Campbell in his attempt to restore the ancient order of things. We need to return to the New Testament church, but not as a fixed model according to which the church is rigidly to conform.

In the third place, when we speak of the plan of salvation we must not think of it as a rigid system according to which God is bound in his reception of the sinner. We should think of it rather as a guide to help the one who is seeking to come into right relation with God.[13] . . .

Another periodical dedicated to the liberal movement among the Disciples was the *Christian Century*, which began in 1908, edited by Charles Clayton Morrison. W. E. Garrison says of the *Century:*

. . . Almost immediately it became the exponent of a more liberal theology than had ever found expression in any Disciple periodical. . . . It promptly became the champion not only of more liberal theological views and more advanced social attitudes than were commonly accepted, but also of "open membership." This last . . . constituted then, as it does now for conservative Disciples, the ultimate heresy.[14]

---

[13]A. W. Fortune, *Adventuring With Disciple Pioneers,* pp. 38, 39.
[14]W. E. Garrison, *op. cit.,* pp. 300, 301.

The next problem considered is directly related to this one. The two are usually discussed together.

2. *The Fight on Open-membership.*

The extent of the swing from extreme conservatism of the middle nineteenth century to this extreme liberalism of the middle twentieth century is well illustrated by the fact that Isaac Erret, founder and first editor of the *Christian Standard,* was considered a "liberal" in those early days. The position he held then is the position of the *Standard* today; but that position now represents the position of the "conservatives" among the Disciples. The greatest fight the *Standard* is making among the denomination at present is against "rationalism" and "open-membership." The latter has been of concern to the Disciples since 1873; it relates itself to the admission of the un-immersed into fellowship of the church. The question is an outgrowth of the controversy over "open" and "closed" communion, already alluded to.

In tracing the history of open membership in a thesis submitted to Drake University for the Master of Arts degree, which was later published in the *Christian Standard,*[15] Mr. Carl S. Ledbetter says of the origin of the question: "L. L. Pinkerton, it seems, was the earliest open advocate of the practice. In the *Christian Standard* of 1873, appeared a series of articles over Mr. Pinkerton's name entitled, 'No Immersion—No Membership in a Church of the Reformation.' . . ." Pinkerton's position was that if left to him, he would admit the un-immersed, yet he himself felt that baptism and immersion meant "one and the same thing."

Dr. DeGroot says that the first time the question came up as a problem was in 1885, when W. T. Moore, who was supported by the *Foreign Christian Missionary Society,* began preaching in London for a congregation which included both

---

[15]*Christian Standard,* August 31, 1940-February 8, 1941.

the immersed and the un-immersed, although Moore himself practiced only immersion. The *Old Paths Guide* attacked him for "not representing the cause he was sent to represent," whereupon the *Christian Standard* defended him, claiming for him the right to decide such matters on the field.[16] R. L. Cave was the first to lead the way in the actual practice of open membership, in the Central Christian Church, St. Louis, in 1889.[17] However, since he was forced to withdraw, little came of it at the time. "The earliest publicized practice of open membership," says Ledbetter, "was that of the Lenox Avenue Church, of New York City, in 1892 or '93, under the ministry of James M. Philputt."[18] As can be seen, this followed in the wake of instrumental music's being introduced without Scriptural authority, and is another fruit of the same attitude.

A second congregation to practice open membership was the Cedar Avenue Church, Cleveland, Ohio, in 1895. This congregation sought an endorsement of the brotherhood by sending fifty dollars as a contribution to the Foreign Christian Missionary Society, thinking that if it were accepted, it would constitute an apparent endorsement of the program. The secretary of the Society was instructed to return the offering.[19]

Discussing the five men most responsible for the "open membership" movement among the Disciples, against whom the greatest fight has been made, Ledbetter says, "These men then—Ames, Morrison, Willett, Garrison, and Ainslie—represent the most vital and forceful proponents of the open-membership program of the century."[20]

---

[16]Alfred Thomas DeGroot, *The Ground of Division Among the Disciples of Christ*, p. 187.

[17]*Ibid.*, p. 188.

[18]*Christian Standard, op. cit.*, p. 943.

[19]*Christian Standard*, September 14, 1940, p. 912.

[20]*Ibid.*, September 21, 1940, p. 944.

It is difficult to discuss the question of open membership and the organization of the United Christian Missionary Society separately, as the two have been so closely related in the controversy among the Disciples. In tracing the history of the attitude toward open membership, it is necessary to introduce just here the uniting of the various boards.

As early as 1917, the *Christian Standard* called for a special congress of the conservatives among the Disciples to meet in St. Louis early in October of the following year, in order to organize their forces to fight against the organization of the United Christian Missionary Society. As the time drew near for the meeting, the *Standard* carried a bitter fight against what it called "insidious rationalistic propaganda among the Disciples of Christ." The delegates were assembling in St. Louis when the Health Department forbade any assemblies to meet because of the influenza epidemic then raging. Consequently, the meeting had to be cancelled. With the meeting postponed until the following fall, the *Standard* continued its attack against modernism, calling for the meeting of the "Restoration Congress" prior to the general meeting in 1919. The congress met at the appointed time and drew up fourteen resolutions to be presented to the Convention in Cincinnati, October 13-20. The purpose of the Convention was to unite all the Disciples' organizations under one general head. The *Standard* made its fight against such an organization on two grounds: the fact that it would be dominated by the liberal group, and on the ground of too great centralization of power.

We are concerned only with the controversy in the meeting over open membership. Debates were warm, and personalities entered heartily into the discussions. On Sunday, October 19, Z. T. Sweeney preached a stirring sermon in Richmond Street Church, Cincinnati, entitled "Should Churches of Christ Receive Unimmersed Into Formal Fellowship?" in which he showed the scriptural grounds for immersion, and how the plea of the Reformers would be forfeited should that policy be departed from. The article was published in the *Standard* at that time, and reprinted in January and February, 1942. In commenting editorially upon Sweeney's speech, the *Standard* sets forth in a few words the ground for its contention:

> . . . Here is the issue of Jesus' authority and the issue of the authority delegated to the apostles. If we can dismiss the statements of Jesus that enjoin baptism, we can ignore all the authority of Jesus and of His apostles at will.[21]

The *Standard* continues to lead in a fight against the practice, while those congregations referring to themselves as the "Disciples Church" have little scruples in the matter, generally. Since the practice began among those advocating the missionary societies, and oftentimes among the missionaries themselves, it looks as if the prophecies of some of the older opponents of the societies might be reaching fulfilment.

3. *The United Christian Missionary Society.*

William Robinson Warren has well said: "On some subjects the Disciples of Christ have been unanimous but missions was never one of these subjects. . . ."[22] A study of the early period of the controversy on this point reveals an unfavorable attitude toward societies by many on the ground of insufficient scriptural authority, while by a few others, the opposition was on the ground of inefficiency. In 1874, the Christian Woman's Board of Missions was organized, and the year following the Foreign Christian Missionary Society was born. Various other boards were created during the years that followed, leading to the desire by some for the combining of all these as one society under one general

---

[21]*Christian Standard*, February 14, 1942, p. 147.

[22]William Robinson Warren, *The Life and Labors of Archibald McLean*, p. 263.

board. The General Convention for such a purpose was called to meet October 13-20, 1919, having been forced to postpone the meeting in 1918 because of the influenza epidemic.

As previously stated, the *Christian Standard* and its leaders began the fight against such a move a year or two before, and by the time the Convention met they were well organized to oppose leaders in the movement. Those opposing such a merger were afraid of the soundness of the men who would undoubtedly be in power; they likewise had their doubts about the loyalty of many who would be in the employ of the society, for many missionaries sent out by the Foreign Christian Missionary Society had been charged with practicing open membership. In reporting the procedure of the convention, the *Christian Evangelist* summarizes the charges as follows:

> The "Restoration Congress," which met at the beginning of the convention and overlapped its first day had devised a well formulated order of procedure and were in the convention hall practically in a body to protest, if not to defeat, the movement.

> It was like two conventions contending for supremacy. The abuses charged against the societies—often in almost cruel personalities—ranged from personal grievances and strifes like the "Transylvania matter" to such allegations as "open-membership," "infant dedication" on the foreign field, unjustifiable meddling with the local churches and pastors by the secretaries, the ignoring of the deity of Christ, and the willingness to see our own church work supplanted by others.[28]

The United Christian Missionary Society was created in spite of the opposition; however, opposition to it has never ceased. The conservative wing of the Disciples is not op-

---

[28]*Christian Evangelist*, October 23, 1919, p. 1108.

posed to missionary societies, but they are opposed to the one representing the Disciples at present. This meeting led to another, which assembled in Louisville, December 6-8, 1921, to organize forces in opposition to the liberal tendencies of the Society group. The New Testament Tract Society, organized for this purpose, was the result of this last Congress.

Although no definite break has appeared among them, there are definitely three groups, with little fellowship between the conservative element and the other two groups. The condition is the consequence of an attitude developed in earlier years and another which came later. In an effort to be liberal, for some, no stopping point was to be found along the road. Another quotation from Mr. Fortune well summarizes some of the differences to be found between the liberals of today and the pioneers of yesterday:

> There have been some radical changes in the church since the days of Barton Stone and the Campbells. If they were to come back and visit our churches today, they would not feel at home. They might feel that we have departed from the faith. There have been many changes in the organization. They would find societies, especially of the women and young people, of which they had not dreamed. Instead of the elders and deacons managing the affairs of the church, they would find administrative boards, of which the heads of departments are members. They would perhaps be amazed when they found that there are women on these administrative boards.
>
> . . . . .
>
> If these pioneer leaders were to enter one of our finest church buildings they would indeed by surprised. They would not see any stoves. They would see electric lights. They would see stained-glass windows. They would see a chancel with a pulpit on one side and

the reading desk on the other. They would see seats on either side, a baptistry at the end, with the communion table just in front.

When the service started, they would be amazed from beginning to end. They would hear a pipe organ playing a prelude to the service. They might hear the chimes striking the hour eleven. Then perhaps they would hear voices singing a call to worship. They would wonder what was going to happen next, when to their amazement they would see a choir enter, singing a processional hymn, and the members of this choir wearing vestments. They would wonder if they had not gotten into the wrong church when they heard the choir sing an anthem, and especially when they heard it sing the responses in the service. They would perhaps feel there is something lacking in the sermon, which they heard, just as we feel now about their sermons.[24]

---

[24]A. W. Fortune, *op. cit.*, pp. 76, 77.

Chapter XI

THE "NON-PROGRESSIVES"

It is needless to say that a group of people just emerging from a division in which the majority were separated from them, taking with them a large number of the meeting-houses which the minority had assisted in building, should be extremely jealous of their position, which jealousies would inevitably give rise to controversies among themselves. The division proper can be said to have taken place between 1880 and 1890, although it was well under way by 1875. The conservatives, who were called "non-progressives" by others but who called themselves "churches of Christ," viewing the effects of liberalism in the departed churches, and the trend toward rationalism and open membership, became even more determined in their efforts to follow the Scriptures and to keep out anything that looked like innovation. No doubt the recent controversy and division caused many of the minority to swing to a more literalistic view, to assume an attitude bordering on the radical fringe. This, however, was not the attitude of the majority of the conservatives.

Three major questions have confronted the churches of Christ since the separation, which have tended toward division in their own ranks: Sunday Schools, Colleges and Orphan Homes, and Premillennialism. These shall be noted briefly as the fruits of an attitude.

1. *The Sunday School Question.*

The question of teaching the Bible in classes on Sunday morning, and the use of women teachers, became an issue among the churches of Christ after the turn of the present century. The *Apostolic Way*, a periodical published in Dallas, Texas, became the organ of expression for the group opposing such an arrangement of class teaching. It was argued by those objecting to such a method of teaching that the division of the assembly into classes is a violation of the Scriptural example of assembling in one body, while the use of women teachers is a violation of 1 Corinthians 14:34 and 1 Timothy 2:11, 12. These do not oppose teaching, but they oppose what they call the "class system" of teaching.

This group is strongest in Texas and adjacent territory. In a yearbook, privately published by Paul S. Knight, they list two hundred twenty preachers. Four papers are published among them: *The Church Messenger*, Booneville, Arkansas; *The Gospel Tidings*, Abilene, Texas; *The Truth*, Wichita Falls, Texas; and the *Old Paths Advocate*, Lebanon, Missouri.

The breach between those opposing the class system of teaching and those practicing it, is not so great as it was a few years ago. With a younger group of preachers being developed within both parties, among whom bitter personal feelings toward each other are wanting, it is hoped that complete fellowship will be restored at a not too distant date. On all points of doctrine, worship, and organization they are agreed; it is about classes and women teachers in such classes that they differ.

2. *The College and Orphan Home Controversy.*

The second subject which has divided the churches of Christ has been that of Bible colleges and orphan homes. Daniel Sommer bought the *American Christian Review* in 1887, which had been founded by Benjamin Franklin and had played such an important role in the missionary society and instrumental music controversies. Mr. Sommer became a bitter opponent of Bible colleges, and led in the fight against them. The burden of the attack was based on the claim that Bible colleges and orphan homes were unscriptural as agents through which the church should do its work. It was argued that they were in the same catalogue with missionary societies, and Mr. Sommer charged his opposition to them on that ground. He objected, not to educated preachers, but to the churches going into secular business and asking congregations to support the business. The effectiveness of Sommer's work was felt most keenly in the Central States and in the Northwest section of the Nation. It was in those two sections that he and his followers did most of their evangelistic work.

Supporters of colleges have denied that they are "church schools," but adjuncts to the home and permissible only on the ground that they be supported by individuals as such, who are interested in them as good works. It has been a rare thing for congregations to support the colleges as congregations, and very few individuals have advocated their support by church contributions. Looked upon as adjuncts to the home and not to the church, the policy has been for them to be supported by those interested in such education for their young people.

Another ground on which the colleges were opposed was that of the danger which could come of them through the development of a "clergy," a "pastor system," instead of what has been conceded generally by churches of Christ as the scriptural plan of organization and work. Connected with this danger is the fear that modernism or a general "softness" might invade the ranks of the churches. At present this is one of the chief fears to some, as they consider the trends in educational circles of the present and compare them with the experience of the colleges founded by the Reformers of a past generation.

Before his death, Mr. Sommer sought a reconciliation of the two groups, those supporting Bible colleges and those opposed to them. He made a tour of the southern states in 1933, visiting the various colleges, speaking in their chapels, and doing much to break down the old feeling of enmity which had existed. While in Nashville he spoke several times in the church services of various congregations. In the same year, 1933, and later, he did much writing through his paper, and the papers with which he had carried on many heated battles in other years, seeking peace among the brotherhood. Through the effort of young preachers from the South, who have gone into the northern and central states to preach, much is being done to remove the feeling that has existed. Except for a vigorous campaign still being conducted by D. Austen Sommer, a son of Daniel Sommer, through his paper, the *Macedonian Call*, little is ever heard on the subject any more. It bids fair to take its place in the historical past before many years have gone by.

3. *The Pre-Millennial Issue.*

Probably the most serious of the issues to confront the churches of Christ has been that of pre-millennialism. The two differences mentioned have been questions respecting methods of doing things; this third is doctrinal. R. H. Boll, who for many years was associate editor of the *Gospel Advocate*, began vigorously to advocate theories of the second coming of Christ and a millennial reign on earth, which was opposed by the great majority of the brotherhood. Writing on the subject, "The History of the Boll Movement," Foy E. Wallace, Jr., said:

> The history of the case dates from the clash R. H. Boll had with the *Gospel Advocate* twenty years ago over his teaching. He was at that time its front page editor. Because of his visionary teaching he was dismissed. Later, upon his agreement with the management of the *Advocate* not to teach his theories, he was restored to his place. But instead of respecting his agreement he began again to feature his theories. He was again removed from the *Gospel Advocate* staff. He then denied that he had ever made any such agreement,

and preferred some very serious charges against the *Gospel Advocate* editors.[1]

. . . . .

He continued this denial for four years, when in 1919 he admitted there was an agreement in a sense, and his admission was published in the *Gospel Advocate* of October 2, 1919.[2]

In 1916 Mr. Boll began publishing his own magazine, *Word and Work*. Strong opposition to his theory of the establishment of a millennial kingdom of Christ on earth, the restoration of the Jews to Palestine, and the personal reign of Christ from Jerusalem, existed from the beginning of Boll's teaching on such matters. But in spite of the opposition, Mr. Boll has succeeded in building up a small but devoted following.

The *Gospel Advocate* entered vigorously into the controversy in the early thirties when Mr. Wallace became its editor. In 1935 Mr. Wallace began editing a monthly from Oklahoma City, Oklahoma, the *Gospel Guardian,* which was devoted primarily to the opposition of the popular premillennial theory. This paper was not long-lived, but it did a definite work in clarifying the issues and in bringing before the brotherhood the question and dangers involved. In 1938 the former editor of the *Guardian* began the publication of the *Bible Banner,* from the same city, which continues to the present as the avowed opponent to Boll's theory of the millennial reign of Christ on earth. In many respects the *Gospel Guardian* and *Bible Banner* remind one of the old *Christian Baptist,* and like it, they have wielded great influence in molding a definite attitude among preachers of today.

The division over this question promised to be more serious than the questions of Bible classes and colleges.

---

[1]*Gospel Guardian,* January, 1936. Foy E. Wallace, Jr., in an editorial, "The History of the Boll Movement," p. 1.

[2]*Ibid.,* p. 7.

Already, however, the heat of controversy is subsiding; yet there appears to be little hope of reconciliation because of departure in many other points considered by the anti-pre-millennial churches as fundamental to New Testament teaching. At least there will be no reconciliation until the theory has lost its appeal as a present-day fad.

4. *Recapitulation and Conclusion.*

The aim and effort of this work has been to follow the development of an attitude within a specific movement; an attitude that began with the longing desire of a man for Christian union among those professing to be the children of God, union based on the Scriptures and not on some creed of men. This attitude toward union developed into the belief that the Scriptures are all-sufficient, and present a divine plan of salvation, church organization, worship, and purpose in the world. This belief crystallized in a definite attitude of producing a "thus saith the Lord" for all that pertains to the Christian life. As the frontier changed, and the movement became more settled, there was voiced the desire by some for an organization through which to do mission work. The question arose, "Do the Scriptures authorize such an institution?" Controversy followed. There was no question relative to the need for mission work; the question centered in the Scripturalness of a society other than the church through which to do the work. Added to this was the desire of many congregations to introduce instruments of music into the worship, that they might keep pace with the growing social standards. The question of Scripturalness again confronted them, this time being, "Do the Scriptures authorize the introduction of mechanical instruments into the worship of God?" One group held that since the Scriptures did not specifically forbid their use, they were permissible as an expedient; the other group held that inasmuch as there was neither direct command, approved example, or necessary inference for their use, they were thereby excluded. Had the Holy Spirit wished them to be used in worship, the latter contended, they would have been specifically authorized in the New Testament. Division came as the result of the development of the first named attitude.

As a result of division two camps now occupied the field. In the one, liberality did not stop with instrumental music, but introduced other things which brought strife and confusion among them; the new controversies being over open membership, modernism, and the centralizing of power in one great society, under one board. The other, driven by the developed attitude of Scriptural precedent, command, or necessary inference for all work and worship of the church, developed factions contending over the teaching of the Bible in classes divided according to age and grade, women teachers, and Bible colleges, and one doctrinal question, that of pre-millennialism.

The conservative group has just recently recuperated sufficiently from the shock of the division to get its forces organized and begin work in earnest. It is too close to the period in which it operates to say much about its impression upon the world, or of the possibility of the greater bulk of the congregations ever merging with the conservative bodies of the Disciples. A movement is under way at present, led by James De Forrest Murch of the *Christian Standard*, and Claud F. Witty, a minister of one of the churches of Christ in Detroit, to get the churches of Christ and the conservative wing of the Disciples together. What will come of it remains uncertain. It is doubtful if the Disciples will give up instrumental music; it is almost certain the churches of Christ will not, in any appreciable number, engage in fellowship with them so long as it is retained. Although many among both groups would like to see unity realized, it cannot but be recognized that the issue is clear and fixed: either those using the instruments must give them up, or those opposing them must compromise their position. There appears to be no alternative.

In the midst of modern rationalism and the attitude that the Scriptures are of human origin, being the result of a general evolutionary process of development, the position of the churches of Christ appears antique. So far as is known, only a few liberalists have appeared among them, and they soon departed, finding a more congenial fellowship in other groups. The several thousand preachers, and several hundred thousand members, believe with the pioneers of the movement, that the Scriptures present a definite plan of salvation, a Scriptural guide in all matters of faith and doctrine, and a divinely ordained church pattern, which will be sufficient to meet the needs of all men, in all lands, throughout all the ages of the human family. So long as that attitude is maintained, they will be found earnestly contending for what they believe to be "the faith once for all delivered unto the saints." The movement was the development of an attitude—the division came about as the result of another attitude growing up beside the first. The two bodies are separated today, not over instrumental music *per se,* nor over missionary societies, but as the result of an attitude toward the authority of the Scriptures.

A statement by A. S. Hayden may well serve as a fitting close to this study, as it sums up the genius of the nineteenth century Reformation and that of churches of Christ today. In speaking of the pioneer preachers then departed, Mr. Hayden said:

. . . They preached the gospel. They were no mere essayists. They were not theorizers, nor specialists. They preached Christ and Him crucified. In this they were a unit. The same gospel was preached in every town, county, and school district. They used their Bibles. They read quoted, illustrated and enforced the Holy Scriptures. This lesson is all-important. We must "preach the Word," not something about the gospel, but the gospel itself. Some of our preachers should sit at the feet of the departed veterans, and learn to speak and enforce Bible themes in Bible words. Let us have more Scripture, in its exact meaning and import; more gospel, more of Jesus, His will, His mission, and His work. This was their power. It will be ours. . . . Therefore, be not weak, nor ashamed of its facts, commands, and promises, as delivered to us by our fathers; and to them by the holy apostles.[8]

This is the only basis on which the restoration of the New Testament church can be accomplished. If young preachers of this generation can be influenced to contend for the ancient order of things, to formulate in their own minds a definite attitude toward truth, and be led to manifest a Christian spirit toward those who differ with them, by a study of the things presented within these pages, this work will have been justified and the author richly rewarded.

_____

[8]A. S. Hayden, *Early History of the Disciples in the Western Reserve*, p. 464.

CHAPTER XII

1945 - 1975
By
FANNING YATER TANT

Thirty years have passed since the first printing of this book. These three decades have demonstrated once again the truth of the major thesis of the work: religious divisions and separations come from basic differences in attitude toward the nature of God's revelation rather than from any differing interpretations or understandings of the word itself. The author outlined the attitude toward the word held by the early disciples, then traced the developing changes as they emerged through the centuries in the Roman Church, the German Reformation, and the early American denominations. The specific thrust of the work has been to demonstrate the basic difference in attitude which was responsible for splitting the Restoration Movement into the "Progressive" and "Non-Progressive" segments.

In the last chapter of his original work, Mr. Hailey said: "Three major questions have confronted the churches of Christ since the separation, which have tended toward division in their own ranks: Sunday Schools, Colleges and Orphan Homes, and Premillennialism. These should be noted briefly as the fruits of an attitude" (page 239). A generation later, two of these problems have generally subsided, but the third (Colleges and Orphan Homes) has burgeoned out into a major issue, though somewhat different from the way it was first envisaged.

In this short addendum to the original work, we trace briefly the unfolding of this problem, particularly as it has manifested itself among the "Non-Progressive" (anti-instrumental music, anti-Missionary Society) churches. The "Progressives," meanwhile have undergone a major division in their ranks, the culmination of an internal struggle that actually goes back to the early years of the Twentieth Century. They divided slowly into moderate and liberal doctrinal groups vigorously debating such things as higher criticism and open membership. A struggle for control of the General Missionary Society in the early decades of this century ended with the withdrawal of the conservatives, led by the *Christian Standard,* and the formation of the *North American Convention of Christian Churches.* The liberal element was the larger and stronger of the two groups, and kept control of most of the denominational institutions. *The North American Convention* remained active and vigorous, however, and when an effort was made to "restructure" the "Progressives" into a more denominational stance in the 1960's about 4,000 congregations withdrew from the *International Convention of the Disciples of Christ (Christian Church)* to join the *North American Convention of Christian Churches.* According to recent estimates the *International Convention*—having now changed its name to the *General Assembly of Christian Churches (Disciples of Christ)*—has about 1,000,000 members and the *North American Convention* about 1,500,000.

1. The "College in the Budget"

In the mid-1930's the "College and Orphan Home" problem began to emerge as an issue which was destined eventually to rupture the unity of the "Non-Progressives" as irreparably as "restructure" had ruptured the unity of the "Progressives." The Bible colleges have traditionally been hard pressed for funds, and there has always been a strong desire on the part of some advocates of the schools to solicit church support for such institutions. Ever since the days of Campbell, articles have appeared from time to time in the various religious journals suggesting that churches should make contributions to the schools. Invariably other articles have quickly followed such appeals voicing strong protest to the idea.

The coming of World War II, and agitation over whether or not Christians could participate in carnal warfare, diverted attention from this question for about a dozen years. But the problem reappeared in 1947 when Abilene Christian College undertook to raise $3,000,000 in an expansion program. Robert M. Alexander was put in charge of the fund-raising activities, and immediately began a campaign which was interpreted as an effort to secure church contributions to the colleges. *The Bible Banner*, edited by Foy E. Wallace, Jr., and with such men as Cled E. Wallace, Roy E. Cogdill, W. Curtis Porter, C. R. Nichol, and R. L. Whiteside as regular contributors, quickly took up the challenge, voicing strong opposition to the churches' becoming involved in the campaign. Defending the church contributions were G. C. Brewer, N. B. Hardeman and others. The controversy was intense, but short-lived. Advocates of church support soon sensed that the majority of the churches, including both preachers and members, did not look with favor on such support. The aged W. W. Otey had been a strong opponent of church contributions, and he wrote to Foy E. Wallace, "It gave me a thrill of encouragement that you called N. B. Hardeman's hand on putting colleges in the church budget. I began this fight sixty years ago. . . ." [1]

In summarizing his own firm opposition to such a development, Wallace wrote, "Beginning with 1930, the first year of my editorship with the *Gospel Advocate,* I began to write articles on the subject 'Concerning the Church and the College'. These articles appeared in the *Gospel Advocate* every year until the last. During the period of discussion of the organizational question, John T. Hinds, C. R. Nichol, and F. B. Srygley all wrote articles taking opposite views from those of Brother Brewer, and taking the same stand that I had repeatedly taken editorially . . . After severing con-

---

[1] *Bible Banner,* March, 1947, page 1.

nection with the *Gospel Advocate* in 1934, the *Gospel Guardian* was launched in 1935, and again my position on the institutional question was expressed." [2]

2. Injection of the Orphan Home Issue

When it became apparent that the churches would not accept the idea of church support for Bible Colleges, the discussion suddenly took a new and unexpected course — injection of "the orphan home issue" into the picture. The matter of church support of orphan homes had not been seriously discussed although C. R. Nichol, F. B. Srygley, John T. Hinds, A. O. Colley and others had written occasionally urging caution in such matters. C. R. Nichol had written in 1933 contending that such financing of benevolent institutions was comparable to the support of a missionary society. In spite of such occasional and sporatic articles, however, most churches were favorable to the idea, even though most of them actually were not making contributions to the few small orphanages which were then in existence. The care of orphaned children was something all the brethren favored, and little thought had been given as to the specific arrangements under which such care was provided.

N. B. Hardeman saw a clear parallel between church support of an orphan home and church contributions to a college. So he wrote, "Why will these brethren support an orphanage and fight the schools? The possible answer is that there are too many of our best churches that support the orphan home, and these brethren are afraid to attack them." [3] A few weeks later he wrote further, "If the church can do part of its work (caring for orphans) through a human institution, why can it not do another part of its work (teaching the Bible) through a human institution?" [4] He pressed the point vigorously, contending "the orphan home and the schools stand or fall together." Support of one

---

[2] *Bible Banner,* September, 1947, page 21,22.
[3] *Gospel Advocate,* August 28, 1947.
[4] *Ibid.,* October 23, 1947.

justified support of the other. There could be no logical or scriptural reason to support the homes and withhold support from the schools.

Wallace acknowledged the parallel, but contended that the homes "do not offer the threat or power or danger of domination that exists in the colleges." He went on, however, to extend the argument so as to embrace the Missionary Society: "If the church can do its benevolent work through a 'board of directors' (a benevolence board), why not its preaching work or 'missionary work' through a board? And certainly if the church can do its education work through a board of education, there can be no logical reason why the same church could not do its missionary work through a board of missions." [5]

3. The "Sponsoring Church Cooperative"

Following World War II a great enthusiasm developed among the churches for evangelization in the countries with whom America had been at war — Germany, Italy, and Japan. This brought on much discussion as to how best to realize the common goal or objective. As early as 1943, when it became apparent that the tide of war was turning in favor of the Allies, efforts were begun to create interest in reaching the enemy nations. It was in 1943 that the Broadway Church of Christ in Lubbock, Texas, began to build a special fund for evangelizing in foreign countries. In a lectureship three years later M. Norvel Young, minister of the congregation, reported: "For several years there has been among the churches of Christ an increasing interest in doing missionary work in foreign countries. Since the war many people have been particularly concerned with Germany. While Brother G. C. Brewer was minister of the Broadway Church of Christ he wrote some articles on the subject of preparing for foreign mission work during the war. The Broadway Church opened a special fund in 1943 and seven thousand dollars were given

---

[5] *Bible Banner*, July, 1947.

into this fund by members of the congregation." 6

The Broadway Church about this time began to solicit
regular contributions from other churches to augment the
special fund established through contributions from her own
members. The entire fund was to be administered by the
Broadway elders in carrying forward the evangelization of
Germany. This marks the first serious effort of "Non-
Progressive" Churches of Christ to mount a viable alternative to
the Missionary Societies of the "Progressive" churches. It was
the beginning of the "Sponsoring Church Cooperative," and was
a very logical extension and development of the ongoing
controversy over church support of colleges and orphan homes.
They were all logically tied together.

In reality the "Sponsoring Church Cooperative" was only
a modern revival of the plan which had been developed in
Texas following the War between the States, and which had
finally been laid to rest mainly through the unrelenting opposition of David Lipscomb and his co-workers on the *Gospel
Advocate*. This plan called for the accumulation of funds
from many churches to be placed under the control and
direction of the elders of a single church, and to be administered by them in the support of gospel preachers. Dr.
Carroll Kendrick, a Kentuckian who had migrated to Texas
before the War, gave the sponsoring eldership a name which
he felt described its function. He called it a "Receiving,
Managing, and Disbursing Evangelistic Committee."

David Lipscomb saw this clearly as a kind of Missionary
Society, a method by which to activate the church universal,
and fought it vigorously. Through his strong opposition the
plan fell into disuse in Texas, but an effort was made to
revive it in West Tennessee in 1910. The venerable Lipscomb,
then nearly eighty years of age, once again took up the
cudgel to oppose any revival of the arrangement. He wrote,
"Now what was that but the organization of a society in the

------
6 *Lubbock Lectures on Mission Work*, 1946, page 5.

elders of this church? The church elders at Henderson constitute a board to collect and pay out the money and control the evangelists for the brethren of West Tennessee, and all the preachers are solicitors for this work. This very same course was pursued in Texas a number of years ago. The elders at Dallas were made the supervisors of the work, received the money, employed the preachers and directed and counselled them. For a number of years they employed C. M. Wilmeth. He then dropped out of the work and the Texas Missionary Society took the place. Other experiments along the same course have been made. All of them went into the society work."[7]

The "sponsoring church" concept, had been practiced by some congregations all along, from the very beginning of the Restoration Movement. But it had never been very widely used, and did not actually become an issue probably due to the few churches which participated in it. When the Broadway Church began its vigorous efforts to raise funds from other churches, however, the question came to the front for considerable discussion. Money began to come in slowly at first, but rapidly climbed into the hundreds of thousands of dollars' being given through a dozen or more "sponsoring churches" which sprang up.

4. *The Herald of Truth*

While many antagonistic forces and inner tensions had been developing among the "Non-Progressive" churches, the thing which finally ruptured the fellowship, apparently irrevocably, was the inauguration in the early 1950's of a nationally broadcast radio program bearing the name *Herald of Truth*. Originating in Iowa under the vigorous promotion of two young preachers, the program was moved to Abilene, Texas, in 1952 under the "sponsorship" of the Fifth and Highland congregation of that city. The controversy over the orphan home and the sponsoring church for foreign mission

---

[7] *Gospel Advocate*, 1910, page 364.

work had now widely publicized the idea of a "sponsor," and the churches generally seemed willing to accept the arrangement as scriptural so long as it was done "under an eldership." But the very magnitude of the *Herald of Truth* began to create some uneasiness, and to raise some questions in the minds of many.

The first writer to seriously question the scripturalness of the *Herald of Truth,* as it was being promoted, was Robert H. Farish, who asked, "Does any individual or local congregation have the right to plan and promote a program larger than that individual or congregation can support. This is a thing that needs attention. More and more individuals and local congregations are planning super programs of work, which exceed the bounds of the possibilities of that individual or congregation, and then calling on 'the brotherhood' to support their programs. . . . The work of the church is to be under the direction of the local eldership, but the work of the church which the eldership is to plan and direct is restricted to the resources of the local church." [8]

In reference to the *Herald of Truth,* Earl Irvin West, who had gained a degree of recognition by his two-volume *Search For The Ancient Order,* wrote, "Forty-two years ago" (his reference point is the Henderson, Tennessee, plan of 1910 for a 'sponsoring church' to promote evangelism in West Tennessee) "David Lipscomb, F. B. Srygley, E. A. Elam, and J. C. McQuiddy would have said this would have been 'a step in the wrong direction' and 'the organization of a society in the elders of a local church'." [9]

The *Gospel Guardian* magazine became the chief instrument of criticism and opposition to the *Herald of Truth.* Scores of preachers expressed themselves through its pages. E. R. Harper, preacher for the Fifth and Highland Church had a series of fourteen articles over a period of about six

---

[8] *Gospel Guardian,* June 26, 1952.
[9] *Ibid.,* Vol. 5, page 284.

months defending the *Herald of Truth* and criticizing the *Gospel Guardian* for its opposition. Tensions continued to grow, until finally a definite campaign began to be mounted to ostrasize and "quarantine" all preachers who were opposing the work. A letter appeared on the editorial page of the *Gospel Advocate,* and was given editorial endorsement by the editor of that journal, B. C. Goodpasture, suggesting that "the writers for the *Gospel Advocate* might wisely spearhead a movement to quarantine those preachers today who are sowing the seeds of discord among the brotherhood."[10] Thus encouraged, many churches began to cancel meetings and refuse support to preachers who were known to be in opposition to the *Herald of Truth.*

Several major debates were held within the space of four or five years discussing both the Orphan Home and the *Herald of Truth* problems. Chief among these were the Holt-Totty debate in Indianapolis, Indiana, two debates between E. R. Harper and Fanning Yater Tant, held in Lufkin and Abilene, Texas, and two debates between Roy E. Cogdill and Guy N. Woods held in Birmingham, Alabama, and Newbern, Tennessee. The basic question was the "sponsoring church,"and whether or not such an arrangement was scriptural either in the field of benevolence or evangelism. Church support of the colleges (which was really the thing which had triggered the whole exchange) was not debated. Dr. A. T. DeGroot, of Texas Christian University in discussing the impending division within the ranks of the "Progressive" Disciples of Christ, made a passing reference to the problems of the "Non-Progressives," indicating that he had a clear understanding of what was happening among them. He wrote, "The Church of Christ is developing the first forms of these (missionary societies) very rapidly, one of which spends over a million dollars annually on broadcasting sermons. . . . In April and June, 1955, one Church of Christ minister will

---

[10] *Gospel Advocate,* December 9, 1954.

debate another at Lufkin and Abilene on the subject of Missionary Societies which have emerged in the Church of Christ." [11]

In the 1950's several other journals began to join the *Gospel Guardian* in opposition to the sponsoring church concept, all of them being initiated among brethren who felt the arrangement violated New Testament principles. Among these journals were *The Preceptor, Truth Magazine,* and *Searching the Scriptures.* They were joined in the mid-1970's by *Vanguard.* These journals centered their attack on this one problem, correctly identifying this as the major cause of concern. And inevitably the question of one's "attitude toward authority" emerged as the crucial point of difference, the anti-*Herald of Truth* churches' contending that "there is no authority for such an arrangement," and those who favored it arguing that "there is no pattern" for church cooperation, and therefore, any sensible plan would be acceptable to God.

By the mid-1960's the lines of division were fairly well drawn; the rupture was complete and the fellowship was broken. There would continue to be some shifting back and forth by both preachers and churches, but this would be in an ever diminishing flow. When the final estimate could be made with some degree of accuracy, it was found that of the 14,000 congregations among the "Non-Progressives" in the early 1950's, approximately 2,000 of them had taken a stand against church support of Orphan Homes, Bible Colleges, and the *Herald of Truth.*

5. *Other Issues*

Other issues began to emerge to still further trouble the beleaguered "Non-Progressives," chief among them being the development of a charismatic movement among some few congregations, and an ominous tendency toward classical liberalism. These problems were chiefly seen among those congregations favoring the sponsoring church-type of

---

[11] *Detour from Unity,* A. T. DeGroot, 1955, page 4.

congregational cooperation, and the ultimate end of such difficulties is yet to be determined.

But thirty years after Mr. Hailey's first writing of *Attitudes and Consequences,* the moving finger of history has written still another chapter confirming his thesis that "attitudes" toward the Scripture, rather than understandings or interpretations of it are the basic root of divisions and separations.

9 781584 273349